Praise for the first edition of

"*A Silent Sorrow* speaks powerfully with practical advice and pene-
trating understanding of the suffering, loneliness, and despair of
pregnancy loss. It's a valuable resource for those who work with the
bereaved and a comforting companion to those grappling with
their own sorrow."
—Rabbi Dr. Earl A. Grollman, author of *Living When a Loved One
Has Died*

"The book not only validates the grief bereaved parents feel, but
also lets them know they are not alone in their confusion and
heartache. It offers practical coping strategies for grieving parents
and suggestions on how family, friends, and medical institutions
can help."
—San Diego *Blade-Citizen*

"This is not just a book about sharing one another's grief . . . it is
filled with accurate and helpful information on the subject of pregnancy loss. The appendices alone cover practical issues from managing to creating rituals and resources on virtually everything that
might influence a pregnancy."
—*Human Services News*

"Parents and caregivers will find this book informative and sensi-
tively beneficial in working with the many issues involved in perinatal losses. What a gift to all of us."
—Sister Jane Marie Lamb, OSF, founder of SHARE

"Nothing can erase the sense of loss when a pregnancy doesn't
come to fruition, but this book . . . provide[s] comfort and hope as
well as . . . guidance for those who have lost a wanted child."
—*Publishers Weekly*

"The best thing to say to a friend who has lost a pregnancy is 'I'm
Sorry. I know how much you wanted this baby,' [or] give her a
book, like *A Silent Sorrow*, that can help her cope with the pain she's
feeling."
—Barbara Burgower Hordern, First for Women

A SILENT SORROW

Pregnancy Loss

Guidance and Support
for You and Your Family

2nd Edition

Ingrid Kohn, MSW, and Perry-Lynn Moffitt
with Isabelle A. Wilkins, MD

Routledge
New York and London

Published in 2000 by
Routledge
29 West 35th Street
New York, NY 10001

Published in Great Britain by
Routledge
11 New Fetter Lane
London EC4P 4EE

10   9   8   7   6   5   4

Library of Congress Cataloging-in-Publication Data

Kohn, Ingrid.
    A silent sorrow : pregnancy loss : guidance and support for you and your fam-ily / by Ingrid Kohn and Perry-Lynn Moffitt, with Isabelle A. Wilkins.
        p.   cm.
    Reprint. Previously published : New York : Delacorte Press, 1993.
    Includes bibliographical references and index.
    ISBN 0-415-92481-2 (pbk.)
    1. Miscarriage—Psychological aspects.   2. Perinatal death—Psychological aspects.   3. Fetal death—Psychological aspects.   4. Bereavement—Psychologi-cal aspects.   I. Moffitt, Perry-Lynn.   II. Wilkins, Isabelle A.   III. Title.
    [RG631.K64   1999]
    618.3'92'019—dc21   99-25720
                                                                              CIP

To Miriam and Tova, with love
I.K.

To Edward, David and Justine, with love
P-LM

Contents

Preface to the Second Edition

Since *A Silent Sorrow* was first published, mothers and fathers have written us to express their thanks for helping them through the great and gradual task of rebuilding their lives after the death of an unborn or newborn baby. Professional caregivers have been grateful for *A Silent Sorrow* because the book enables them to understand and guide the families in their care.

Over the past seven years we have noted a growing awareness of the emotional needs of families who endure pregnancy loss. In the late 1980s, the month of October was designated Pregnancy Loss Awareness Month, which has increased public sensitivity to this issue.

However, there is still much to be done. Too many bereaved parents suffer in silence and alone, fearing that their grief is a weakness rather than an expression of the courage to cry. And too few hospitals and medical staff members are aware of bereavement issues and protocols, leaving parents unsure where to turn for help.

We thank Routledge for responding with such enthusiasm, professionalism and commitment to the need for an updated edition of *A Silent Sorrow*, ensuring that bereaved parents, and those who care for them, will continue to have a comprehensive source of support at their time of loss.

The roots of *A Silent Sorrow* reach back to 1983, when Ingrid, drawing on her experience as an obstetrical social worker at Mount Sinai Medical Center in New York City, as well as on her personal ordeal with a miscarriage, cofounded the Pregnancy Loss Support Program at the National Council of Jewish Women, New York Section. Perry-Lynn, who had just endured two consecutive miscarriages, was a member of the program's initial support group and trained to become one of their first lay counselors.

Over the next several years we each led support groups and

wrote and spoke publicly about pregnancy loss. In the process, our own personal grief was transformed into a message for bereaved parents: Expressing sorrow is the first step toward surviving sorrow.

In writing *A Silent Sorrow,* we grappled with how to validate the grief mothers and fathers feel in a world that lacks patience with sorrow. We have praised caregivers who treat grieving parents with understanding, and we still hope to enlighten those whose lack of specialized training may have kept them from being more compassionate.

Throughout *A Silent Sorrow* we have chosen to refer to women and men who have suffered pregnancy losses as "mothers," "fathers" and "parents." This reflects the feelings of many bereaved couples who believe they became parents through the love they gave their unborn or newborn children, no matter how briefly they knew them. We have tried to avoid sexist concepts by referring to each member of a couple as a "partner" instead of a "spouse," "husband" or "wife." We hope that whether you are female, male, single, married, gay or heterosexual, you will find solace within these pages. We also hope you will feel free to pass *A Silent Sorrow* along to a friend, relative or caregiver who you feel will find its stories and suggestions useful.

A Silent Sorrow was written to provide guidance, comfort and hope to all parents who have experienced an unwanted loss, whether in the first few weeks or final days of pregnancy, including those who have ended an impaired pregnancy. We refer to the "unborn or newborn baby" throughout the book because we felt compelled to acknowledge this common grief: No matter what the cause of their loss, bereaved parents mourn for their baby, who was dear to them. If the words we have chosen are imperfect, they still represent our sincere attempt to give expression to this universal sorrow.

In our first support groups, we talked about "getting over" the grief of pregnancy loss, of "completing" the mourning process and providing "closure" to our sorrow. Now we know that these terms are inaccurate, that our losses are integrated into our lives as we learn to accept our grief. Neither the sorrow nor the children lost are ever truly forgotten. Thank you, our readers, for being an ongoing part of this process.

INGRID KOHN   PERRY-LYNN MOFFITT
San Diego, California   New York City, New York
October 1999   October 1999

Acknowledgments

We wish to extend thanks jointly to a number of people for their part in the creation of this book: Heidi Freund, publishing director of Routledge, who recognized the importance of this topic and the need to update the book; Shea Settimi, who answered all questions eagerly and deftly; Liana Fredley and Krister Swartz, who guided this edition through its production; Sue Warga, who won our gratitude for her excellent copyediting; Isabelle Wilkins, who patiently and expertly advised us on the medical issues; Laurie Stone and Morris Bernstein, who gracefully but emphatically dragged us into the computer age; Margot Zobel, who solved every computer problem that cropped up along the way; Edward Rogoff, who managed to keep us communicating by e-mail; and Lee Feltman, who kept his advice clear and concise. A special thank you goes to the SHARE staff, Sister Jane Marie Lamb, the founder of SHARE, and Cathi Lammert, the current executive director of SHARE.

Health care professionals who offered invaluable expertise include Robert Barish, Ph.D.; Albert Feldman, M.S.W.; Joann Galst, Ph.D.; Laurie Gottlieb, Ph.D.; Madelyn Hoffman, M.S.W.; Michelle Marcus, Ph.D.; Barbara McGuire, M.S.W.; Linda McQuade, M.S.W.; Elyse Morgan, Ph.D.; Jill Nooney, M.S.W.; Lucille Perrotta, M.D.; Victor Reyniak, M.D.; Laura Robb, M.S.; Valerie Rubin, M.S.W.; Susan Schept, M.A.; and Allan Weingold, M.D.

Several members of the clergy contributed personal and professional wisdom, as well as the rituals presented in Appendix B: the Reverend Dr. Vienna Cobb Anderson; Rabbi Nina Beth Cardin; Rabbi Diane Cohen; Rabbi Stephanie Dickstein; Sister Mary Donohue, M.S., M.A.; the Reverend Catherine F. Garlid; Imam Yusuf Hasan; the Reverend Michael Mannion; the Reverend Walton D. Moffitt; Imam Feisal Abdul Rauf; the Reverend Carol

Ripley-Moffitt; the Reverend Matthew Ripley-Moffitt; Sister Mary Claire VanOrsdal, OSU, M.A.; and Rabbi Chaim Wasserman.

We have many friends, family members and colleagues who read various portions of the original and revised manuscripts. Through their expertise with writing or their own familiarity with grief and loss, their input and guidance proved invaluable: Helayne Baron, Linda Bernstein, Jane Brown, Becky Bunnell, Deborah Dokken, Arline Duker, Robin Fleischner, Holly Hafendorfer, Leah Garchik, Judith Garson, Paula Kascel, Holly Kromer, Dr. Jeri Little, Susan Marchese, Susan Margolis, Ethel Moffitt, Rick Moranis, Linda Myers, Dr. Barrie Raik, Dr. Stephen Rudin, Vicki Thorn, Janet Weingarden and Mitchell Weingarden.

Librarians were helpful in aiding and abetting our research, especially those at Barnard College, the New York Public Library, the New York Academy of Medicine, Columbia University and the McGill University Health and Sciences Library.

The Pregnancy Loss Support Program of the National Council of Jewish Women, New York Section, brought us together in 1983 in their first group for grieving parents and provided an entrée to many of the people we interviewed for this book. Without the National Council's commitment to helping bereaved parents, no matter what their religious background or financial means, this book could not have been written. Their dedication to seeing the program prosper has enabled it to serve more than two thousand individuals since its inception. A special thank-you goes to former staff member Rabbi Nina Beth Cardin, who conceived the idea and cofounded the Pregnancy Loss Support Program, to New York Section presidents Nancy Rubinger and Ernestine Rasch, to executive director Helen Caplin Heller and to staff and board members Amy Gershenson, Valerie Rubin, Renee Ritz, Ruth Hyman, Tem Weisman and Alicia Driks for their enthusiasm for this project and their hours of help.

We must also thank the dozens of lay counselors in the Pregnancy Loss Support Program who have devoted time and talent to handling phone counseling and leading support groups over the years. Through their dedication, they have helped hundreds of bereaved parents to heal emotionally.

We are grateful to each other for surviving this odd arrangement called coauthorship with a working relationship and friendship enriched through the mutual commitment to seeing this project completed, in spite of many competing demands.

Most important, we thank the mothers and fathers, grandparents and children who were willing to be interviewed for this book. Although their names have been changed to preserve their privacy, they have shared their stories, their sorrows, and their hopes so that you, our readers, could benefit from their experience, survival and growth. We hope you are as moved by their honesty and their courage as we have been.

We also have individual acknowledgments to make, which are listed separately.

INGRID

Special thanks to my family, Lois Kohn, Walter Kohn, Marilyn Kohn and Rosalind Dimenstein, for their sustaining enthusiasm and support throughout this project. I am grateful to Jill Borg Spitzer, M.S.W., and Louis Vener, M.A., for the flexibility and enthusiasm they have shown me at Jewish Family Service. I wish to express special appreciation to Professor Laurie Gottlieb for her professional and personal wisdom so generously shared, and to Virginia Walther, M.S.W., and Dr. Barbara Morrison, who first encouraged me to write. Most of all I am indebted to my daughters, Miriam and Tova Katz, for their enduring patience and preciousness.

PERRY-LYNN

I wish to extend my thanks to Kathleen Watts, for knowing I would write a book, any book, someday, and to Bill Tredway for knowing it would be this book, even before I did; to David Roberts and Carolyn Lewis, who taught me more about hoping and coping than any individuals deserved to; to Jerry Babbitt, who gave so much love and life to the world, particularly to his tiniest patients; to all of my friends who supported my involvement in this project and made it such a part of their lives, especially (in alphabetical order) Helayne Baron, Arline Duker, Dr. Perry Elfmont, Leah Garchik, Paula Kascel, Susan Margolis and Elyse Morgan; to Mary Pickering, Hank Lauricella and their children, Nicolas and Natalia, whose willingness to spend so much time with my children enabled me to finish much of the original draft of this book; to Deborah Dokken, Tom Tourish and their children, Abigail, Jonathan and Jeremy, whose love of life and determination to live it are a constant inspiration to me; to Dylan Siobhan Morrisey, for reminding me and so many others of why we continue to do this work; to Selma Rogoff and Walton and Ethel Moffitt, for loving all their grandchildren, even the ones they never met; to Edward Rogoff, my husband, who is always there for me, no matter what; to my children, David and Justine Rogoff, who have put all of my personal struggles into perspective and made them worthwhile, over and over and over again; and to all of my unborn children, whose brief lives continue to have a most profound effect on my own.

Foreword

I am honored to write the foreword to this second edition of *A Silent Sorrow: Pregnancy Loss,* a book I have turned to often in my practice. Years ago, few resources were available to obstetricians as we struggled to understand and console patients who experienced a miscarriage, stillbirth or newborn death. Eventually, bereaved mothers and fathers turned to each other for comfort, and pregnancy loss peer support groups proliferated. Grieving parents learned to speak about their right to mourn, and physicians, nurses, social workers and members of the clergy learned to listen. But this battle for awareness and understanding is never fully won. It requires constant vigilance and commitment. Fortunately, we have *A Silent Sorrow* to guide us.

We need a guidebook because as advances in science and technology continue to reveal the medical mechanics of pregnancy loss, our sense of compassion must keep pace. Too frequently miscarriages are still treated as matter-of-fact events that are "meant to be," rather than as the loss of a much-anticipated dream they actually are. Medicine rightfully proclaims that prenatal tests are diagnostic breakthroughs, but it needs to provide enough emotional support for parents as they face the agonizing choices these new techniques create. Artificial reproductive technologies have given thousands of families the gift of children, but have also increased the risk of multiple conceptions in a single pregnancy, leading to further medical complications and increasingly difficult parental decisions. When a pregnancy ends in tragedy, both medical professionals and bereaved couples often feel uneasy confronting the grief they endure together. *A Silent Sorrow* shows us how to understand each other as caregivers and as patients.

The second edition of *A Silent Sorrow* builds on the comprehensive foundation of the first. In addition to discussing the causes of pregnancy loss, the authors examine such important topics as the differing ways in which men and women grieve and the impact pregnancy loss can have on a couple's relationship. The book also explores how pregnancy loss can affect the entire family, from siblings to grandparents, as well as friendships and work relationships outside of home.

A Silent Sorrow clearly explains how each individual pregnancy loss occurs, within a framework I have termed the "triangle of caring." First of all, parents need to develop compassion for themselves as they move through their grief. The medical professionals who care for them must also understand and accept the process of mourning. And, thirdly, the surrounding community must learn to tolerate expressions of grief which so often seem to embarrass, rather than ennoble, us. *A Silent Sorrow* sets forth how essential this triangle of caring is to healthy grieving, which in turn leads to recovery and the ability to plan effectively for the future.

No matter what our medical advances may achieve, we will never completely eliminate the chance or the sorrow of pregnancy loss. Nor can obstetrical patients and their physicians ever be entirely prepared for the emotional, social and physiological impact a pregnancy loss can have on their lives. But *A Silent Sorrow* enables us to find a path through our shared grief to a destination of both healing and hope.

> Michael R. Berman, M.D.
> Clinical Professor of Obstetrics and Gynecology
> Yale University School of Medicine
> New Haven, Connecticut
> May 20, 1999

Dr. Berman created the Hygeia Foundation for Perinatal Loss and Bereavement, whose mission is to institute international multimedia resource centers for pregnancy loss in medically and economically underserved communities. His most recent collection of poems is included in his forthcoming book, Parenthood Lost, A Gathering of Hope.

Section I

The Grief of Pregnancy Loss

Parents who endure any form of pregnancy loss share a common bond: They have all lost the reality of bringing a new baby into the world. Yet each bereaved parent suffers individually and must cope with the present sorrow as well as anxieties about the future.

Pregnancy loss and infant death have been with us since the birth of humankind. However, it has been only in recent years that we have devoted much medical scrutiny and emotional honesty to this frequent and sorrowful event. In this book, the term "pregnancy loss" encompasses the entire spectrum of misfortune during pregnancy, including miscarriage, ectopic pregnancy, losses following medical crises, stillbirth, newborn death and ending a pregnancy when the baby's or mother's life or health is compromised. The term embraces all losses that occur whenever a wanted pregnancy has ended.

Section I examines the grief you may feel as a mother or father when you suffer a pregnancy loss. By exploring these different responses to your loss, you can begin to find solace and the will to face your future again with hope.

I

When an Unborn
or Newborn Baby Dies

Experiencing a pregnancy loss can make you feel as if your world has turned upside down in the space of a few hours. You had expected a new life and instead were confronted with death. Whether you suffered a full-term loss or a first-trimester miscarriage, the hopes and plans you had for your future and your baby were wrenched from you. Instead of feeling expectant and special, you may be left with a sense of frustration and even failure. Your life and goals may seem totally beyond your control. The love and hopes you had nurtured for your baby have turned into grief.

Reminders of your tragedy may be all around you. If you experienced an early loss, the unworn maternity clothes hanging in your closet can reflect your shattered dreams. If you suffered a full-term loss, friends and relatives may have already sent you baby presents. Perhaps you had moved to a larger home or set up a room for the baby, and your loss renders all your plans meaningless. With any pregnancy loss, you may suddenly find yourself painfully jealous of other expectant couples, even if they are close friends or family. Loved ones who were caring and attentive while you were pregnant may suddenly avoid you after your loss, or say things that are well-meaning but hurtful.

No matter what kind of pregnancy loss you experienced, you are probably unprepared for the anguish you feel. This sorrow may take a long time to heal, as you have lost a baby who was a real part of you and your hoped-for future.

BONDING WITH YOUR UNBORN BABY
Of all life events, having and raising children are among the most significant. You may have taken for granted from childhood that you would have a family of your own someday. No matter what your career

3

orientation may be, your womanhood or manhood can be powerfully affirmed by bearing or fathering a child. Pregnancy and parenthood are passages into adulthood that bestow a special status on you within both your family and your community. Pregnancy even represents a chance to overcome mortality, as you contemplate the continuation of your family line.

Until recently, popular wisdom held that parents were incapable of caring deeply about their unborn baby because they didn't really know their child. But in the 1970s two pediatricians, John Kennell and Marshall Klause, showed through their research that parents' emotional attachment, or bonding, actually begins early in the pregnancy.

Perhaps the baby became real for you the moment the conception was confirmed. As your pregnancy progressed, the baby's place in your family may have become more firmly established. You may have wondered whom the baby would look like and imagined your child in your extended family, playing with cousins and grandparents. You may have dreamed about the baby's future, wondering if your child would go into your profession or attend the same schools.

Your attachment to your unborn baby might have been enhanced by medical technology, which allowed you to hear a heartbeat ten to twelve weeks after conception and to see your unborn baby by sonogram as early as seven or eight weeks into the pregnancy. If you had prenatal genetic tests, you may have discovered the baby's sex and may have even named your child. Experiencing the pregnancy in these personal ways can make your unborn child very real and dear to you.

Even if your pregnancy was unplanned, you still had a relationship to your child and will probably go through a grieving period. Mourning can be especially difficult under these circumstances, because you may feel burdened with guilt as well as sorrow.

GRIEVING FOR YOUR BABY

Grief is a healthy human response that helps us cope with crisis and loss. If sorrow, anger, jealousy and resentment are not expressed, they don't disappear. Instead they merely go underground to resurface in more debilitating forms later. Grief is a natural reaction to your loss, but if you are unprepared for its power, you can become frightened and overwhelmed. When allowed to run its course, your grief will gradually lessen.

Mothers and fathers often experience and grieve a pregnancy loss differently. The mother usually forms an earlier and stronger bond than the father because she physically carries the baby. When the pregnancy ends in loss, a mother typically grieves more intensely and for a longer time. A father can also grieve deeply, although he may hide his emotions because he feels socially constrained or wants to appear "strong" for his partner.

As you become acquainted with your grief, try to be patient. The mourning process is very individual, and it takes time. Expressing your feelings about your loss is an important part of grieving. You may be helped by having someone to talk or cry with, whether it is your partner, another family member, a friend, a member of the clergy, a psychotherapist or other bereaved parents in a support group. If you wish, try keeping a journal, tape-recording your thoughts or writing a letter or poem to your baby. You may also want to read comforting literature, such as a pregnancy loss support program newsletter. Expressing your sorrow does not lessen your loss, but it can help you mourn and allow you to heal emotionally.

Respect your own inclinations about whether to put away baby things yourself or have others do this for you. If you feel a religious ritual would be meaningful, consider planning a ceremony to mark your loss, even if it is a simple service at home just for your immediate family. Try to pamper yourself for a while. Ask for help with household chores or with your other children, and avoid social situations with infants or expectant couples until you are ready to handle them.

Grief is hard emotional work and is physically depleting, so try to eat regular, balanced meals and schedule some form of exercise every day. Get lots of rest, even if you have trouble sleeping. As tempting as sleeping pills, antianxiety medication or alcohol may be, avoid them, since they can impede the grieving process. Alcohol in particular is a depressant and will only make you feel worse.

If you cannot sleep, eat or take care of daily tasks, if your upset is not improving or if you begin to feel worse several weeks after your loss, consider seeing a psychotherapist for bereavement counseling and a physician for a medication consultation. Suitable antidepressant medication, in conjunction with counseling, can provide a degree of relief and give you the emotional and physical strength to grieve. Antidepressant medication usually takes about three weeks to take full effect, and doctors most often prescribe it for at least six months. Please refer to Appendix D for help in finding a qualified psychotherapist.

Although you may long for a change in your life immediately after your loss, you should keep in mind that grief impairs judgment. If at all possible, avoid making major decisions, such as a job change or move, until both you and your partner feel more emotionally settled, usually about a year after your loss. With time, as you mourn, you should begin to feel better and to look forward to your future with hope.

THE PHASES OF GRIEF

If you could step back from your grief, you would see it as a process with different phases that can last many months and change over time. No two people will respond to a loss in the same way. People grieve at different rates and intensities. They may skip some of the phases or go through them in a different or overlapping order.

At the moment of your tragedy, you probably felt initial shock and denial, followed by acute emotional distress, including anxiety, guilt and anger. As the grieving process continues through an intense stage called grief work, you may experience feelings of ardent envy and yearning for your baby.

No matter what form your grief takes, you will eventually sense a gradual lessening of emotional pain as you come to terms with your loss. This final phase of mourning is often referred to as grief "resolution," which some bereavement counselors prefer to call grief "integration."

Whatever phase of grief you are in right now, you will probably go through various other stages in the months ahead. Phases of grief can pass and then return again. Although you will grieve in your own unique way and your grief will have its own life, rhythm and eventual integration, you may find it helpful to learn more about the typical phases of grief and the feelings each may bring.

Initial Shock

When you lose your pregnancy, you may cry uncontrollably at first and then experience emotional shock and denial, feeling numb and detached, unable to believe that your baby has died. Emotional shock is probably a self-protective response that allows you to mobilize internal strength to cope with your loss. It may last several hours or days, or it may come and go over a few weeks.

During the phase of initial shock, you may feel you are in the midst of a bad dream from which you hope to awaken to find a healthy pregnancy or a live baby. Although you probably remember exactly how you learned about your loss, you may not recall other conversations or events that took place while you were in this initial state of grief.

Adam experienced shock as soon as his wife's doctor diagnosed their baby's severe genetic defect two weeks before her due date:

> He told us that our baby was anencephalic, that she didn't have a fully formed skull or brain and would not survive long after birth. Lisa shrieked and broke into tears, crying hysterically. She fell into my arms, and I started crying with her. Everything we had hoped for in the nine months was taken away in that split second.
>
> While we made the arrangements to have a funeral and bury the baby, my attitude was one of total shock. And that time period between our daughter's death and when she was buried is a complete blank for us both.

If you suffered a loss early in your pregnancy, you can feel equally stunned, even if only a few days or weeks have elapsed since you

learned about the conception. The baby you had just begun to anticipate is suddenly no longer there. Being jolted from the elation of the
initial news to the sorrow of the loss can be staggering at a time when
you already feel vulnerable from a new pregnancy.

Ellen was in the ninth week of her first pregnancy when she awoke in
the middle of the night, bleeding profusely. As her husband searched
the early-morning streets for a taxi to take her to the hospital, she
waited alone in the lobby of their apartment building:

> At that point I was just astounded by what was happening. Even the ride to
> the hospital, with the cabdriver rushing through red lights, seemed surreal. It
> wasn't until the next morning, after the miscarriage was over, that I fully real-
> ized we were not going to be bringing a baby home.

A mother who experiences a midterm or late pregnancy loss can
develop disturbing symptoms during this initial stage of emotional
shock. She may imagine she hears the hungry wails of her baby, a phe-
nomenon called "phantom crying," or she may feel a kicking sensation
in her womb after delivery. The bereaved mother knows these sensations are impossible, and she may wonder if she is losing her mind, but
they are natural reactions and should subside with time.

Dr. Kenneth Kellner, an obstetrician who has researched the needs
of bereaved parents, found that mothers who heard phantom crying or
imagined the baby kicking usually stopped having these sensations
when they were allowed to see, hold and say good-bye to their babies.
Some caregivers have also noted that if a mother no longer has these
options, she usually stops hearing phantom crying when she can at
least see her baby's photograph.

You may find that episodes of emotional numbness and denial come
and go, but they will diminish with time, especially if you are given the
chance to grieve your loss openly.

Anticipatory Grief

If you learn that your baby has died before the actual miscarriage or
birth, you may experience a phase of sorrow called anticipatory grief,
in which you begin to mourn while the baby is still in the womb. Yet,
even as you start to mourn, you may be unable to believe fully that the
pregnancy has ended until it is physically over. One woman, whose
baby stopped growing at twelve weeks, had a dilatation and curettage,
or D&C, to remove the pregnancy. "I was in mourning from the
moment I knew the baby had died," she explained. "But it really hit me
after the D&C. Then it was final."

If your baby was born gravely ill or dying, you probably began to
grieve when you learned about your child's condition. If prenatal

testing indicated a severe abnormality in your unborn baby and you decided to end the pregnancy, you probably began to mourn immediately. As you awaited the procedure, your feelings of anger, anxiety and depression likely intensified.

With the pregnancy finally over and your remnants of hope gone, you may feel a confusing mixture of sadness at the loss and relief that your uncertainty has ended. As the reality of your loss sinks in, you can begin to mourn fully.

Acute Grief

As shock and denial recede, the enormity of your tragedy may hit you full force, plunging you into the phase of mourning called acute grief. This emotional and physical upheaval can be all-consuming and may last from several days to several weeks. Crying jags and nightmares are common during acute grief, as are physical complaints such as insomnia, extreme fatigue, digestive problems, tightness in the throat and shortness of breath.

Some parents develop symptoms of a severe stress reaction during the stage of acute grief. They respond to their pregnancy loss with the same intensity as do victims of physical and emotional traumas, such as fires or plane crashes. These parents may relive the events in great detail, have recurrent nightmares and suffer extreme anxiety. It is vital for parents to have outlets for their feelings and fears, so that their symptoms are expressed and do not persist and become chronic.

During acute grief you are still emotionally raw from your loss and may find you cannot function well. You may be unable to concentrate on even simple tasks and may feel little energy for your usual activities, including work, care of your other children or maintaining your personal appearance.

After Sally's first baby was stillborn, all she could manage to do was watch TV and lie in bed:

> I wasn't able to do anything else. We cut ourselves off from others, folded into ourselves. I wouldn't eat, wouldn't get dressed, couldn't function. I couldn't even get out of bed to make myself breakfast! This lasted three or four weeks.

You may find that all you think about is your pregnancy loss as you review in your mind all the details, over and over again. You may also experience a sense of failure. As one woman who had two consecutive miscarriages put it, "Everyone can have babies, and I can't. I feel it is a terrible defect in me."

The overwhelming emotions of acute grief can be frightening. At times you may feel so upset and out of control, you may begin to wonder if you are losing your mind. Most likely you are experiencing a normal, albeit distressing, aspect of acute grief.

Amy had an early miscarriage, which she never mourned, followed quickly by a subsequent pregnancy, which ended in another early loss. "There were a few times after the second loss when I felt like I was going crazy," she said. "I would sit on my bed and stare for hours and cry uncontrollably. It was scary."

Many bereaved parents have outbursts of irrational anger that can stun them because it feels so foreign. No matter what caused your loss, you may condemn yourself, your partner, your doctor, or even God. This struggle to comprehend your sorrow by assigning responsibility usually has nothing to do with any real fault; it is an understandable attempt to make sense out of a senseless tragedy.

Hilary conceived twins in her first pregnancy and felt fine until she noticed slight bleeding in her sixth month. When she learned at the hospital that her cervix had opened and the delivery could not be stopped, she became furious with the doctor who told her the babies could not be saved:

> The doctor said, "There is nothing we can do. One baby is in the birth canal." I hated this man. I lashed out at him every time he came into the delivery room. I thought, "Maybe he's wrong." I needed someone to be angry at.

Some parents have transient thoughts of wanting to die during acute grief, as if it were a desperate expression of wishing to rejoin their baby. Although these thoughts are frightening, they are not unusual. It is very important, however, for bereaved parents to share these feelings with a supportive family member or friend. If troubling thoughts continue, or if you feel you might act on them, it is crucial to seek psychotherapy immediately.

You may also feel angry at how unfair your loss is. You may read about neglected children, or unfit parents, and feel the injustice of not having the child you want so badly while others have children they don't seem to want. As one bereaved father admitted:

> I had a lot of hostility. I felt deprived of my baby and of fatherhood. Looking at other people who had what I didn't have made me wonder, "Why can this idiot have a family and children and I can't?" This was a question I asked myself a lot.

Guilt is another powerful and nearly universal reaction to a pregnancy loss, and you may instinctively blame yourself for your baby's death. You may wonder, for example, if your loss is a punishment for not planning your pregnancy or for ending a previous pregnancy. You may worry that ambivalence about being pregnant, or your preference for a child of one sex or the other, caused the loss. Wishes and ambivalence have never caused a pregnancy loss, but these worries can torment you.

Stuart, whose wife experienced an early loss in their first—and unplanned—pregnancy, recalled. "We were young, we hadn't been married very long, and we were worried that we might have caused the loss because we hadn't wanted the baby enough," he said.

In struggling to comprehend your loss, you may fault yourself for taking a trip or having sexual relations immediately before your pregnancy ended, neither of which is likely to cause harm. Your feelings of self-blame may be so strong that you become convinced you should be punished in some way.

Sally intentionally refused medication through the painful delivery of her stillborn son because she felt she deserved to suffer after his death was confirmed. Only later did her husband, Roger, learn her reasons:

> The labor took a long time, even with Pitocin, and Sally was in a lot of pain. The doctor said, "Don't be a hero, take something for the pain," but she refused. Later she told me she felt she had to punish herself. If I had known that, I would have demanded she take some medication. It seemed so unfair for her to be blaming herself like that.

It is natural to wonder if you could have somehow protected your pregnancy. Unfounded guilt can intensify, especially if your need to grieve and talk about your loss goes unacknowledged. While feelings of guilt are common, it is highly unlikely that anything you did or neglected to do caused your pregnancy loss. It is crucial for you to raise any questions with your doctor, because the medical facts are often reassuring.

Ellen was sure she had caused her first miscarriage when she started bleeding after vacuuming her apartment. "I was relieved when I went in for an examination," she recalled, "and my doctor confirmed that the baby had died a couple of weeks earlier."

A mother who experiences a loss from a medical condition she didn't know about, such as cervical incompetence or an undiagnosed hormonal imbalance, may feel guilty that her body did not sustain the pregnancy. It is important for her not to fault herself for something neither she nor her doctor knew to prevent. Finding out what precautions to take during any subsequent pregnancy can help her guilt feelings subside.

Guilt can also be a major source of distress if you underwent prenatal testing and chose to end an abnormal pregnancy. No matter how strongly you feel that you made the right choice, being forced to choose places an additional burden on you. This is a particularly agonizing experience, which is explored more fully in Chapter 8, "Prenatal Diagnosis and the Burden of Choice."

Parents who engaged in activities or who were exposed to substances that can actually harm a pregnancy may feel additional guilt. A man may feel responsible if he discovers his exposure to toxic substances at work could have caused his partner's miscarriages. Similarly, a woman who smoked heavily during her pregnancy and lost the baby due to prematurity may worry that her smoking was a contributing factor.

If you feel responsible for a loss because your baby was exposed to harmful substances, your guilt can paralyze you emotionally and prevent you from grieving. Try to make any necessary changes that will allow you to take realistic precautions for your next pregnancy. It is important to realize you don't have to handle this difficult situation by yourself. Psychotherapy can enable you to make changes and to forgive yourself for dangers you were unaware of before the loss, or for behaviors that were out of your control.

Within two or three months of your loss, you may find your physical and emotional turmoil begin to subside. You no longer constantly picture the details of your loss, as you did in the early weeks. You might be able to resume work and household responsibilities; perhaps you cry less often, and your eating and sleeping patterns become more regular. You may still feel waves of anger, but you lose your temper less often. However, it may seem that you are merely "going through the motions" rather than being fully involved with your activities. Preoccupation with the loss and feelings of depression can continue to dominate your life.

Unfortunately, you may find that many people expect you to be over your grief within a couple of months. They may interpret your return to work or other activities as a sign that you are feeling fine. You might encounter remarks such as "Put the loss behind you and get on with your life" or "It's been three months already. Why are you still depressed?"

Although intense feelings of grief are usually less constant and debilitating within several weeks after a loss, waves of emotion can continue for months and may last a year or more. The lack of understanding from others may add to the isolation you already feel, a topic explored more fully in Chapter 11, "The Response of Your Family and Friends."

Grief Work

As the overpowering emotions of acute grief subside, you start to function a little better, but your heart is still with your baby and nothing seems quite right. You have trouble focusing for any length of time, and you probably feel less pleasure and interest in relationships and activities you treasured before. Instead, you are overcome by longing for your baby and by envy of other new mothers and fathers. These emotions are part of the stage of mourning called grief work.

Grief work is aptly named. It is hard and it is exhausting. During this phase of bereavement, you may experience particularly strong feelings of envy. Suddenly it seems as if babies and pregnant women are every-where, triggering an immediate, gut response of both jealousy and hurt. "At the beginning it seemed that every time I turned on the TV someone was having a baby—on the news, on shows," admitted Maggie. "The world was full of pregnant women. Everything reminded me of the baby." Even if you had never paid attention to children before, you may find you have become painfully aware of babies everywhere you go. Bennett, who lost premature twins, remarked, "Every place I went I saw twins, which never happened before."

You may be especially troubled by your envy because it does not fit your self-image and can alienate you from friends or relatives you care about. You may criticize yourself for feeling angry with a pregnant sis-ter-in-law or for avoiding friends with new babies. It is important for you to realize that most bereaved parents have these feelings. Jealousy of expectant parents after a loss is no reflection on your character, but rather an understandable and temporary aspect of grief.

You cannot avoid seeing babies and pregnant couples on the street sometimes. But you can take care of yourself by explaining to friends or relatives who are either pregnant or new parents that you cannot see them for a while because of your loss. If they care about you, they will respect your wishes.

It is also natural to feel vulnerable during this phase of grief, con-stantly fearing that other loved ones will come to harm. You may become exquisitely aware of the fragility of life and overreact to the smallest challenges.

Christine's anxiety seeped into other areas of her life after she suf-fered a full-term stillbirth:

> At first I was afraid whenever someone left the house that they would die, both children and husband. I felt overprotective. It was a real struggle to let my son even ride his bike to school.

During the stage of grief work, you might find yourself searching and yearning for your baby weeks or months after the loss. You may constantly imagine what you would now be doing with the baby and become uncomfortably aware of every infant you encounter who was born near your own due date. Longing for your child can be a way of wishing to undo the finality of the loss. This happened to Hilary, whose premature twins died at birth:

> For a long time I would fantasize about the babies, putting them into situa-tions. I would go into a grocery store and think, "I couldn't fit a double stroller in here." When driving, I would think the twins should be in the backseat.

Once on a business trip I told a fellow passenger I had twins. I'm really embarrassed about this. I engaged in this fantasy and pretended they had lived. It was
so nice. The man was kind, and I knew I would never see him again.

Yearning for your baby can also take the form of longing to become
pregnant again quickly, which is a natural response to the void created
by a loss. But when either you or your partner desperately wants to conceive again, you may be wishing that the loss could be undone rather
than feeling ready for another pregnancy. One woman conveyed her
urgent desire for a baby after two miscarriages when she told her husband, "I have waited for such a long time to have kids. I have to have
one! Get me one!"

While the wish to replace the baby is understandable, it is important
for you to mourn your loss before embarking on a new pregnancy. If
you conceive right after a loss, you may be unable to grieve, because
mourning your loss and bonding with a new pregnancy are demanding
and opposite emotional tasks, difficult to do at the same time. If you
give yourself time to grieve your loss, you will eventually realize that
another pregnancy will not replace the baby who died, enabling you to
welcome the baby who follows as a new and unique individual. You may
read more about pregnancy following a loss in Chapter 16, "Becoming
Pregnant Again."

Integration of Your Grief

A time will eventually come when you begin to feel true relief and are
no longer constantly reminded of your loss. In the course of remembering your tragedy, you will gradually come to terms with it, a process
that can take months or even longer. "Time helped," recalled Bennett.
"It took at least one year before we could talk about the loss without
getting all emotional."

Once time has passed, you may start to feel as if a weight has been
lifted from you. You find your appetite and sleep patterns are returning
to normal. You may take renewed pleasure in family, work and recreation and may once again enjoy socializing. You can expect to continue
thinking about your loss, but daily activities and plans for your future
will become important as well. The painful emotions of mourning will
reemerge from time to time, but the feelings may be short-lived and
less intense.

You may experience guilt as you start to feel better, as if grief were
loyalty to your baby and relief tantamount to abandonment or betrayal
of your child. It is important to realize that you can let go of your pain
and still be faithful to the special place that baby has in your heart.

Your loss may become more integrated into your life only when you

become a parent, through either childbirth or adoption. While the
new baby cannot replace the one you lost, the demands and pleasures
of having an infant, and your affirmation as a parent, may help you
continue the healing process that began with active mourning. But
memories of the pregnancy loss remain. Joel found this to be true
when his healthy son was born:

> Everything has changed for me since Sam was born. The pain of losing our
> daughter diminished more. However, there are times when I see Sam and
> think of our daughter. It is bittersweet.

Couples who do not have the solace of becoming parents may need
to find other ways to resolve their feelings of loss. They face special
emotional challenges that are discussed in Chapter 15, "Pregnancy
Loss and Infertility: A Twofold Sorrow."

Anniversary Reactions

Anniversaries of the due date, birth or death of your baby often bring
on a brief resurgence of grief, known as an "anniversary reaction."
Other reminders of the baby, including another pregnancy and birth,
can have the same effect. "I still cry around her birthday," explained
Lisa three years after her infant daughter died from congenital defects.
"I cried for her when my son was born, and at Christmas. Sometimes I
cry when I see baby things in stores, tiny dresses for little girls. Things
like that."

As an anniversary approaches, you may become depressed, tearful
and preoccupied, much as you felt immediately after your loss. An
anniversary reaction can be disconcerting, especially if you are unprepared for it. "I was doing much better," said one woman. "Now I am irritable and tearful again."

If you suffered an early loss, you may experience two anniversary
reactions in a year, one at the due date and the other a year after the
loss. Karen remembered all five due dates from each of her first-
trimester losses. "I think of the babies as each due date comes and
goes," she admitted. "I think of how old those babies would be now and
how close or far apart they would be in relationship to my two children." Most often, once the anniversary has passed, the upset also sub-
sides and you again feel better.

GRIEVING LOSS IN A MULTIPLE PREGNANCY

Parents develop special grieving issues when they experience a multiple
gestation in which one or more babies die spontaneously or through a
procedure called pregnancy reduction. Multiple pregnancies are statistically more prone to certain problems, including genetic abnormalities

and a circulatory anomaly called twin-to-twin transfusion syndrome. Occasionally an early sonogram indicates that there is more than one amniotic sac, but one fetus disappears as the pregnancy progresses—a spontaneous event referred to as vanishing-twin syndrome. Up to one-half of all pregnancies that begin with twins result in a single birth.

If you experienced a loss that involved a surviving baby or babies, your love and wish to care for the living babies, and the infants' demands on you, make it especially difficult to mourn the ones who died. Kristen Swanson-Kauffman, R.N., explains how confusing and ambivalent new parenthood can be in this situation, especially when it occurs at birth:

> Congratulations and condolences, birth and death announcements, baptismal gowns and caskets are all a part of the first few postpartum weeks. While trying to attach to the surviving [babies], parents are also experiencing the need to grieve the dead [infants].

If you are the parent of a surviving baby or babies, you may be confused and angered by people who tell you that you should be happy that some of your babies lived. You may also find you cannot grieve effectively because you are caring for the surviving infants. "I feel I'm in mourning all the time," explained Nora after one of her twins was stillborn. "But I can't really let myself mourn because I have my son to tend to."

Special grieving problems continue for you as your baby grows. Every joy for the surviving babies, every milestone and holiday is a happy occasion with a shadow cast over it because of the absent siblings.

If you lost one or more babies during a multiple pregnancy, you need and deserve support with the constant challenges you face. Psychotherapy and bereavement support groups can help. For support during and following a pregnancy reduction procedure, please read Chapter 8, "Prenatal Diagnosis and the Burden of Choice." There is a publication entitled *Our Newsletter*, issued by the Center for Loss in Multiple Births, that offers specific advice and information for loss in a multiple pregnancy. Please see Appendix D for more information.

IF YOU HAVE DIFFICULTY MOURNING

It is natural to grieve after a pregnancy loss, but it is not altogether automatic. Mourning can be either supported or inhibited by your own tendencies to express or contain feelings. Your ability to grieve can also be greatly affected by the reactions of others. If you do not mourn effectively, your grief may go underground and interfere with your mood, relationships or functioning for a long time after your loss.

If you fail to grieve, the symptoms of mourning can become chronic.

Feelings of depression and worthlessness as well as nightmares or over-activity can continue for many months without improvement. If you become chronically bereaved, you may experience persistent crying spells, irritability or anxiety, and you may sleep and eat too little or too much. Unrelenting grief can lead to a breakdown in your relationship with your partner, including sexual problems, and it can leave you functioning poorly at work or unable to enjoy recreation. You may even develop stress-related medical problems.

Symptoms that persist for many months without improving significantly probably indicate that your grief is blocked. This can happen if you do not have outlets to express your grief. You may even be unaware that your troubling symptoms are related to your pregnancy loss, because you have suppressed your thoughts and feelings.

Laurel delivered a very premature baby in the hospital, but no staff were in the room with her at the time. After the birth, a nurse arrived and removed the infant without speaking to Laurel or showing her the baby. The nursing staff continued to avoid her until her discharge.

In retrospect, Laurel realized it took her a long time to begin to grieve because of the lack of support in the hospital. "I went home feeling like a freak because no one wanted to talk to me," she explained. "The hospital tried to make it all go away. I kept feeling that was what I had to do: make it all go away."

You can also develop a chronic grief response if you had a midterm or late pregnancy loss but did not see your baby or say good-bye. Ruth had suffered an early miscarriage and then a pregnancy loss at five months. When her second loss occurred, she did not look at her baby, and she plunged into a busy work schedule right afterward:

> After losing the baby, I thought I was doing okay and threw myself back into my old routine. But then I started having sudden crying spells and angry outbursts and I didn't know where the feelings were coming from. Then I realized things *weren't* okay, and I tracked down the hospital social worker, who told me about a pregnancy loss support group. I finally allowed myself to grieve.

With the help of the group, Ruth's suppressed feelings surfaced. She needed to grieve her losses and to mourn not having seen or held her baby. She also had to deal with worries about having a successful pregnancy in the future. As she and her husband talked out their feelings in the group and at home, Ruth's crying jags and temper outbursts subsided and eventually stopped.

Another circumstance that can complicate grief occurs when the pregnancy loss rekindles sadness over an earlier emotional trauma, such as the previous death of a loved one. Caroline plummeted into a severe depression when she lost a premature baby boy and became terrified that her healthy older son would also die. Her depression improved when she sought psychotherapy and worked through old fears stemming from her childhood, when her younger brother had died in a drowning accident. "The loss of my baby son brought back my childhood nightmare," she recalled, "that little boys die."

If you think you might be experiencing a form of chronic grief, seek additional help. You need an environment in which you can safely express your sorrow, whether by opening communication with your partner, by joining a bereavement support group, by engaging in psychotherapy or by a combination of these outlets. You may need to talk about earlier sorrows that have resurfaced as a result of your pregnancy loss. With time and adequate understanding, you can be helped to tolerate your grief and integrate your loss.

PREGNANCY LOSS CHANGES YOU

You may discover that your pregnancy loss leaves a permanent mark on you. In addition to the sadness, you may notice other changes that are positive and meaningful, such as a greater sensitivity to others who experience a loss, or a deeper appreciation for loved ones. You may reevaluate your personal goals and make a career change, or you might make new commitments to community responsibilities you feel are worthwhile.

Susannah found that she experienced many changes after her miscarriages and the subsequent birth of her son:

> A loss changes you, it touches you forever, and you never forget it. It makes you appreciate your children more. Having a child is so much more important than other things in life.
>
> Even going back to school to get my degree in early childhood education is a gift from my "other children" and grew out of my losses. People who haven't experienced losses just never really understand this. It has been a real character—well, addition, for lack of another word. I am more forgiving of people.

As time passes and as the more active stages of mourning diminish, you will likely feel renewed energy and interest in yourself, your family, and your daily activities. But the loss remains a permanent part of your life and history, and you will always remember your baby.

KEY POINTS TO HELP YOU GRIEVE

Grief is a natural and necessary response to your pregnancy loss and is a physically and emotionally exhausting process. It is important that you give yourself permission to grieve and that you have adequate support during this difficult time. The grieving process takes longer than most people expect, and it is often six months to one year or more before the pain and preoccupation with the loss subside.

Here are some suggestions to help you manage the painful and sometimes overwhelming emotions of grief:

- Express your grief by talking, remembering or crying over your loss. Try to find understanding listeners—a loved one, a friend, a member of the clergy, a psychotherapist or a support group. Write down or tape-record your thoughts and feelings, or compose a letter or poem to your baby.
- Take care of your health, as grief is physically depleting. Eat regular, balanced meals, avoid alcohol and take medication only under a doctor's supervision. Maintain your usual rest patterns even if you have trouble sleeping, and try to get some exercise daily.
- Postpone any major decisions, such as a job change or move, for about one year after a loss, if at all possible. The emotional turmoil of grief may make a change seem appealing, but grief impairs judgment, and it is preferable to avoid significant changes until you feel better.
- Read comforting literature such as support program newsletters or poetry by other bereaved parents. Parents who have lost a multiple pregnancy, please refer to the resources for multiple gestations listed in Appendix D.
- Consider bereavement counseling if you need more support than you can find informally, or if your depression is worsening or not improving several weeks after your loss. It is vital to locate a psychotherapist who understands pregnancy loss. For further help, see Appendix D.
- Be patient. Gradually your mood should improve and you will be able to feel pleasure without feeling guilty. You will eventually enjoy increased interest and energy in your daily activities and relationships.

2

The Mother's Experience

When your pregnancy ended in loss, both you and the baby's father grieved. However, your experience of the loss, as well as your emotional expression, are probably quite different from his. You physically carried this baby and felt the major hormonal changes that follow a loss. Moreover, your deep-seated childhood expectations of becoming a mother may have nurtured your dreams of parenthood for years. You have to deal with the loss of those childhood dreams, at least for now, as well as the emotional and physical impact of losing your expected baby. Because of your unique relationship to the pregnancy, you will probably grieve more openly and for a longer time than the baby's father.

FACTORS THAT AFFECT YOUR GRIEF

Physical, hormonal and emotional factors all contribute to the deep sorrow and the relatively lengthy grieving period you may experience following your pregnancy loss. You physically carried and nurtured your baby from the moment of conception and probably bonded to the pregnancy in both conscious and unconscious ways. You may not have realized that your body responded to your conception immediately with major hormonal shifts, so you were probably unprepared for the sudden physical changes triggered by your loss, even an early miscarriage. Your morning sickness suddenly disappeared, your breasts were no longer tender and that mysterious and wonderful glow people may have mentioned to you had gone from your face.

The further along you were in your pregnancy, the more complicated your body's response to your loss. These changes may continue for weeks afterward and may be associated with such real events as your milk letting down—a devastating reminder of the absent baby—or the onset of your first menstrual period following your loss.

These abrupt hormonal shifts are the same ones that often provoke normal postpartum "blues" following the delivery of a healthy baby. When your loss occurred, your body went through the same sudden reduction in hormones, but there was neither a baby to rejoice in nor happy relatives and friends to offer congratulations and help. As Lisa recalled following the birth of her full-term baby who lived only a few hours, "I remember standing in the shower when my milk came in and I just stood there crying. The baby had died, but my body didn't know it."

Your desire to nurture and parent your baby, the bond that was built hour by hour as you felt your growing baby's presence, continues after your loss as a bond of grief. You may feel you have lost not only your baby but also part of yourself. Your sense of emptiness can be especially overwhelming if you have no other children, because then you have lost the dream of motherhood, at least for a time, as well as this baby.

When you suffer this double loss, of baby and motherhood, a sense of failure can spill over into other areas of your life and affect your entire self-concept. Natalie had two early miscarriages and then a loss at nineteen weeks:

> I feel constantly preoccupied by the losses. I have this yearning for mother-hood. I have this feeling of deprivation, inadequacy, sadness. I need constant reminders that this doesn't declare me incompetent as a person because I am not a mother. The desire, the wanting to have a baby and not being able to have one, is excruciating.

If your loss is made worse by a sense of failure, try to focus on the ways you took care of your unborn baby. Perhaps you gave up smoking or alcohol when you decided to conceive, or as soon as you learned you were pregnant. You may have improved your diet or sought the best obstetrical care possible. If you endured a medical crisis, your sacrifices of time and effort to maintain the pregnancy may have been enormous. Even though you couldn't prevent your loss, the commitment you gave your pregnancy is proof that you were a good and loving mother to your unborn child.

You can help nurture a positive sense of yourself after your loss by concentrating on your strengths. Even small accomplishments can bolster your self-confidence without denying your need to grieve and may allow feelings of loss, not failure, to come forward. Reread a work report you are proud of, or have lunch with a friend. Try to draw on your talents, even though doing so may seem frivolous at first, and take the time to reach out to others.

After her fourth miscarriage, one mother recalled writing a series of letters to friends she had not been in touch with in several months:

I pride myself on my letter writing and found that sending the letters had a very positive effect on my mood. I didn't even mention my most recent loss in all the letters. I wasn't looking for sympathy. I was looking more for a small feeling of fulfillment that involved people I loved.

Taking the time to pamper yourself can also help you maintain a positive attitude toward yourself. If you usually wear makeup and enjoy dressing nicely, try to continue taking care of your appearance. Treat yourself to a facial or a massage. Think about simple activities that have given you satisfaction in the past, such as going to the movies, baking or exercising, and do your best to make time for them. Positive outlets and activities are important aspects of self-care for you to maintain following your loss.

FEELING YOU FAILED THE BABY'S FATHER

Both you and the baby's father may have planned to share the responsibility for the upbringing of your children. The significant changes in societal expectations about child rearing and sexual role models that came about in the 1960s and 1970s may have had a profound effect on your decision to adjust each of your careers to make room for a baby in your lives.

Yet like many women, you may have found that pregnancy conferred on you a special status. No matter how equally you and your partner shared decisions about having and raising a family, you may have felt very special as you carried, nurtured and felt love for your child, experiencing at the same time a deepening bond between you and the baby's father.

With the loss of your pregnancy, you may miss this special bond. Julia and Ian had one little boy and were expecting their second child when Julia's uterus ruptured almost at term, causing the infant's death. Although her life had been endangered by her medical condition, she still felt guilty because she thought she had deprived her husband of a second child. "I feel terrible," she explained. "He's a wonderful father. He should have had a second son, and I feel it's my fault that he doesn't have one." Sometimes a childless woman even contemplates divorce so her husband could remarry and have children more easily, regardless of the husband's devotion to her and commitment to the marriage.

Feeling as if you "failed" as both mother and partner can intensify your grief and complicate your emotional recovery from the loss. It is important to keep communication open so that you and your partner talk about these concerns and deal with them, rather than keeping them private and letting them fester.

THE WAYS WOMEN GRIEVE

As a woman, you may feel a compelling need to talk or cry about your pregnancy loss. Talking can help you express your grief, leaving you deeply appreciative of others who listen and understand you.

But coping with a pregnancy loss may leave you feeling selfish for concentrating on your own preoccupations. Our society encourages women to care for others, often before themselves, so it may be difficult for you to make time for your sorrow. Although it may seem self-centered to focus on your own distress, this is an important step in coming to terms with your grief.

Women who grieve openly may notice that their emotional style is different from their partner's more reserved response. This tendency is reinforced by our culture, which expects women to be emotional, while men are not supposed to show feelings. Maggie observed that she and her husband had very different reactions to their premature baby's delivery and death:

> We both felt very sad about the loss, but as a woman, I was more emotional and I would cry and Bert would be comforting. I also did more of the talking and initiated most of the conversations about my feelings.

Regardless of your partner's way of expressing his sorrow, if you feel the need to talk about your loss, by all means seek out an understanding family member, close friend or member of the clergy who will listen. If you don't know anyone you can talk to, you may find meeting with a sensitive psychotherapist helpful. Attending a bereaved parents' support group can be especially beneficial, as it provides the companionship of others who understand.

YOUR RETURN TO THE COMMUNITY

Returning to work or your usual activities can be difficult after a pregnancy loss. With an early loss, if you had not yet told colleagues or friends you were expecting, you may feel awkward telling them you miscarried. Nevertheless, you will probably feel better if you tell some friends about your loss so that you can get support during the difficult weeks ahead. If you are back at work, it may be a good idea to let a few sympathetic colleagues know what you have been through so that they can make allowances for your being moody or distracted.

One mother, who was physically well enough to return to work a few days after her miscarriage, found the emotional pressure of feeling alone with her misfortune almost unbearable. "I'd be sitting at my desk and want to stand up and scream, 'I had a baby and was pregnant and now it's gone!'" she recalled. "I wish I had told people earlier along. I needed that extra support."

If your pregnancy was showing, your return to work or other activities will probably involve frequent reminders of your loss. Colleagues and storekeepers may ask about your baby, and you will have to tell the sad news, sometimes when you have no desire to discuss it.

Hilary lost premature twins and was so upset by questions when she returned to work that she stopped trying to give polite answers:

> I went back to work six months after our loss. I work for a large firm, so most of my coworkers only knew I had been out on maternity leave and said, "Oh you're back. What did you have?" Sometimes I was mean and just bluntly said, "I had twins. They died."

Once back in your usual routine, you will inevitably encounter pregnant women, mothers and infants, and each confrontation can reawaken feelings of hurt and failure. Sylvia, whose full-term baby died shortly after birth, worked for a company that maintained several offices in her city. She arranged to switch locations when she returned to work, so that her colleagues wouldn't know about her pregnancy or her loss and she could tell only those she wanted to. But this did not protect her as much as she had hoped:

> They changed my location, but they put me in an office where many young mothers and babies came in. One mother came up to my desk with her newborn and asked if I wanted to hold the baby. I said no and ran crying to the bathroom. I spent a lot of time crying in that bathroom over the next six months.

Once you accept that your emotional response to these awkward situations is to be expected, you can begin to forgive yourself and allow your grief to surface. For a fuller discussion of how to handle these predicaments, please read Chapter 11, "The Response of Your Family and Friends."

KEY POINTS FOR BEREAVED MOTHERS

Grief over your pregnancy loss includes sorrow for your baby and your lost chance to mother this child, as well as grief for an aspect of your womanhood. You should not have to face these feelings alone. You deserve opportunities to share your thoughts about the loss and what this baby meant to you. You need others to listen who appreciate the magnitude of your loss. When you talk about your loss, you make a statement that the pregnancy was important and real.

Here are some additional suggestions to help you cope with your sorrow:

- Give yourself the time and outlets you need to express your grief, especially since your sorrow may be more prolonged and intense than your partner's.
- Concentrate on your areas of competence as you continue to grieve, allowing the feelings of loss, rather than inadequacy, to come forward.
- Make good self-care a priority. You can take better care of your loved ones if you take good care of yourself. Remember that expressing your grief is an important part of coming to terms with your loss.
- Do not assume that your partner's preoccupation with your health or keeping the household running means that he lacks feelings about the loss. It may simply be hard for him to express his sorrow.
- Acknowledge the difficult feelings aroused by seeing pregnant women and mothers with young children. These are understandable reactions that should diminish with time.

3

The Father's Experience

As a partner and father, you may have felt helpless and frustrated in the face of your family's loss. You may see yourself as a provider and caretaker who must focus his energies on constructive action, such as returning to a busy work schedule to maintain insurance coverage or caring for other children at home. Although these activities are an important help to your family during the crisis, they may divert you from your own sorrow and powerlessness, emotions that can seem unacceptable to men. You may naturally focus on your partner's recovery as she physically regains her strength, but in the process you may neglect your own grief.

If you are a father who expresses feelings openly to family and friends, you may have encountered uncomfortable reactions to your emotions. At a time when you needed understanding, this unspoken criticism may have felt like an added injury.

You may be troubled by having to take care of practical details following the loss, leaving you guilt-ridden for worrying about mundane problems when faced with such a monumental sorrow. Watching your partner suffer may only increase your sadness and frustration. "It was so hard for me to deal with my wife's milk coming in," remembered Simon, whose first child was stillborn. "It made me feel so completely helpless."

BONDING WITH YOUR BABY

As a bereaved father, your experience of the pregnancy and the loss can be quite different from the mother's. If you had a first-trimester loss, hearing the heartbeat and seeing an early sonogram could have brought home the reality of the pregnancy, but you may have had no other direct experience of the baby. Your feelings of loss may have related more to the disruption of your plans for a family and to your partner's distress, and less to feelings about the baby. With either a miscarriage or a late loss, you may be like some fathers who feel the full impact of the pregnancy only as the birth—and death—occur.

If you suffered a stillbirth or newborn death, you probably had to pull yourself together quickly to make needed arrangements with the hospital or mortuary and to plan for your partner's sad homecoming. Whether your loss was early or full-term, your attachment to the baby may not be the same as your partner's, because hers was physical as well as emotional. As one bereaved husband explained to his wife after their full-term baby died:

> You carried her and knew her the best for nine months. I didn't feel every kick and turn. It's not that I didn't love her or have hopes for her, but I didn't live with her the way you did.

While the mother's bond with the baby is usually stronger than the father's, there are important exceptions. Some men develop powerful attachments to their infants by attending prenatal appointments, by touching the mother's abdomen, and by talking to their babies throughout the pregnancy. After birth, a father may form a strong connection to his baby, especially if he is involved with an ill newborn's medical care while the mother is confined to her hospital bed.

Cecelia recalled how her husband became very attached to their dying baby while she was in bed recovering from an emergency cesarean delivery:

> Mark was with the baby the whole nine hours of his life, when I couldn't be. I had tremendous concern for him because he was so bonded with the baby. He isn't someone who expresses his emotions easily. He wasn't hysterical or anything, but I could just see it in his face.

YOUR GRIEF AND THE PRESSURE TO MOVE ON

Like many fathers, you may have felt most overcome by grief immediately after the loss occurred. You may mourn intensely for a few short weeks and then make a deliberate effort to move beyond your loss by immersing yourself in work. While you probably want to support your partner emotionally, you may also feel a desire to keep functioning and get on with your life.

Joel mourned openly when his infant daughter died, but quickly felt a need to move past the loss:

> We cried the whole first week, and talked. In the process of crying and grieving, each time I had another way to look at it, why our daughter came, why she left, the growth she brought to us.

> The day of the cremation came. I am fuzzy about the dates. Maybe one and
> a half weeks after her birth. By that time I felt cried out. I made the decision to
> put it behind me. The day we picked up the baby's ashes was a rough day for
> Sylvia, but I felt a lot was behind me.

Although your desire to move on may be powerful immediately after the loss, if you put aside your grief too quickly, you may find it resurfaces in troubling ways long after your loss. If you are concerned about this happening to you, please see the section "When Your Grief Is Unfinished," toward the end of this chapter.

YOUR CONCERN FOR THE BABY'S MOTHER

As a father, you were a bystander to an event that not only took your child but also may have made you fear for your partner's safety. The loss itself may have created a high-risk medical condition, making this fear unavoidable. But even if there had been no serious medical danger, you still may have worried about the well-being of your baby's mother due to an unexpected delivery or her need for sudden sedation or surgical procedures. You also may have been so caught up in worrying about your partner's dramatic grief reactions that you neglected your own feelings.

When Hilary started bleeding in her second trimester of a twin pregnancy, she and her husband, Bennett, rushed to the hospital in an unsuccessful effort to save the babies. Hilary recalled that her own medical condition was stable, but her husband doubted this from what he saw in the delivery room:

> I will never forget Bennett watching me. I had fetal monitors and intravenous
> lines attached to me. It must have been terrifying. He said to me, "If it comes
> down to a choice between you and the babies, I am not going to ask what you
> want to do. Your life is more important." Bennett was afraid of what he saw. It
> looked terrible.

This dual threat you experienced—for partner and child—gives you a different perspective on the loss. If you were worried about your partner's health, let her know this, so that she doesn't misinterpret your relief as meaning that you didn't care about the baby or the loss.

THE URGE TO BE STRONG

After your loss, you may have been influenced by the societal expectation that men are supposed to be "strong" and not overly emotional. Karen Reed, a nurse who has researched the impact of pregnancy loss on fathers, has pointed out that men not only feel this initial need to be "strong," but are often so conditioned by their male roles that they cannot even let themselves cry. This expectation is reinforced if you are obliged to make practical arrangements following your loss.

Joel, whose newborn daughter died shortly after birth, described this period:

> The hospital staff came to me about permission for an autopsy. I arranged for my wife to be taken off the maternity floor so she wouldn't be hurt more by exposure to other babies. I called our relatives with the bad news. I packed up the baby clothes and dealt with the mortuary. In the first few days, when I was taking care of the details, I had to put my grief aside.

Even when you were hurting badly, you may have tried not to look upset, in the belief that this would be best for your partner. You may have seen her falling apart emotionally and felt responsible for being the functioning member of the family while protecting her from upsetting thoughts or feelings. "If Hilary and I were out walking and I saw a double stroller, I would try to avoid it," explained Bennett following the death of the couple's twins. "I was trying to protect Hilary and myself."

You may also be struggling to suppress the urge to blame the baby's mother for not providing you with the child you had successfully conceived. Even though you may know she is not at fault, your own anger, coupled with hearing her doubts about her ability to carry a child and listening to her say she feels like a "failure," can make you prone to blame her.

But your efforts to spare your partner by skirting the subject of the loss and your own reactions to it can lead to misunderstanding, as she may think you are no longer sad. It is usually helpful, instead, for you to admit that you feel angry and unhappy. Your honesty won't always allay her fears, but sharing feelings and recollections can bring you closer to each other. When Bennett finally admitted to Hilary that he was upset whenever he saw a double stroller, she was relieved. "I had assumed he hadn't felt the same way I did whenever we saw twin babies," revealed Hilary, "when all along it was a sorrow we could have shared together."

In contrast to the open grief of the baby's mother, you might be actively avoiding mention of your loss with friends and family. You may have found other people to be unsympathetic or embarrassed, so you prefer to manage your feelings alone.

Jeff became socially withdrawn after he lost three babies to early miscarriages:

> I just didn't feel like being with people. I avoided friends with kids. I wanted to talk to certain people, but talking didn't do me any good. I would be more

concerned about them. I would fill in all the clichés for them. They didn't know what to say.

Societal assumptions that the loss is primarily the mother's and not the father's probably reinforce your sense that you should not express your grief. Friends, family and colleagues may concentrate on the mother's health and recovery and forget to ask how you are feeling. This neglect can reinforce your sense that you must contain or avoid your own sadness, making your mourning more difficult.

Once you become aware of this imbalance, you may find yourself responding gratefully when you are included in a friend's expression of concern. After Roger and Sally had suffered a full-term stillbirth, Roger recalled that everybody kept asking him how his wife was coping. "Finally a friend of mine at work asked me how *I* was doing," he confessed. "It really meant a lot to me."

Like many bereaved fathers, you may have immersed yourself in work soon after your loss in an effort to do something active and constructive. You probably welcomed the chance to return to a routine and to focus on work instead of on your tragedy. "Going back to work and my regular routine was almost a blessing," revealed one father. "I was able to go on with my life and think about the future, instead of dwelling on the loss or living in the past."

Sally Brosz Hardin, a nurse who has done research on the emotional aftermath of pregnancy loss, points out that the father's return to work may provide "an immediate escape from grief and sadness." But it is important to remember that this may be very different from the woman's experiences of returning to work, which usually entail constant, painful reminders of her loss.

While you may tend to be less demonstrative about your grief than your partner, you may be affected by your loss in a way that changes your entire outlook on life. Jeff explained that he returned immediately to a demanding job after his wife's third miscarriage and that grief never took over his life. But feelings about his losses remained:

> Today I found out a colleague's wife is pregnant. One secretary is expecting. I say congratulations. But I wonder why this is so easy for them and not for me. I feel it's not fair.

Another father, whose premature twins died and whose wife then had two miscarriages, felt his losses had made him a more cautious person:

> I am more reserved in life about things that would have excited me before. The losses put a lid on things for me. The disappointment is overwhelming. I lost my innocence.

WHEN YOUR GRIEF IS UNFINISHED

The many demands placed on you as a bereaved father by the hospital, your partner and your family may allow you to grieve only briefly. You might lack outlets for your sorrow and may feel a strong inner need to get past the pain. All these factors contribute to the likelihood that your mourning will be cut short to some degree.

Yet for many fathers, grief does not end quickly. You may have expressed your feelings of loss only partially and then let them become submerged as your energies were diverted into work and taking care of the baby's mother. Your grief may take the form of anger that your basic assumptions about having a family have been upset. You may find yourself becoming jealous and resentful of friends and family who are in the process of having babies or raising small children. Your loss can even leave you doubting your ability to set and achieve important goals in your life.

Grief may reemerge with anniversaries of the birth or loss, or during holidays and family gatherings, often taking you by surprise. While upsetting, this resurgence of memories and feelings about your pregnancy loss can enable you to continue the mourning process that was left unfinished. Take this opportunity to talk with your partner, family, friends, a member of the clergy or a psychotherapist. Joining a pregnancy loss support group or a men's group can help give expression to your frustration and sorrow. As one bereaved father said:

> I've never had to grieve before. I've had grandparents pass away. But that's different—it's part of life to grow old and get sick and die. But not a baby. Our baby's death was so unfair. And this loss was so close to us—so personal. Talking enabled me to express the grief and come to terms with it. It made me a better person.

KEY POINTS FOR BEREAVED FATHERS

Like most bereaved fathers, you probably feel you must be "strong" for your family and may be denying yourself the chance to demonstrate your sorrow openly and effectively. Immediately after the pregnancy loss occurs, you may have many burdens to carry, such as worry about the baby's mother and responsibility for practical but upsetting arrangements related to the loss, all of which may put your grief on hold. But if you do not express your grief now, it can reemerge in damaging ways later.

Here are some suggestions that can enable you to deal with the demands placed on you without repressing your own grief response:

- Include your partner in decisions about the baby if she is able to participate. This will help both of you feel connected to each other as well as to your child.
- Give yourself time to express your feelings with your partner, with another loved one or alone, even though you may wish to appear strong.
- Let your partner know if you were worried about her health, so that she doesn't misinterpret your relief at her recovery to mean you did not care about the baby.
- Consider setting aside a limited time during each week to recall, write about or talk about the loss, even if you experience a welcome feeling of relief after returning to work. Though difficult, expressing your grief can allow you to integrate your loss and move on.

4

Pregnancy Loss and Your Relationship: Grieving Together and Apart

I don't remember our sex life being different after the loss. Our sex life was good before and after. There was no change, really.

—Mark

When we talked about the loss we got into trouble because we would fight. We just got on each other's nerves over other things, too.

—Lisa

I felt like someone had pulled a plug. We were both so drained.

—Bennett

Your pregnancy loss forces you and your partner to grapple with a tragedy, perhaps the first you have shared. Your relationship is put to a test that can either draw you together or drive you apart. If you are fortunate, family and friends are there to listen, but more likely you have been left to manage your grief with little outside help. Even compassionate friends and relatives might not reach out to you for nearly as long as you need them. Aware of this lack of understanding, you and your partner may isolate yourselves and turn to each other as your primary—or only—source of comfort.

YOUR RELATIONSHIP DURING THE CRISIS

During and after the immediacy of your loss, you and your partner probably felt close to each other. Together you lived through the anxiety, the fear, the emergency medical care and ultimately the loss of your baby. Having shared this ordeal, you likely turned to each other for solace, each of you feeling grateful for the physical and emotional presence of the other. "There was this sense that we've gone through this experience together," Jeff said after his wife's third miscarriage. "There was this very strong feeling that at least we had each other and should hold on to that."

When Maggie and Bert's premature baby daughter died, Maggie was grateful that they both stayed at home and grieved together at first:

> Bert had wanted the baby very badly, and he took her death very hard. He couldn't share my physical pain, but as much as he could share without actually carrying the baby, he was there. His being home with me for a few days helped us to be loving together and be miserable together. He was very supportive.

You may each take turns mourning and supporting each other immediately after your pregnancy loss. When one of you is most out of control, the other holds together and is the consoler, and then your roles switch. "I think it was too much for both of us to fall apart," one bereaved father remarked. "I was relieved that my wife was more in control when I went to pieces. Then I took the ball when she was grieving."

A bereaved mother often finds she is still nonfunctional during the first few weeks after a loss. She may cry constantly, have insomnia and nightmares and feel unable to get out of bed. Although the baby's father is probably back at work, perhaps after only a few days' leave, he may continue to care for her and help her, sometimes in thoughtful, touching ways.

Lisa credited her husband for gently prodding her out of her lethargy after their newborn baby died:

> After our loss, I just vegetated in front of the TV. Adam was great. He finally wrote me lists. "Do two things on this list today," he said. Then the next day he said, "Do three things on this list." Eventually I could do things and get out of the house.

Sometimes the baby's father responds to the mother's continuing depression by sympathetically insisting that she engage in an enjoyable activity, whether an exercise class, a regular outing to the movies or a hobby. As long as he is also respectful of her need to grieve, this type of persuasion can work very well.

Months after her premature son died, Cecelia refused to go out of the house at all, except to work. Her husband became impatient and worried until he hit on an idea. He knew that Cecelia had always enjoyed singing, and before losing her baby, she had planned to join a choral group. She remembered the night her husband literally dragged her to one of their rehearsals:

Outside in the hall I heard them singing and said to my husband. "I'm not that good. Please don't make me go in." But with his encouragement, I not only went in, but I sang with that group for two years. It was very therapeutic.

After the initial crisis has passed, parents may become acutely aware of the differences in their grieving. By this time their families expect them to be getting on with their lives. Visits and phone calls from friends become infrequent or stop. The baby's father is back to his work routine, and although he may still be grieving, he might not express his feelings openly or even be aware of them. Yet the mother is probably still in active mourning, whether she is at home or back at work, and she may continue to grieve openly for many months.

This is when a bereaved mother can begin to find the baby's father unfeeling and unsupportive, while he begins to tire of her extreme emotions and wonder if she will ever get better. And this is when incongruent grief—the very different courses mourning can follow—begins to take its toll.

INCONGRUENT GRIEF

He wondered why I wasn't feeling better; I wondered why he wasn't feeling worse.

—Sylvia

The differing intensity and duration of mourning that a mother and father may experience can create stress in your relationship, especially if you don't realize that such incongruent grief is quite common. Instead, you may feel angry and critical of your partner for grieving differently.

Deep fears usually lie at the root of this conflict. A bereaved father can become convinced that something is seriously wrong with his continually grieving partner. She then feels betrayed by the one person she had relied on to understand her, comfort her and share in the loss.

A grieving mother may misinterpret her partner's faster recovery and contained emotions as lack of love for the baby and may mistake his relief at her own physical recovery for lack of sorrow about the loss. Perhaps the baby's father believes he should suppress his grief to remain functional so that he can help her. As misunderstanding builds, marital trust is shaken.

Adam's helplessness and frustration grew as he tried, unsuccessfully, to make Lisa feel better after their newborn daughter's death:

I tried to say things I thought were comforting, but they had the opposite effect. It was also difficult for Lisa to understand what a father would feel under these circumstances, especially since my grief seemed shorter.

Anger, guilt and attempts to place blame for the loss are distressing aspects of bereavement. It is natural for you to direct these negative feelings toward your partner sometimes. If your relationship is strong and you realize that anger is part of your grief, you can tolerate these outbursts and actually help each other. Roger recalled how he and his wife both broke down and yet depended on one another through the delivery of their stillborn son:

> When I first found out, I started punching the pillow on the hospital bed and kept sobbing, "Why? Why?" over and over. I was so angry and out of control. But just being with each other physically at first, literally clinging to each other, was helpful. We knew we could do this in front of each other and it would be okay.

But not all relationships can tolerate such anger. You may feel personally attacked by your partner's outrage and may sense that one of you is blaming the other for causing the loss. Issues that had not been problematic before may suddenly become the focus of conflict.

One couple who hardly ever argued prior to their loss found themselves in constant conflict afterward:

> We had so much anger toward each other. I was so angry I needed to hit pillows and throw things and beat the bed. I was angry about his working with a female consultant at his office. I really had no reason to be jealous of her, but I was. When we talked we got into trouble because we would fight. We just got on each other's nerves.

A bereaved father may avoid bringing up the pregnancy loss with his partner after his own initial upset is over. He may feel that discussing the loss will make her more depressed, or he may be seeking relief from his own painful memories. "As time went on, it got hard to talk," explained Bennett. "I didn't like to see my wife upset. I wanted to talk about other things."

But a father's avoidance of the topic can backfire, because his partner may truly need to talk about their baby, her sadness or her jealousy each time she sees a pregnant woman or a new mother. She may experience her partner's reluctance to talk about the baby as emotional abandonment, especially if she has no one else to turn to. Hilary, Bennett's wife, found that her need to talk about their twins who died and his need not to talk eventually hurt both of them:

> In the beginning we talked about the babies, the grief and when to try to get pregnant again. But then Bennett said, "I want to talk about the loss but not all

the time." I said, "If I can't talk to you, who can I talk to?" We both understood each other but couldn't help each other.

When you feel the need to talk about the loss either more or less than your partner, you may find it helpful to set aside a specific and limited time each day, or later on once a week, to talk about the baby together. In this way you can share your thoughts and feelings with each other without worrying that grief will become an all-consuming preoccupation or that your needs will not be respected. Hilary and her husband finally reached this compromise. "I tried not to talk as much about the loss," she explained. "If he had a decent day, talking could crash it in. And because of our arrangement, I felt he tried to listen to me more."

Psychotherapist Merle Bombardieri proposes "the twenty-minute rule," in which a couple sets a timer and takes turns venting feelings for ten minutes each. After the buzzer rings for the second time, no further discussion is allowed that day. This rule encourages couples to become aware of each other's concerns but not overburdened by the other's turmoil. Later, you may need to invoke the twenty-minute rule only once a week or once a month, but it can still help you start—and finish—discussions about your grief when you feel the need to talk about your loss.

Sometimes your grief reaction is so different from your partner's that you can no longer empathize with each other. You may stop wanting or even trying to talk to each other and may end up feeling angry, misunderstood and emotionally distant.

Amelia found it increasingly difficult to cope with the news of friends' and colleagues' pregnancies when her husband didn't react similarly:

I was consumed by jealousy and bitterness. And worse than that for me was that Charles didn't feel the same anger and resentment I did. I felt he didn't support or understand my rage. I desperately needed someone to talk to about my feelings each time I heard about someone else getting pregnant, but Charles just didn't share my emotions and I couldn't talk to him.

If these sharp differences in a couple's grief responses are not understood, they can lead to a total communication breakdown. As time goes on, the bereaved father may want his life to get back to normal and might blame his partner's continuing distress for the fact that they no longer enjoy shared activities or each other. "I was screaming and having hysterical fits, while Joel was contained and wanted to get on with things," revealed Sylvia. "He got tired of my being so emotional. Both of us felt justified in our feelings and believed the other was 'wrong.'"

Joel felt that their different grief reactions got to the point where mistrust, anger and anxiety began to take over their marriage:

I told Sylvia that I had heard enough crying, that I thought we were getting better. Her reaction was to clam up. Then, when I tried to talk about the baby, she told me that I didn't really want to hear about it and she wouldn't let me bring up the subject, which left me really angry.

Sometimes she would say she missed the baby, or felt defective as a woman, and I would tell her I didn't know she was feeling that way. Then she would snap that she felt this way all the time. It made me feel so out of touch. There were times when I thought Sylvia would never get better.

If you reach this kind of serious but common impasse in trust and communication, it is vital to try to talk to your partner and reestablish contact. By making time to sit down together and taking turns talking to each other, your feelings and worries can be aired and explored. This may enable you to learn that each of you is pulling away from the other due to hurt and fear, not from lack of love for each other or the baby. As your misunderstandings clear, mutual respect and support can again become possible. If you are having difficulty doing this, seek outside help. Once you have reestablished communication with each other, you may be greatly relieved to discover that although your reactions are very different, they are entirely understandable.

YOUR GRIEF AND SEXUALITY

After the miscarriage I didn't have a problem with having sex at all. It was so comforting, so exciting. We had missed each other so much.
—Cecelia

I didn't want to be touched. Sex felt forced. I was sad because the loss had taken the joy out of sex as well as out of pregnancy and childbearing.
—Sylvia

Pregnancy loss can affect every aspect of your marriage, including your sexual relationship. Your reaction to resuming sex will be highly individual and may be quite different from your partner's. Perhaps you are one of the few couples whose loss has increased your physical need for each other. For you, sex is a source of comfort and pleasure, a way of expressing the closeness you feel from having endured and helped each other through your loss. "We had always been very much in love," recalled Adam, "and if anything, our tragedy made us realize how lucky we were to have each other, both physically and emotionally."

But for most parents, resuming sexual relations after a pregnancy loss is highly charged. Although your doctor has probably insisted on a specific period of abstinence, these medical restrictions do not take into account the complicated feelings about sex you may have following your loss. Your reactions to the loss, sex, birth control and conceiving again can become interrelated and extremely upsetting after your pregnancy ends.

Doctors generally suggest waiting two to six weeks, depending on the nature of the loss, before resuming sexual relations. This gives the cervix time to close and heal, limiting the chance of uterine infection or other physical damage. A period of abstinence is also recommended following a cesarean section. Waiting to resume sexual relations allows the uterus to return to its original size and the lining to slough off after the birth, giving any subsequent pregnancy the best chance of implanting properly. If there was an episiotomy, it, too, must have sufficient time to heal.

Once you have abstained the requisite number of weeks and are free to resume sexual relations, you may discover that sex vividly reminds you of the pregnancy that ended. Thoughts about the loss may resurface when you make love as you are reminded of the last pregnancy you conceived. You might urgently wish to become pregnant again, while your partner may be terrified at the prospect of another pregnancy. These memories and preoccupations can make you lose your sexual desire.

Maggie found that both she and her husband approached sex gingerly after losing their premature baby. "It brought out a lot of feelings," she recalled. "Having sex was like getting my period after the loss—I felt sad that I wasn't pregnant anymore. Sex also had the danger of becoming a chore, an obligation. The loss took away all the spontaneity."

A man may worry about physically hurting his partner during intercourse, as he thinks she may be sore after childbirth, an episiotomy, a D&C, or other surgery. His concern about her physical vulnerability may be tied in with guilt for having conceived the pregnancy that put her through the pain and grief of a loss. Taken together, these feelings can make him reluctant to approach her sexually.

Even the use of birth control, which is usually a straightforward matter, can be depressing after a pregnancy loss. You and your partner may realize you need time to heal emotionally before conceiving again. But because you have lost a baby you wanted so much, deciding not to conceive for a period of time can cause making love to be distressing.

Jeff felt there was a lot of sadness around the use of birth control after he and his wife had suffered three miscarriages:

> Birth control became a loaded issue. We needed some time before attempting another pregnancy in addition to the physical wait after the D&C. But the idea of sex with a contraceptive felt horrible. Sometimes I couldn't escape the

focus, and it bothered my wife all the time. It interfered with our sexual pleasure a lot.

Even though sex might be difficult to talk about, it is important for
you and your partner to speak frankly about your readiness to resume
sexual relations or to plan another pregnancy. Although birth control
can be hard to contemplate initially, continue to use it until you feel
prepared for another pregnancy. As each of you heals emotionally, sexual pleasure will gradually return, and the sad associations between
birth control and the pregnancy loss will lessen.

Some couples lose all sexual interest after a pregnancy loss, even for
a long time. If this happens, you may be avoiding intimacy because you
feel so vulnerable. You may feel cheated because sex is not giving you
what you truly want, which is not just physical pleasure but a healthy
baby as well. Mistrust and resentment over the differing ways you and
your partner cope with the loss can also contribute to your lack of interest in sex.

When you feel ready to have another baby, sex may again go "on
hold" once you conceive. Although doctors rarely consider sex to cause
pregnancy loss, in certain instances they may recommend that you
abstain from intercourse as an extra safeguard. Some couples take this
precaution upon themselves because it makes them feel they are doing
something to protect the pregnancy. But this can mean a long period
of sexual abstinence and serious marital strain.

Sylvia's aversion to sex continued for several months after her newborn daughter died:

> I didn't want to be touched. I felt physically damaged, bruised, hurt. I bled for a
> long time. I leaked milk and had a large episiotomy. I turned in toward myself. It
> took me a long time to feel physically better. I didn't want sexual contact for six
> months. I wanted to be left alone, to curl up in the fetal position in a blanket.
>
> In March we wanted to try to become pregnant again. That was the only
> reason for having sex; there was no pleasure in it. These feelings persisted
> until I became pregnant again. Then I wanted to be left alone with this new
> baby. I needed my body for myself. It was even hard to share it with the baby,
> let alone with my husband.

While a period of sexual abstinence may be unavoidable, you and
your partner may pay a price for a long hiatus in your sexual relationship. Sexual tensions can add significantly to the marital stress brought
on by bereavement. Your partner may not always agree that abstinence
after a pregnancy loss is a wise or necessary choice. As one father
remarked, "We were much too cautious, and it wouldn't have made a
difference in our particular case. Abstaining created a strain."

It is important for you to talk honestly about your sexual needs to prevent resentment from building after a loss or during a subsequent pregnancy. You may want to give and receive sexual pleasure without intercourse, so that sexual frustrations do not add to the other pressures you are experiencing. Some women must avoid climaxes during a precarious pregnancy because orgasms can stimulate dangerous uterine contractions; however, physical intimacy is still possible. "Even when I chose not to have a climax," admitted one woman about the pregnancy that followed her miscarriages, "it made me feel close to my husband and better about our sex life if I at least helped him achieve an orgasm."

If you find your sexual needs are different from your partner's after your loss, especially if your relationship is stressed in other ways, you may benefit greatly from outside support or professional help. You may even be harboring unrealistic fears that sexual intercourse contributed to your pregnancy loss. Learning that sexual difficulties during bereavement are common can help you open communication and meet your partner halfway.

You and your partner may decide you need a period of relaxed sexual relations after your pregnancy loss and may delay your plans to conceive because of this. You may feel you have gone through pain and heartache from your loss and are anxious about whether the next child you conceive will be born healthy. You may not want to add to these difficulties by depriving yourself of the intimacy and comfort of sexual pleasure.

Cecelia spent two months in and out of the hospital trying to save her pregnancy, without success, and with tremendous strains on her sexual life:

> It was important that I not have any orgasms as well as not having intercourse. The doctor wouldn't allow any uterine contractions. It was driving me crazy not to have sex. It became a real joke. When I was in the hospital, I remember saying to my doctor, "I can't work, I can't take care of my family, I can't have sex. What can I do? Can I at least take some vitamins?"
>
> I worry about the next pregnancy because it will mean no sexual intercourse. It's a reason for me to postpone it.

HOW PREGNANCY LOSS CAN CHANGE YOUR RELATIONSHIP

Having endured a pregnancy loss, you and your partner may find your relationship has been permanently changed. As you each live through your loss and grief, you may feel estranged from your partner because of your differing responses. You may even experience grave doubts about whether you can count on either yourself or your partner to survive the ordeal with your relationship intact.

Yet, like many couples, you and your partner may discover that your relationship has been strengthened through the sorrow you endured together. You may uncover resilience and resolution in yourself and your spouse that you never experienced before. You can feel you have gained a richer understanding of each other, both as individuals and as partners.

Eric and Annette had tried to have a child for four years before finally conceiving. When the baby stopped growing eight weeks into the pregnancy, Eric was moved by the way Annette handled herself:

> This was one of the worst experiences of Annette's life. She had wanted to be pregnant for so long, and then to lose the baby—it was unimaginable. I remember so clearly the way she set her alarm clock and got up the day of the D&C. She went to the hospital and came home with a manner of acceptance I was unprepared to see. I was incredibly impressed by her bravery.

If you and your partner care for each other in the crucible of bereavement, you may emerge with a deep sense of faith in your relationship.

Karen believed her five miscarriages affected her marriage profoundly:

> I think there is a certain celebration in our relationship because we have been through these losses but are still so close and caring. It's made the good times better and the bad times bearable. Our marriage was tested over and over again, so now we know we will always be there for each other.

If you have other children, you may find that the shared sorrow has left you with a sense of unity and understanding that equips you to handle the crises of parenthood. When your child is ill or in need, you and your partner may know instantly where your priorities lie and may be able to mobilize yourselves with strength and clarity of purpose.

One husband, whose wife had suffered four miscarriages, arranged for a substitute to conclude a vital out-of-town business transaction in his stead, because he wanted to stay with his infant daughter, who required an emergency hospitalization. "My partners told me it would be impossible to find a last-minute replacement," he recalled, "but I found a way to close the deal legally without actually being there. It was more important for me to be with my family."

Parents often find they reorder their priorities and protect what is most important to them. Ellen told how her husband had joined her in the hospital recovery room with their sobbing two-year-old who was just out of surgery, in spite of hospital regulations that permitted only one parent at a time. "His coming in against the rules reminded me of his determination when he stayed in my hospital room all night after my miscarriage," she explained.

But not all couples fare so well after a pregnancy loss, and for some, the crisis of a loss takes a major toll on their relationship. Even if your relationship is good, you may temporarily become critical of each other after your loss. And if your relationship had tensions, conflicts or unaired resentments before the loss, your grief can trigger cruel attacks, accusations of blame or complete withdrawal.

Sometimes relationships do break up after a pregnancy loss. Disappointments that were kept in check when your lives were stable can become intolerable in a crisis. And when your relationship is tested by sorrow, one of you may be devastated when the other fails to come through with needed solace. This happened to Jody and her ex-husband:

My first husband and I were totally thrown apart by the miscarriage. There was no support at all from him. I went in for a D&C and he refused to drive me to the hospital. I was so hysterical about this, the doctor had to tranquilize me. I could hear the nurses talking about why my husband wasn't with me. When I woke up from the anesthesia, I woke up crying. At first I thought I must be in physical pain, but then I realized I was distraught because I needed my husband with me so much, and he wasn't there. When I went home my husband said, "Everyone has D&C's. It's no big deal." That was the beginning of the end.

Your relationship may dissolve after your loss because you see each other at your most needy and vulnerable and may not like what you see. One woman was engaged to be married when she unexpectedly became pregnant and then miscarried. Shortly afterward her fiancé left her:

He said I was no longer the person he knew before the miscarriage. He said when he met me I was strong and beautiful. And here I was lying in the fetal position, weeping. Now I think the breakup was for the best. If it hadn't been the miscarriage, he would have left me around some other crisis. I would have been alone for the hard times.

If your relationship is in serious trouble after your loss, you and your partner must deal with two cataclysmic events—pregnancy loss and potential separation—simultaneously. You need to begin sorting out your feelings about the loss and each other as quickly as possible. Try to have open discussions allotting equal time for each of you to express your concerns, and listen patiently to each other's reactions to the loss. A support group or sessions with a psychotherapist skilled in bereavement issues can be especially beneficial. These steps can help your mutual and individual adjustments following your loss, whether you ultimately decide to stay together or to separate.

Although pregnancy loss can strain primary relationships, most couples remain committed to their union and family. They may even emerge with a special appreciation for one another. Paula found this to be so after losing a baby following a medical crisis in her pregnancy:

> My husband and I were always very close anyway, but the loss brought us closer. Losing the baby reinforced our wonder at the next child and confirmed our wanting to have the next child. We never again took for granted what happens in pregnancy.

KEY POINTS FOR COUPLES

Your pregnancy loss and grief have probably touched every aspect of your relationship. You and your partner may be brought closer, and your commitment to each other may be strengthened, as a result of surviving the loss together. But your relationship can also be stressed by incongruent grief, especially if each of you thinks the other is "wrong" for reacting differently to the loss. Criticism is conveyed and resentment sets in. You may each feel misunderstood, if not betrayed, when you are in critical need of the other's support.

It is important to realize that each of you will experience grief in a unique way. A mother's grief may well be more intense and prolonged, while the baby's father may need help in finding ways to express his underlying sadness.

Here are some suggestions to help you weather the difficult days and weeks ahead:

- Give yourself time to grieve, on your own and with your partner. Expect to need support from others in addition to your mate, who is emotionally depleted, too. It is essential to grieve your loss, because unexpressed grief can emerge later as depression, anxiety, anger or stress.
- Expect your grief response to be different from your partner's. Frankly share your feelings and needs, but do not expect your partner to react the same way. Try to be understanding without judging each other.

- Discuss your readiness to have sex, especially if your needs are different from your partner's. Any sexual problems usually improve as mourning progresses.
- Make sure you both feel ready before you try to conceive again. Use birth control until you are willing to plan another pregnancy.
- Understand that grief is stressful and may aggravate other issues in your relationship. Couple or individual psychotherapy can help you sort out these difficult problems.
- Keep in mind that it takes time to grieve and that gradually your pain will lessen. Surviving a pregnancy loss with your partner can give you a new appreciation for each other and for what is most important to you as a couple.

Section II

Pregnancy Loss Examined

No matter what type of pregnancy loss you experienced, you share with other bereaved parents a bond of sorrow, endurance and hope as you live through your tragedy and begin once again to build a future. Yet each loss remains unique, with its own medical implications and emotional impact.

Following a stillbirth or newborn death, you had to decide whether to name your baby or to say good-bye with formal rituals. If your loss occurred in the first three months, you may have been spared some of these decisions, but loved ones, doctors and clergy were less likely to acknowledge your sorrow and help you mourn.

The medical concerns that now confront you also depend on the kind of pregnancy loss you suffered. If you experienced consecutive miscarriages, you are probably anxious about what caused them and what treatments are available to you. If your baby died from a cord accident in the womb or from birth defects, you must grapple with the heightened uneasiness an unpreventable misfortune brings to any subsequent pregnancy.

Parents face a particularly lonely and painful experience when prenatal diagnosis indicates a severe problem with the baby and they decide whether to continue or to end their pregnancy. And if a loss occurs toward the end of the mother's most fertile years, both parents may be worried about never having another successful pregnancy, a fear that couples in their twenties probably won't share.

Whatever your circumstances, you are not alone. Nearly one-third of all conceptions end in some type of natural pregnancy loss, with almost 80 percent of all losses occurring in the first three months of pregnancy, about 14 percent in the second trimester and approximately 6 percent in the third. Sadly, if you have experienced more than one previous loss, you are at increased risk for suffering another.

But statistics mean very little when you have lost your baby. "No matter what the chances are," said one woman, "if it happens to you, it happens 100 percent." And in spite of the frequency of pregnancy loss, you may find your grief is often overlooked. You may bear the additional burden of having to initiate conversations with your doctor on potential treatments to safeguard future pregnancies.

This section, "Pregnancy Loss Examined," discusses the different emotional and medical issues associated with early losses, stillbirth and newborn death. Also included are losses caused by crisis pregnancies and the choice to end a pregnancy following prenatal testing. By understanding the symptoms, causes, treatments and emotional impact of your loss, you can take steps that will help you grieve and plan any special medical care that you may need for a future pregnancy.

5

Early Losses

I felt devastated after my second miscarriage. From childhood, a little girl is taught she will grow up to be a bride and a mother. Motherhood is revered. This dream of having a baby is from childhood. It was the dream that was being wiped out.

—Amy

A first-trimester loss is a particularly silent sorrow since outsiders often fail to recognize the agonizing emptiness it leaves behind. When you lose a baby early in the pregnancy, you may have to deal with a lack of concrete memories about the pregnancy or your baby and the absence of established rituals to mark this sad event.

You may take some comfort in learning that you are not alone, since most losses occur during the first three months of pregnancy. Miscarriages account for almost 95 percent of all early losses up to twenty weeks' gestation, after which they are considered to be live births or stillbirths. Ectopic pregnancies, in which implantation occurs outside the uterus, make up about 4 percent of the total. The remaining 1 percent consists of rare forms of pregnancy loss, such as molar pregnancies, in which a nonviable egg is fertilized and cannot develop properly.

An early loss ends the pregnancy just as it is beginning, only weeks or even days after you first realized you and your partner were going to be parents. Your joyous expectations were suddenly turned to grief, and the pregnancy, which ended so early, may now seem real only to you.

ISSUES COMMON TO ALL EARLY LOSSES

Although a woman's hormones shift immediately and dramatically to support a new pregnancy, the changes in her body during the first few

weeks after conception are subtle and personal. She may feel nause-
ated and her breasts may be tender, but the pregnancy is still a secret,
locked invisibly inside her body. Friends and family cannot see any
changes until much later in the pregnancy, and she may wish to keep
her secret a while longer, savoring it with her partner. Both parents may
also feel superstitious about telling anyone about the pregnancy too
soon, afraid that their joy may become jinxed.

When a pregnancy ends early in the first trimester, many mothers
immediately feel shocked and bereft, but the impact on fathers is often
delayed. Even fathers who share in pregnancy tests, visits to the doctor's office and early sonograms can have a difficult time absorbing the
reality of a pregnancy that ends just as it is beginning. Eric admitted
that his wife's first-trimester loss seemed real to him only after it was
over. "It was something I hadn't felt part of or emotional about, and
suddenly I was crying about it for days," he confessed. "It amazed me
that this was how and when I knew I cared about the pregnancy—only
once it was over."

The lack of tangible reminders of your pregnancy can keep each
of you from grieving properly. Even the smallest keepsake can help.
Annette cherished her sonogram photographs of the first-trimester
pregnancy she eventually miscarried. Although she didn't look at the
pictures often, it was comforting to have them tucked away. In a subsequent, healthy pregnancy, another sonogram reawakened feelings
about the image of the tiny baby she never knew:

> We learned so much about this current pregnancy after the sonograms and
> the amniocentesis—that we're expecting twins and that they are girls. I kept
> looking at them moving around on the sonogram screen and kept wondering
> to myself, "Who was that first child we lost?"

Tangible reminders of a pregnancy that ended in the first trimester
can also help you and your partner release feelings of disappointment
and grief. After Natalie's third loss, she went home to her living room,
where she had a picture from the sonogram and some congratulation
cards from friends and family. "I was so upset, I took them off the man-
tel," she explained, "and threw them all out."

You may be feeling isolated and alone after your early loss, especially
if your friends and family do not acknowledge how upset you are. They
may not have been aware of your pregnancy until the loss occurred,
forcing them to absorb both pieces of news at once and leaving them
little time to develop a sense of what the events mean to you.

Few people offer enough sympathy after an early loss because they
do not comprehend its impact. This leaves both you and your partner
without help when you most need others to listen compassionately and

let you talk. Eric withdrew from people when he felt they didn't realize how much his wife's miscarriage affected him:

> When people didn't seem to understand, it became a good reason to shut up about the loss and not talk about it anymore. I think people would have understood more easily if they could have seen the pregnancy. People tend to dismiss it if it is an early loss.

Well-intentioned people may utter platitudes such as "It was only an early loss" or "It happened for the best" in an attempt to reassure both you and themselves. They may also assume that because the loss occurred so early, you should recover quickly and have another child right away. But pregnancy losses should be acknowledged and mourned, and these comments only make you feel your sadness is inappropriate because the pregnancy was so brief.

Emotional reactions after an early loss can be triggered by the onset of the woman's menstrual cycle and the arrival of her subsequent periods. Annette was at first ecstatic about getting her period after her early loss and even called her husband at work to tell him the news. "I took it as a sign that my body was back in working order," she remembered, "but every period after that I felt was a sorrow, because it reminded me I wasn't pregnant."

An early pregnancy loss can create two anniversary reactions: one a year after your actual loss and another around the baby's due date. "I was feeling much better about six months after my first miscarriage," said Ellen, "and suddenly I felt just awful again. When I looked at my calendar, I realized why. My baby was due that week."

Your early loss may leave you preoccupied about undergoing medical tests before you plan another pregnancy, or you may feel depressed far longer than you anticipated, especially if you have had more than one loss. "I'm normally a happy, productive person who loves life," professed Karen, "and I resent all this grieving and emotional upheaval following each of my losses."

No matter what type of early loss you suffered, you will need time to recover. Consider joining a peer support group or scheduling sessions with a psychotherapist if you feel the need.

You may also find yourself searching for some meaning to your tragedy, a way of accepting that your baby's presence, no matter how brief, was life-affirming. As Stuart, whose wife suffered three first-trimester miscarriages, said:

> It seems to me we have two choices: One is to become withdrawn and bitter and angry, and the other is to integrate this experience into our lives so it leaves a positive legacy. As hard as it sometimes is, we are trying to make that positive choice.

EXPERIENCING A MISCARRIAGE

My wife, Iris, suffered two miscarriages in one six-month period, one in the spring and the next one in early fall. Nine months later we found out Iris was pregnant again.

We went for a sonogram and there on the monitor was the heartbeat! It was so wonderful to have the pregnancy documented that way. The doctor said that everything looked fine, that everything was great and perfect.

Iris was still nervous and afraid because of her other losses, but she was so happy. The doctor said she could come back anytime she needed to be reassured about the pregnancy. That made us both feel better.

A few days later it was our son's birthday, and we would normally have had a party for him in our backyard. But Iris was trying to reduce stress in our lives, so we held the party in a nearby gym. We came home from the party and our son was opening his presents when Iris said she had to go to the bathroom. When she came back she told me she was bleeding quite heavily. We had a sonogram the next day. The doctor confirmed that the baby had died. We were devastated.

—Patrick

Miscarriage is an unexpected and disheartening experience that turns more than six hundred thousand couples into bereaved parents in the United States alone each year. The statistics on miscarriage in general, and for older parents in particular, are on a tragic rising trajectory. The trend toward late childbearing in our society augments the rate of all pregnancy losses each year. In more than half of all miscarriages a cause cannot be determined, which can add to parents' anxiety about planning future pregnancies.

Symptoms and Diagnosis of a Miscarriage

Signs of a miscarriage can vary from one pregnancy loss to another, even in the same mother, making it hard to recognize potentially serious symptoms. Sometimes all the outward signals are present, such as bleeding, cramping and the loss of nausea and other pregnancy symptoms, but often only one sign appears as a single, ambiguous warning.

Although vaginal bleeding is a symptom in many early losses, bleeding occurs in more than 30 percent of all pregnancies in the first trimester. Half of these bleeding episodes resolve and the pregnancies continue normally, so it is often difficult to determine when concern should become alarm.

Cramping in the early months of healthy pregnancies is also common, making it hard to know when the pain has moved into the strong uterine contractions that often accompany a miscarriage. Ellen recalled waking up in the middle of the night with what felt like severe menstrual cramps during her first pregnancy:

> There was no blood, so I just lay in bed for a while wondering what I should do next. I didn't understand what was happening, but for some reason the word "labor" came to mind, even though I'd never had a baby before. The cramps were becoming stronger and more rhythmical, and I was quite frightened. I finally woke up my husband and we called my doctor, who felt I was probably losing the baby.

Miscarriages can also occur without the common symptoms of bleeding and cramping. Since the mother cannot feel the baby's movements early in the pregnancy, she is equally unaware when they stop. It may be weeks after the baby died before her body attempts to expel the pregnancy with uterine contractions and bleeding. If the pregnancy had been progressing nicely, she may be totally unprepared to discover she has experienced a loss.

A doctor can confirm an early miscarriage by several means. If the pregnancy is beyond eleven weeks, listening for the heartbeat with a Doppler instrument is the first step. If no heartbeat is found, the doctor does both internal and external examinations to see if there is any uterine or cervical change, or if any elements of the pregnancy have passed into the vagina. Tests that determine the amount of pregnancy hormones in the mother's bloodstream are accurate but can take up to forty-eight hours for final results, a long time for anxious parents to wait.

The most conclusive and immediate test is a sonogram, with which the doctor can visualize and evaluate the condition of the womb, embryonic sac and fetus. Because a healthy, developing fetus is visible on a sonogram screen as early as eight to nine weeks of gestation, even earlier if a special sonographic instrument is inserted vaginally, its absence is equally clear.

Treatment of a Miscarriage

Your doctor may have recommended bed rest for miscarriage symptoms, even though no scientific studies have established bed rest as an effective treatment for early spontaneous losses. Once you began to miscarry in the first trimester, you probably ultimately lost the pregnancy whether or not you stayed in bed.

If a doctor finds that all the products of the pregnancy have been expelled—fetus, sac, placenta and uterine lining—she may suggest that the patient go home, rest for a few days and try to conceive again once she has a couple of normal menstrual cycles. If some elements of the pregnancy remain in the uterus, the doctor recommends that the woman wait until everything is expelled naturally, or performs a dilatation and curettage, known as a D&C, to remove the remaining material.

Since a D&C is considered an elective procedure and is not usually an emergency, a woman may have to wait for treatment. The procedure takes about twenty minutes, followed by an hour or so in the recovery room to make sure the woman's pulse, blood pressure, respiratory rate and temperature are stable before she is discharged. Vaginal bleeding that tapers off over several days is common after a D&C.

Causes of Miscarriage

Once the immediate shock of the miscarriage is behind you, you may begin wondering why the pregnancy ended so early. You may be afraid to plan another pregnancy without some medical answers, especially if you have suffered more than one miscarriage.

But the causes can be as numerous as they are elusive, and your physician may only be able to make an educated guess as to why the loss occurred. You can gain an important sense of control, however, by learning about the standard tests that may help identify causes and treatments before you plan your next pregnancy.

Most doctors do not recommend testing after only one miscarriage, since a full medical workup is time-consuming and costly and will probably not yield any significant information. One miscarriage in a healthy woman who has many childbearing years ahead of her is not treated by physicians as a serious medical problem, in spite of the emotional impact it might have. Most women require no further treatment after a single miscarriage and go on to have normal, healthy pregnancies.

Some specialists now recommend that a woman have a complete workup after two *consecutive* miscarriages, especially if she is over thirty. With the recent advances in diagnosis and treatment, there is no need for a woman to suffer three miscarriages before beginning the series of tests that might indicate some underlying and treatable problem.

Once testing has begun, causes can be clearly identified in about half of all miscarriages. A woman could have hormonal imbalances, complex immunological problems, or uterine malformations that triggered her miscarriage. Or she could have several interrelated causes that may require a combination of treatments.

The fact that physicians are not able to determine a cause in approximately 50 percent of miscarriages can be frustrating, especially if you have endured weeks or months of testing. When you do not know the cause of your pregnancy loss, you also lack a specific course to follow in trying to prevent a subsequent miscarriage, so that succeeding pregnancies may be fraught with anxiety. You may have to try to become pregnant again with your questions unanswered and your doubts unresolved. If your losses continue, you might have to seek further medical advice in your search for guidance and answers.

The following causes of miscarriage are presented from the most common to the least common. Because miscarriages are the most numerous and complex type of pregnancy loss, a fuller discussion of both causes and treatments is presented in Appendix A.

Genetic and chromosomal causes. Half of all miscarriages with known causes are triggered by chromosomal and genetic abnormalities. Sometimes a fertilized egg does not develop properly because there is a defect carried in the egg or sperm itself, or the flaw may have occurred spontaneously as the pregnancy began. In either case, the problem is irrevocable from the moment of conception.

The incidence of Down syndrome, the most common chromosomal defect, increases with maternal age, unlike most other genetic and chromosomal abnormalities. Research is being done on the effects of paternal age on pregnancy loss. Studies indicate an increased risk for chromosomal and other defects, although the incidence is small compared to the risk associated with maternal age. Newer research has centered on the manufacture of sperm, which, unlike the mother's eggs, divide rapidly before fertilization and may be subject to genetic mutations as they grow, especially if the fathers have been exposed to hazardous materials or environmental toxins. Sperm that have been subjected to such mutation can still fertilize an ovum.

Embryos that are too abnormal to grow properly are frequently miscarried in the first trimester. This may be the reason why medical professionals often say that an involuntary loss due to chromosomal or genetic errors "happened for the best" or that it was "nature's way."

If a genetic or chromosomal cause has been determined following a miscarriage, the chances of a similar loss occurring in a subsequent pregnancy vary, depending on the age of the couple and simple probability. Although chromosomal problems in the baby account for a high number of first or random losses, only about 6 percent of *recurrent* miscarriages are due to chromosomal causes. Some genetic problems do not originate in the embryo but are passed on by parents and can be determined by a simple blood test. The incidence of recurrence with these types of defects can be quite high.

Hormonal factors. Pregnancy involves a complex hormonal interplay among the mother, embryo and placenta, which can malfunction and lead to miscarriages. Luteal phase defect, or LPD, is the most common hormonal imbalance associated with early pregnancy loss. In LPD, the menstrual cycle is too short and the endometrial lining of the uterus does not develop properly, rendering it incapable of sustaining a pregnancy. Some research points to the inability of the hormones of older women to sustain a pregnancy, which may account for the correlation between early losses and maternal age.

Uterine factors. The uterus, or womb, is the organ that protects and nourishes the pregnancy. If it fails to provide the proper environment, the pregnancy can miscarry. The most common problems are caused by genetic malformations, uterine growths called fibroids, or exposure to the synthetic estrogen diethylstilbestrol (DES).

Immunological problems. Immunological disorders in pregnant women generally take one of three forms: (1) antiphospholipid antibody syndrome, in which the mother's immune system turns against her own cells and tissues; (2) lupus, involving a similar attack mounted against the mother's body by her own immune system; and (3) fetal rejection, currently being researched as a cause, in which the mother's body attacks the fetus as if it were a foreign object. A woman should investigate the possibility of immunological problems if she has had three or more consecutive miscarriages and tests have failed to establish hormonal, genetic or other problems.

Infectious factors. Infections from a variety of organisms may result in early losses by causing serious maternal illness. Recent studies have been unclear as to the correlation between *Toxoplasma gondii* and chlamydia, two microorganisms previously thought to cause miscarriage. Many other infectious agents, such as the ones that cause rubella or syphilis, have an effect on pregnancy outcome but have not been implicated in early losses. There is further discussion on the effects maternal health has on pregnancy in Appendix A.

One infectious agent that has been implicated in early loss is T-strain mycoplasma. Very little is known about this microorganism, and diagnosis is difficult, but it can be transmitted sexually and can be harbored in the reproductive tract of either parent.

Prenatal testing. If chromosomal or genetic problems are implicated in the mother's miscarriage history, or if she is over thirty-five, prenatal testing is encouraged by most physicians. Sadly, the tests themselves may increase the risk of miscarriage. A more complete discussion of prenatal testing and loss appears in Chapter 8, "Prenatal Diagnosis and the Burden of Choice," and in Chapter 16, "Becoming Pregnant Again."

Injuries or accidents. A century ago it was believed that almost any physical or emotional trauma could cause miscarriages. Now doctors generally feel that if an accident didn't harm the mother, it would not harm the fetus, which is well protected. This, of course, does not include direct trauma to the mother's abdomen or to the fetus, which might occur in a fall or car accident.

Emotional Aftermath of a Miscarriage

In addition to the sorrow you already feel following your loss, you and your partner may find that the terminology health care professionals use to describe miscarriages adds to your anguish. Like many parents, you may have chosen the word *miscarriage* to describe your early, unplanned pregnancy loss. However, the correct medical term is *abor-*

tion, which is generally defined as any pregnancy loss, spontaneous or induced, that occurs in the first twenty weeks of gestation.

But the term *abortion* has been so thoroughly adopted throughout our society to refer to intentional terminations that parents who hear the word used by health care professionals may feel it implies a deliberate act to end their pregnancy. This term can be upsetting when you are trying to cope with the emotional impact of having lost a baby much against your will.

One woman found the term *incomplete abortion* distressing, even though she understood the medical definition:

> The phrase was bandied about the emergency room, the operating room and the recovery room. I knew intellectually what they meant, that all of the material from the pregnancy had not been spontaneously expelled from my uterus, but it grated on me every time I heard it. It sounded as if I had tried to get rid of my baby and hadn't done a thorough job. It still irks me. My doctor even used the phrase during my checkup. Medical staff should realize the impact this has on patients and choose words that are not so highly charged.

If you have endured several miscarriages, you may be angry at your doctor for waiting so long before investigating possible causes. Even if you are young, this can be a source of friction between you and your caregivers, but it becomes especially anxiety-provoking if you are older. Iris found a new doctor who immediately identified a potential cause following her third miscarriage, which occurred when she was thirty-eight:

> My other doctors had the nerve to make me go through three miscarriages before they would start testing. It should be standard after a second consecutive miscarriage, especially for women like me who get such a late start.

While sad that a wanted pregnancy has ended, you may be comforted knowing that the pregnancy was probably unhealthy and could not have developed properly. You may agree with the scientists who view early miscarriages as nature's way of dealing with defective embryos. After Annette conceived again following a miscarriage, her husband, Eric, described the feelings he had about her early loss:

> I'm what I'd guess you'd call a biological realist and believe there was something wrong with that first baby so it couldn't maintain life. It seemed right and proper that the baby we lost should make way for something wonderful and beautiful—these two little healthy girl babies we're expecting now.

You may find, however, that you are not consoled by these explanations and feel they dismiss your need to grieve. You may believe that if everything always happened for the best, you would have had a healthy pregnancy from the beginning. You may long for some acknowledgment of your grief and believe you have reason to be sad that your pregnancy ended.

Jody was upset by the superficial reassurances her husband's family offered after her miscarriage, which only made her realize how little they understood her feelings:

> They did the best they could. But they tried to just pat me on the hand while they mouthed all the clichés, like "You can have another baby" or "It wasn't really a baby yet." I could not convince them how badly I was feeling.

Doctor insensitivity on this issue can make you incredibly angry. Physicians tread a thin line between reassuring you that miscarriages are the most common type of pregnancy loss and recognizing that you feel emotional anguish. If doctors consider miscarriages to be so ordinary, they should understand that grief is an equally unremarkable response.

Unfortunately, lack of recognition for your grief can add to your distress. Susannah recalled how quickly she healed physically after her discharge from the hospital. "But it was a horrible experience emotionally," she admitted. "I was so depressed in the pre-op room, and I was crying. I had just lost a child, and no one acknowledged that."

In spite of all the emotional drain you experienced in the first few weeks following your miscarriage, you may feel unexpectedly strengthened simply by having survived the ordeal. "I know the effect on my life is double-edged," said Karen in contemplating her five miscarriages. "I am tremendously sad, but I have also gained compassion and understanding of others because of my losses. Those little babies I never knew still had an impact on my life."

EXPERIENCING AN ECTOPIC PREGNANCY

> My husband and I had been trying to get pregnant for a couple of months. My period was a little late and I thought I might be pregnant, but nothing had been confirmed. One night I was on duty at the hospital where I work and I suddenly had a great deal of abdominal pain. At first I thought it was something I had eaten the night before. The pain got worse and I kept getting hotter and hotter. I was going into shock but didn't realize it. So I went into the bathroom at the hospital and took off my shirt because I was so hot. I was getting dizzy spells, so I lay down on the bathroom floor. Then I started to worry and had this impression that if I didn't stand up and get help, I would die right there on the bathroom floor.
>
> So I used all my efforts to stand up and put on my shirt, but as I opened the door, I fainted into the hallway. This saved my life. Otherwise

I would have gone into shock, lost most of my blood supply into my abdomen and died. But I fainted on a hospital floor, and doctors and nurses came to help. If I had been out shopping, I would never have had made it to the hospital alive.

My tubular pregnancy had ruptured right into an ovarian artery. Forty minutes after fainting in the hospital bathroom, I was in surgery. I eventually lost 60 percent of my blood volume from the ovarian artery. This near-death became the unfortunate backdrop to my trying to become pregnant again.

—Tracy

Ectopic pregnancy—from the Greek *ektopos,* "out of place"—occurs when a fertilized egg becomes implanted anywhere outside the uterus. Ectopic pregnancies are no longer rare, and the incidence is increasing dramatically. In 1970 there were 17,800 ectopic pregnancies in the United States alone. By 1992, the latest year figures were available, the number of women who endured the emotional and physical anguish of ectopic pregnancy had reached 108,800, a rate of 19.7 for every 1,000 women who gave birth that year.

Close to 98 percent of all ectopic pregnancies occur in the fallopian tubes, but rare cases have been documented in the ovary, in the cervix, or elsewhere in the abdominal cavity. The embryo cannot survive away from the protective, nourishing environment of the uterus, although it continues to develop for several weeks. The greatest danger occurs when the ectopic pregnancy remains undiagnosed and the growing embryo ruptures surrounding tissue, causing severe internal bleeding, which can be fatal.

Women who have experienced one ectopic pregnancy have little more than a 40 percent chance of having a successful pregnancy afterward. This is because of the extensive damage usually done to the fallopian tubes and the increased risk of experiencing a second ectopic pregnancy with any subsequent conception.

Symptoms and Diagnosis of an Ectopic Pregnancy

The symptoms of an ectopic pregnancy can be well masked and varied, leaving you and your partner completely unprepared for the diagnosis. Your doctors may have been equally misled by the symptoms. In fact, misdiagnosis occurs in roughly 50 percent of all cases of ruptured ectopic pregnancies.

The most common symptom is intense abdominal pain, which usually increases just prior to the rupture of the fallopian tube, but then can decrease until either infection sets in or the volume of internal bleeding causes severe abdominal pressure. About 25 percent of women feel a sharp pain in their neck or shoulder, due to the pressure of hemorrhaging blood on certain nerves. Some women have described a sudden faintness caused by the loss of blood, even before the onset of pain.

The earlier an ectopic pregnancy is properly diagnosed, the more likely you will be able to conceive and carry a future pregnancy. If the doctor can treat the ectopic pregnancy before it ruptures, the chances of salvaging damaged tubes and other reproductive organs are greatly increased.

Once an ectopic pregnancy is suspected, the doctor can perform several procedures to confirm it. These include a pelvic examination to check for tenderness, a sonogram to look for the misplaced pregnancy, and blood tests to determine pregnancy hormone levels and to check for appendicitis. The doctor may test for blood in the abdominal cavity with culdocentesis, which involves inserting a needle through the vaginal wall to see if blood is drawn out. But these tests may still not be conclusive.

The most definitive diagnostic test is a laparoscopy, which requires anesthesia. The doctor makes a small incision in the abdomen and views the fallopian tubes and ovaries with a small optical instrument. Laparoscopy enables the doctor to see an ectopic pregnancy or abnormal bleeding that could indicate a rupture.

Treatment of an Ectopic Pregnancy

If an ectopic pregnancy is discovered or strongly suspected, the doctor will move directly into surgery. This is an extreme emergency, and action must be taken immediately to remove the pregnancy, save as much of the reproductive organs as possible and safeguard the mother's life. In some situations, doctors use the medication methotrexate to dissolve an ectopic embryo.

If the pregnancy has developed within the fallopian tube but the tube has not yet ruptured, it is possible that the pregnancy can be removed and the tube repaired. But once the tube has ruptured, chances are far greater that it must be removed. New microsurgical techniques and laser technology have increased the success of reconstructive surgery following a rupture, but statistics indicate that only about 60 percent of women conceive at all following an ectopic pregnancy, and of those, 15 percent have another ectopic pregnancy.

Causes of Ectopic Pregnancy

Several conditions can cause ectopic pregnancy. Fallopian tube problems are the most common factor in the 60 percent of ectopic pregnancies with known causes. Hormonal imbalance, reproductive tract malformations and infections can all impair the tubes' normal functioning and result in ectopic pregnancy.

Another factor is DES, a synthetic estrogen given to pregnant women from 1945 through the early 1970s because it was erroneously thought to forestall miscarriages. In fact, DES created health problems in the offspring it was supposed to save. Women of childbearing age whose mothers took DES when they were in utero have an increased risk of fallopian tube and uterine abnormalities.

About 2.5 million women were exposed to DES in utero, and approximately 13 percent of them have ectopic pregnancies. If a woman suspects she was exposed to DES in her mother's womb, she should check with her mother for an accurate medical history and inform her doctor.

In more than 40 percent of ectopic pregnancies a cause is never determined. Unfortunately, no matter what the cause, this is a dangerous medical condition that can recur, and which can create a difficult emotional aftermath.

Emotional Aftermath of an Ectopic Pregnancy

It is upsetting to know that once you have endured one ectopic pregnancy, with each subsequent conception you run the risk of another ectopic pregnancy, surgery and infertility. But a far graver concern is that another ectopic pregnancy could put your life in jeopardy again.

The extensive planning required to contemplate a subsequent pregnancy can affect every aspect of your life. You and your partner may avoid work-related trips or vacations to be sure you remain close to medical facilities while trying to conceive.

Tracy had experienced two ectopic pregnancies and felt as if she couldn't plan anything about her life or work for fear of having another. "Once I realized how vulnerable I was, it spilled into my whole life," she confessed. "Just planning the next pregnancy was a daunting task."

Ectopic pregnancies can also leave you and your partner upset by the loss of privacy when your personal misfortune becomes a medical crisis. Lack of privacy continues to be a problem when you try to conceive again because close medical monitoring is so important. One woman, who was anxious to become pregnant again, described how unsettling it was to have a pregnancy test early in each menstrual cycle. "I kept thinking I shouldn't have to expose all my hopes and feelings like this once a month," she admitted. "I did it because I had to, but it was like watching a pot that never boiled."

Because ectopic pregnancy is a life-threatening condition, a couple's sexual relationship is often affected. One woman described how the thought of possibly dying as a result of conception was "very unarousing" to both her and her husband. "Although we did other things to give each other pleasure and have climaxes," she recalled, "we simply were not able to have intercourse for almost a year after my ectopic pregnancy."

You may find that people who recognize the potential dangers in a subsequent pregnancy can make unusually presumptuous and vexing comments. "People just didn't want to hear that we were planning another pregnancy," explained one woman. "They thought my husband and I were crazy and irresponsible and didn't hesitate to tell us that."

Vera was equally annoyed when people asked her if she was ready to adopt after her second ectopic pregnancy. "At the time, my husband and I had different feelings about adoption," she admitted, "so we didn't feel like discussing it with outsiders." While you can't avoid the intrusion of other people's comments, you may feel better if you frankly explain that you need comfort more than advice.

Many people regard an ectopic pregnancy as a medical emergency only and refuse to realize that no matter where your baby was growing, it was still your baby. As Tracy explained:

> I couldn't shake the feeling that the first ectopic was a real baby. She was even a girl to me. She would have been born in June, and every summer I think about how old she would be now and what grade she would be entering in the fall.

Your ectopic pregnancy was a real pregnancy that ended in the loss of your baby. Although your feelings of grief may be complicated by serious medical concerns, you still need to mourn your loss as you recover from your physical and emotional ordeal.

EXPERIENCING A MOLAR PREGNANCY

> We had been married for three years when we decided to start a family. When I became pregnant and it appeared to be a normal pregnancy, everything seemed fine. Toward the end of the first trimester, the doctor couldn't find a heartbeat. I should have followed this up with blood work, which would have indicated the problem. I know I should have, but I have extremely small veins and refused to have the blood work done. I also felt fine and didn't think anything was wrong.
>
> At that point I changed doctors, and the new one insisted that I immediately go for a sonogram, and I went that day. I don't remember looking at the sonogram screen—I have blocked out so many of these painful memories—but I remember being told that there was nothing in the uterus. But they had to have seen the molar pregnancy, even though they didn't say anything to me. I felt so lost.
>
> —Sonia

A molar pregnancy—or as it is known medically, a hydatidiform mole—is a pregnancy in which the placenta develops into a mass of fluid-filled sacs that resemble clusters of grapes. There was initially a conception that triggered the formation of the hydatidiform mole, but no fetus was ever present in the womb.

A molar pregnancy grows at a regular rate, sometimes even faster than a normal pregnancy, and the uterus expands to accommodate its size. Although this condition is rare, occurring once in every two thousand pregnancies in the United States, it appears to be on the rise.

Women who suffer a molar pregnancy also face an increased risk of developing a rare form of cancer, which although highly treatable is still extremely serious and requires vigilant follow-up medical care.

Symptoms and Diagnosis of a Molar Pregnancy

There are very few physical symptoms of a molar pregnancy that serve as accurate warning signs. Most women experience bleeding, and some have nausea and vomiting, but these symptoms can occur in both normal and abnormal pregnancies. Severe nausea accompanying a hydatidiform mole may be caused by high hormone levels resulting from the rapid growth of the placenta. The sudden onset of high blood pressure can also be an indication that a hydatidiform mole has formed. But many women, like Sonia, have no outward symptoms at all. "It really seemed like a picture-perfect pregnancy up until the point when the doctor couldn't find a heartbeat," she recalled.

A molar pregnancy can be confirmed by a sonogram, which may indicate the lack of a fetus and fetal heartbeat as well as the particular shape of a molar tumor. A hydatidiform mole tends to produce excessive amounts of the pregnancy hormone HCG at a time when the levels should be falling, or at least leveling off, so a series of blood tests is another important diagnostic tool.

Treatment of a Molar Pregnancy

Molar pregnancies, like ectopic pregnancies, are among the few pregnancy losses that pose a severe threat to maternal health. Even if the molar pregnancy spontaneously miscarries, it will be necessary to remove remnants of the growth from the uterus, generally by a D&C procedure.

But the real danger comes later. In about 15 percent of molar pregnancies, the woman develops a rare form of cancer from the placental tissue, called gestational trophoblastic neoplasia, or GTN, which is nearly always curable with intensive chemotherapy. Doctors generally ask patients who have experienced a molar pregnancy to wait a year before conceiving again to make sure the molar pregnancy has not left a cancerous legacy behind. Levels of the pregnancy hormone HCG are measured weekly following a molar pregnancy, because if a certain level of HCG is still present, the suspicion of malignancy is high.

If you and your partner have experienced a molar pregnancy, you should be assured that this is a rare form of pregnancy loss. As long as you continue to have thorough checkups, you are likely to have other, healthy pregnancies.

Causes of Molar Pregnancy

Although the causes remain obscure, scientists have studied the genetics of molar pregnancy and have uncovered some important clues. A molar pregnancy appears to result from fertilization of an "empty egg," one in which the nucleus is absent or inactive. Doctors suspect there may be other factors as well, such as genetics and ethnic origin, which may explain the higher incidence of molar pregnancy in Southeast Asia. African-Americans, for example, have far fewer molar pregnancies than do white Americans.

A few reports have noted that a molar pregnancy is more likely to develop in the sister, especially a twin, of a woman who has already had one, and there is a documented risk for women over forty. If a woman has developed one hydatidiform mole, she has a slightly increased risk of having another and should be monitored carefully during subsequent pregnancies.

Emotional Aftermath of a Molar Pregnancy

Although you and your partner have suffered a molar pregnancy, you still have a very good chance of carrying a healthy baby to term. But succeeding pregnancies are tense and anxiety-ridden. One woman succinctly described her subsequent pregnancy as "probably the worst time of my life." Sonia felt she could relax more once she had a healthy baby who was born a year and a half after her molar pregnancy. But even with the pregnancy that produced her second healthy child, Sonia harbored doubts:

> At that point I knew I was capable of having a normal child, but I still worried that the second baby would turn into a molar tumor, even after I heard the heartbeat and saw the baby on the sonogram and knew she was a real baby.

You may also have to confront the reactions of family and friends, who are often misinformed about the dangers and risks of molar pregnancies. And because a baby was not actually growing, your need to grieve the loss of the child you had hoped for is often completely overlooked. As Sonia said:

> When people are ignorant they don't know what to say. Some people thought I would definitely get cancer and they were afraid of me. It was hard for me to accept that my conception was a hydatidiform mole, but in my mind the molar pregnancy was still a pregnancy and I grieved that loss.

KEY POINTS FOR COPING WITH YOUR EARLY LOSS

When you lose a pregnancy in the first trimester, you struggle to gain acknowledgment of a baby who was real primarily only to you. You may be stressed by having to seek medical tests or plan for special medical care during your next pregnancy. These additional demands make it especially important for you to acknowledge and mourn your baby.

Here are some suggestions that can help you give expression to your grief:

- Allow yourself time to grieve. Talk about your loss and your feelings with your partner; keep the lines of communication open. Be honest about what the pregnancy meant to you, no matter how brief it was.
- Ask your physician directly for medical information about your loss. If you think you should see a specialist, ask your doctor for a referral or seek a medical consultation with a specialist on your own. See Appendix D for help in locating a specialist.
- Don't be surprised if you suddenly feel sad again around the baby's due date or the anniversary of your loss. Many bereaved parents experience this "anniversary reaction."
- Seek out other sources of emotional support if you are not receiving acknowledgment of your loss from family, friends and medical staff. Read Chapter 10, "Finding Solace in Your Religion," and Chapter 11, "The Response of Your Family and Friends," and consider meeting with a psychotherapist or a pregnancy loss support group in your community.

6

Crisis Pregnancies and Loss

W hen your loss follows a serious complication during pregnancy, you and your partner have urgent medical decisions thrust upon you. The later your pregnancy loss, the more time and energy you both committed to becoming parents. Since some complications can be treated if detected early enough, you may feel additionally upset if the cause of your loss was not identified in time to save your baby.

Doctors are usually quick to intervene in crisis pregnancies because most result in premature birth. Babies born before thirty-four weeks' gestation have low birth weights and underdeveloped vital organs, which create complications that often lead to newborn death. But treatments for preventing threatened losses are often complex and sometimes experimental, compelling you to make medical and ethical decisions you may feel ill-equipped to handle.

The three most common causes of a crisis pregnancy are preterm labor, premature rupture of the membranes and cervical incompetence. Other losses may be related to a condition called placenta previa, in which the placenta grows over the opening of the cervix, triggering early delivery and other complications. If a woman's uterus is weakened from scarring or structural defects, it may rupture as the pregnancy progresses or labor begins. Diabetes, high blood pressure and certain infections such as listeriosis, caused by a common gastrointestinal bacterium, may bring on a medical crisis that can lead to pregnancy loss.

Although all crisis pregnancies share certain issues, the three most common causes of loss have particular treatments and emotional consequences which are discussed in this chapter. More detailed information regarding specific treatments can be found in Appendix A.

ISSUES COMMON TO ALL CRISIS PREGNANCIES

If your medical crisis progressed to delivery before the thirty-fourth week of your pregnancy, you faced the birth of an extremely premature baby. If labor began before twenty-five weeks' gestation, you faced the likelihood of your infant's death shortly after birth. You were probably unprepared for either a very ill infant or your baby's death, even if your condition had been accurately diagnosed and the prognosis explained to you.

Perhaps you and your partner had the chance to speak with a neonatologist or a specialist in maternal-fetal medicine who could realistically assess your baby's condition and chances of survival before delivery. Amelia and her husband, Charles, had lost a baby daughter due to prematurity. They met with two neonatologists while Amelia was in labor during the twenty-third week of her next pregnancy. The doctors explained that this baby would not be viable if delivered, which allowed Amelia and Charles to decide against intervening in their tiny infant's life should he be born that day. "Knowing in advance that Ethan wouldn't live long after birth," acknowledged Amelia, "helped us say goodbye to him."

Treatments for preterm labor, premature rupture of the membranes and cervical incompetence often involve bed rest and hospitalization, which profoundly affect all aspects of a patient's life. Extended bed rest and family separations during hospital treatments can take their toll on the most loving relationships, and children at home greatly miss their once active, involved mother.

Paula underwent treatments for premature rupture of the membranes and found them to be a physical and emotional ordeal:

> I had my legs up, and my head was lower than my feet. I couldn't eat solid food in case I went into labor at any moment, and I felt I was getting weaker and weaker every day. I couldn't move or go anywhere. I missed my daughter, who wasn't allowed to visit so she couldn't expose me to germs. It was awful, like being trapped while waiting for disaster to strike.

If you and your partner tried to maintain a crisis-ridden pregnancy, you may have been surprised when a sense of relief overcame you once the delivery was over, even though it resulted in your loss. If you did not know that relief is a natural response, you may have found it disturbing.

Relief after the delivery does not mean you didn't want or love your baby, but rather that you welcomed your release from the anxiety, uncertainty and, for mothers, the physical pain of enduring a crisis pregnancy. Feeling relief does not negate your sense of loss or your need to mourn. Accepting that both relief and sorrow are natural reactions to your loss can help your emotional recovery.

When a crisis pregnancy requires bed rest or hospitalization, both parents must adjust to the loss after enduring major disruptions in their family life and work obligations, ultimately in vain. Mothers are physically weak from their immobilization and need ample time to exercise and regain their strength. They may find it useful to ask for extra emotional and practical help during this adjustment period.

You and your partner will also have special medical and emotional needs when you begin to plan a future, possibly high-risk pregnancy. Reading Chapter 14, "The Impact of Pregnancy Loss on Your Career," and Chapter 16, "Becoming Pregnant Again," can help prepare you for the special challenges involved.

The physical and emotional strains of facing a future high-risk pregnancy may ultimately affect your dreams for the number of children you and your partner plan to have. Marianne, who had lost three children to crisis pregnancies, felt strongly about the difficulties of maintaining a pregnancy with bed rest. Her feelings intensified once she had a child to care for; she and her husband decided not to have any more children after their second healthy daughter was born:

> I went for a checkup when my youngest was about two years old, and the doctor was talking to us about birth control methods. He turned to us and said, "You know, there is no reason why you can't have another baby." But my husband and I just looked at each other and then at him and said, "No, two is just great!"

In addition to all the stresses you endured, you may be struggling to find some purpose to your sorrow that will enable you to mourn and go on with your life. Sometimes this takes the form of an added appreciation for a child born after the loss. "I think about the fact that we would not have Max if I had been able to keep that other baby," Paula explained. "And Max is so special and so wonderful."

You may also find you are more able to be comforting when friends and family experience sorrow and disappointment. Caroline admitted that her pregnancy loss following a medical crisis enabled her to reach out to others more effectively:

> I talk to people who have children with problems or who have experienced pregnancy losses. I feel we are all in it together and that I am more helpful because I truly understand what they are going through. I had good support from family and friends when I went through my loss, and I want to be there for others now.

EXPERIENCING PRETERM LABOR

> *During my first pregnancy, I was supposed to stop work and rest at home around the twenty-eighth or twenty-ninth week because of my double uterus, but I went into preterm labor three weeks before my last scheduled day at work.*

I thought something was happening, but it was my first pregnancy and I didn't know what to expect. The doctor examined me but couldn't feel anything or see anything, so he thought I was okay. I went on oral ritodrine just in case, but I only had time to take one pill before hard labor began.

My husband was out of town on a business trip, but I was in too much pain to drive myself to the hospital, so I called one of my best friends to drive me. I lay down in the backseat of her car, and even though I had never experienced childbirth before, I suddenly felt that the pain had changed, that something more dramatic was happening. We had just pulled into the parking lot of the hospital when I felt the baby being born. Suddenly it seemed like there were dozens of doctors and nurses and machines all around the backseat of the car.

Olivia was so premature, she only lived a few weeks. We had a memorial service for her, which concluded in the parking lot where she was born. We released a Mylar balloon from that spot, just like the ones we used to bring to her every week to attach to her isolette.

—Amelia

As Amelia discovered, preterm labor is both frightening and frustrating. Most parents desperately want their doctor to stop the process, to do anything to save the baby, but unfortunately this is not always possible.

Despite many medical advances in the past three decades, the incidence of preterm labor leading to birth has increased slightly, to approximately 9 percent of all live births in the United States. Preterm deliveries that are not due to congenital malformations or genetic problems are responsible for almost 75 percent of all neonatal deaths.

Symptoms and Diagnosis of Preterm Labor

Preterm labor is generally defined as at least six to eight uterine contractions per hour, accompanied by progressive change in the opening or thinning of the cervix between the twentieth and thirty-seventh weeks of pregnancy. But many women find the symptoms of preterm labor to be unclear, especially in a first pregnancy, when they are not sure what contractions or other warning signs should feel like. Because early contractions of preterm labor are not necessarily painful, some women may not even realize they are in labor.

Even if a woman is not sure what is happening, she may expect her doctor to make a precise diagnosis. But there is so much individual variation in cervical change and uterine contractions that physicians may not identify the condition. This is especially true in the very early stages, when doctors may overtreat contractions that are not necessarily a prelude to labor in order to avoid undertreatment of true labor.

Internal examinations are the best way to see whether the cervix has dilated or effaced. However, doctors usually keep such exams to a minimum because of the risk of introducing infection. Uterine monitors that indicate the strength and frequency of contractions are also employed to help diagnose preterm labor. Some doctors prefer to treat most symptoms rather than wait and run the risk of labor progressing so far that it is irreversible.

In spite of the high incidence of preterm labor and the opportunity physicians have to observe it, doctors are usually unable to predict when it will occur. As a result, physicians have focused their efforts on trying to prevent preterm labor in women at risk and on trying to stop, or at least slow down, the symptoms once they begin.

Treatment of Preterm Labor

If there is any possibility of stopping preterm labor, the doctor will impose bed rest and drinking of fluids at home, hoping that the contractions will slow or stop as soon as pressure is taken off the cervix and the woman is properly hydrated. If this fails, the woman is usually hospitalized for intravenous hydration with saline solution, which can also curb contractions. If labor stops and the woman is discharged home, her doctor may recommend that she use a small home monitoring device to pick up any recurrence of contractions.

If the contractions do not stop, the next line of defense is treatment with either oral or injected drugs, called tocolytics, to control contractions. Ritodrine is the only drug currently used to manage preterm labor which has been approved for this purpose by the FDA. A more complete discussion of these tocolytic agents is in Appendix A.

Because all tocolytics have dramatic side effects, including racing heart and low blood pressure, they are used only in clear cases of preterm labor and must be carefully regulated. It is a challenge for doctors to balance the efforts to prolong the pregnancy for the baby's safety against the mother's physical stress caused by such powerful drugs. As one doctor expressed it, "We have to remind ourselves that we are treating a mother here, too."

Causes of Preterm Labor

In most cases, the causes of preterm labor are unknown. Sometimes a woman simply begins the process of labor long before the baby is due. As Dr. Allan Weingold, for many years the chairman of the Department of Obstetrics and Gynecology at the George Washington University Medical Center, points out, "As much as we understand labor, no one knows exactly what triggers the strong contractions that help propel the baby into the world." This makes it hard simply to shut down the triggering mechanism until the baby has been in the uterus long enough to develop sufficient lung power and other critical functions necessary for survival.

Doctors do know that certain wombs cannot expand properly during pregnancy. This may be due to a structural malformation the woman is born with, such as Amelia's double uterus. Some women develop fibroid tumors, which can fill the space within the uterus so that a pregnancy does not have room to grow. A multiple pregnancy or excess amounts of amniotic fluid can also occupy more space than usual in the uterus and may trigger preterm labor.

Maternal illness, such as urinary tract, uterine and vaginal infections, has also been implicated in preterm labor. As the bacteria are destroyed in the body, by-products can include potent substances such as prostaglandins, which can cause uterine contractions.

Emotional Aftermath Following Preterm Labor

If the cause of preterm labor is related to a physical problem, many women are burdened with guilt following a loss. Amelia recalled feeling culpable at the moment of her second premature delivery:

> It crystallized for me when Ethan was born at twenty-three weeks and we knew he wouldn't survive. When I held him I cried and said, "Ethan, I'm really so sorry." I guess I held myself responsible. I was aware of my double uterus and knew it figured in these premature births and that part of the problem was intrinsic to me.

But not knowing the cause can be equally painful, rendering you and your partner fearful and anxious about future pregnancies and your hopes for having a family. Kimberly struggled with the fact that she never discovered the cause of the preterm labor that triggered her midterm loss:

> I started to question whether or not I was ever going to have a second child. The sense of futility, of having the loss happen so fast, of going through the high of making it to the second trimester, where I thought I would be safe, overwhelmed me. We were back to zero again.

Losing your baby after such a tremendous investment is heartbreaking. And once you know you are at risk for preterm labor, you must take extraordinary precautions the next time you become pregnant. Although this may include weeks or even months of bed rest and hospitalization, many carefully monitored subsequent pregnancies do result in the birth of healthy babies.

Even with the stress of your loss, you and your partner may still find some consequences to be surprisingly positive. After losing her baby to preterm labor, one woman said of her subsequent high-risk pregnancy:

> Our family and friends really worked together to help me manage this last pregnancy. Even with all my problems, I would definitely go through another pregnancy again, especially if I believe I can have a healthy baby at the end.

EXPERIENCING PREMATURE RUPTURE OF THE MEMBRANES

A couple of days after Paula's amniocentesis, she joined me in Florida for a vacation. She took a nap right after her plane landed, but when she awoke and stood up, there was a gush of fluid, and suddenly a pool of blood appeared on the floor. We rushed her to a nearby hospital, but the bleeding stopped by the time we got there. They did a sonogram and everything looked fine. The baby had a strong heartbeat.

This gave us an enormous sense of relief, but we decided to cut our vacation short and return home. Once home, Paula had a transvaginal sonogram and the doctor couldn't see a tear in the sac at all. The doctor felt if Paula kept her feet up and took it easy, everything would be fine. At that point I felt we had been spared and were lucky. We hadn't lost the baby and felt optimistic.

A few days later, Paula woke up in the middle of the night complaining of a warm rush of fluid. We were terrified she was hemorrhaging again and were relieved when we saw it was clear liquid. But she had to keep changing her sanitary pads all day and finally called the doctor, who told her to go to the hospital immediately. A sonogram showed almost all of the fluid gone, and they assumed Paula would go into labor immediately or would spike a fever from an infection. But she didn't do either and the fluid reaccumulated.

What followed then were several weeks of hospitalization. The fluid would accumulate and then leak again. The doctor thought the rip in the membranes might heal itself, and we clung to that hope. We were having frequent sonograms to test the fluid levels, and finally, one day, the fluid was all gone. A neonatologist told us that the baby's lungs could not develop properly from that point, that it was over. Paula still hadn't gone into labor, so she had to be induced. It was a harrowing experience.

—Ted

Like Paula and Ted, you and your partner probably knew that bleeding during pregnancy can be a sign of trouble, but you may not have realized that a loss of clear fluid could be a danger signal as well. Premature rupture of the membranes, or PROM, occurs when the fluid-filled membrane, or amniotic sac, that holds the growing baby breaks before the onset of labor. If the sac tears at term, 80 percent of women will go into normal labor within the next twenty-four hours. But if PROM occurs before thirty-four weeks' gestation, it can pose severe problems to both the baby and the mother.

The danger to the baby is threefold. First, preterm delivery is a major concern, usually occurring within a few days of the onset of

PROM. Second, once the protective sac has been torn, infection can set in rapidly. Third, once amniotic fluid starts leaking, the baby's lung and bone development may be compromised. Risks to the mother include uterine infection and fever, both of which can be managed with antibiotics and delivery of the baby.

Premature rupture of the membranes is responsible for 30 percent of all cases of premature birth in the United States. Usually the cause can never be discovered, but certain infections or specific conditions, such as excess amounts of amniotic fluid, multiple gestations or cervical incompetence, have been implicated in episodes of PROM.

Symptoms and Diagnosis of Premature Rupture of the Membranes

The most pronounced symptom of PROM is a sudden gush of fluid from the vagina followed by persistent, uncontrolled leakage, but other outward signs can be much more subtle. A woman may notice wetness and assume she is having trouble controlling her bladder or experiencing larger amounts of normal vaginal discharge, both of which are common during pregnancy.

The doctor should confirm the diagnosis by examining samples of the fluid and visually inspecting the cervix. There are several laboratory tests that can help distinguish amniotic fluid from other vaginal secretions or urine. The doctor may also monitor the woman to check for any signs of fetal distress or uterine contractions, or use a sonogram to determine the amount of amniotic fluid still within the sac. A pelvic examination with a sterile speculum should be done as soon as possible. An examination by hand is usually avoided unless the doctor expects delivery within twenty-four hours, because it increases the chance of infection.

Because of the difficulty in distinguishing between normal vaginal discharge and leakage of amniotic fluid, good communication between the woman and her doctor is especially important in cases of PROM. This can be a problem if she is cared for in a prenatal clinic or by a group of doctors in private practice, in which a different physician examines her at each visit. If this is your situation, you should be aware of the potential for missing a clear diagnosis and insist on thorough testing and as much continuity as possible in any future prenatal care.

Treatment of Premature Rupture of the Membranes

Once a diagnosis of PROM has been made, the doctor generally recommends complete bed rest in the hospital until delivery. The woman may be placed in the Trendelenburg position, in which her head is lower than her feet, allowing amniotic fluid to pool. Daily monitoring of both the mother and her unborn baby tests for the onset of possible infections. As a pregnancy advances, the amniotic fluid develops its own antibacterial properties, which can help ward off infection. But once an infection has developed in the uterus, it poses a danger to the mother and can cause the death of her baby.

PROM may also cause the umbilical cord to become compressed, which can be fatal for the baby. This can be checked carefully with a fetal heart monitor and nonstress tests administered to the mother.

If neither infection nor labor occurs, the doctor may ask the couple whether they want labor induced, to minimize risks to the mother, or if they want to wait to see what develops, in the hopes of increasing the baby's chance of survival. The parents are then forced to balance the risks to the mother's health against the baby's life in the face of great uncertainty.

No matter what the circumstances are, eventually a resolution does come. If sonograms indicate that too much fluid has leaked and the baby cannot be saved, labor is induced. Labor *must* be induced if laboratory analysis shows that infection has set in or if the mother develops a fever. Although induction or natural labor both provide a clear conclusion to the crisis, laboring for the birth of a baby who cannot survive is both an emotionally and physically painful event.

Causes of Premature Rupture of the Membranes

No one knows what causes premature rupture of the membranes, but several factors have been identified as contributing to the problem. Infectious agents such as chlamydia may ascend from the vagina through the cervix to attack and eventually weaken the amniotic sac, while also infecting the fluid and the growing fetus. Group B streptococcus organisms, which are routinely found in the vaginal mucus of 20 to 25 percent of all pregnant women, can also cause a weakening of the membranes, which could lead to their rupture. Since some of these conditions can be identified and even treated during pregnancy, a thorough medical examination is mandatory following any episode of PROM.

As a baby grows, the stress on the sac increases. If the structure of the sac is defective, its ability to recover from the impact of the baby's growth and movements may be reduced, and it could tear. Genetic and chromosomal abnormalities in the baby can also trigger premature rupture of the membranes.

Sometimes a combination of conditions could be responsible for PROM. Exposure to DES may cause abnormalities that alter the uterus, rendering it overly sensitive to invasive prenatal tests such as amniocentesis, triggering episodes of PROM. Most women never discover what caused their fluid to leak, and are left anxious and uncertain about what will happen in a subsequent pregnancy.

Emotional Aftermath Following Premature Rupture of the Membranes

If you experienced PROM that involved weeks of hospitalization, you lived through a physical ordeal and emotional extremes of hope and fear. If labor was eventually induced, you may have felt a sense of relief when there were clear medical reasons for ending your uncertainty. Paula and Ted were forced to accept that their baby was no longer viable after spending weeks trying to save their pregnancy. "It was like a great sense of relief washed over us," Ted recalled. "We were grateful it wasn't a marginal situation anymore, that it was now clear-cut. The decision was finally taken out of our hands."

Once you have suffered from premature rupture of the membranes, you must face the chance of encountering episodes in future pregnancies. Since you will have a 21 percent chance of experiencing PROM again in each subsequent pregnancy, you must be prepared for the possibility of extensive hospitalization and difficult choices following each conception.

Losing a baby following premature rupture of the membranes may cause you to search for some consolation that will give you hope and rekindle your desire for another baby. Your priorities may shift to accommodate new goals. Bert felt that his twenty-six-week loss related to PROM and other factors put much of his life into perspective. "The most important thing to me was my wife, that she was okay," he admitted. "And we realized how much we truly want to have a child and only hope that it will be possible."

EXPERIENCING CERVICAL INCOMPETENCE

I had lost babies at seven weeks, twenty weeks and twenty-seven and a half weeks. There were a combination of factors in the losses, but after the third loss, of our son who lived just a few minutes, my doctor and I decided to send me to a team of high-risk specialists. They felt that one of my problems was an incompetent cervix and told me that I would have to have a stitch put in my cervix to keep it closed once I was pregnant again.

I had the stitch put in at fourteen weeks in my next pregnancy. I went home and saw the doctor about a week later. The stitch had torn loose and ripped my cervix. At this point, it started to get to me. It seemed that up until our pregnancy losses, everything else in our lives had fallen into place. This seemed so frustrating and unfair.

After they fixed the stitch, I stayed in the hospital five months. My legs were up and my head was lower, so as the pregnancy advanced I started to do less and less. I played a mental game with myself. There

was so much time ahead of me. After so many losses, I tried to think
how lucky and temporary my current situation was. It all seemed worth
it when our healthy daughter was born at thirty-eight and a half weeks.

—Marianne

The cervix is a narrow, ring-shaped structure at the base of the uterus that opens into the vagina. The cervix consists mostly of nonmuscle fiber called collagen, and opens during labor in increasing amounts that are measured in centimeters of dilation. During this time it also goes through the process of effacement, becoming shorter and thinner. However, in a diagnosis of cervical incompetence this ring of fiber begins thinning and opening long before the pregnancy reaches full term, usually without contractions.

This condition generally appears during the second trimester of pregnancy and is surprisingly difficult to diagnose accurately. Calculations of how many women are afflicted with cervical incompetence vary widely. One estimate states that up to 20 percent of all losses in the second trimester of pregnancy are related to cervical incompetence.

Symptoms and Diagnosis of Cervical Incompetence

The symptoms of cervical incompetence fall into two categories: those that a woman can feel or see and those that are observed by her doctor. It is important that both sets of symptoms be monitored constantly, beginning with the second trimester of any pregnancy at risk for this condition.

Symptoms that a patient can see or feel include vaginal bleeding, or increased vaginal discharge, especially if it is mixed with mucous. A woman may also feel pressure in her pelvis or experience pain similar to cramping. A classic case of incompetent cervix will *not* be accompanied by the strong uterine contractions associated with labor.

Signs that the doctor checks through an internal examination all involve determining the condition of the cervix, such as effacement and dilation, especially if these signs are not accompanied by uterine contractions.

If a woman has had one or more second-trimester losses of undetermined causes, but without labor having to be induced, her doctor should regularly check the condition of her cervix during any subsequent pregnancy by looking at it with the aid of a speculum and performing internal examinations. If the cervix is slightly effaced or opened, or if any of the membranes seem to be showing through the cervical opening, cervical incompetence should be suspected. Sonography can be used to measure the length of the cervix, but it is not always conclusive.

Since there are no straightforward criteria for diagnosing cervical incompetence, it is important that the doctor have an understanding of the patient's complete medical history, especially if she has had a second-trimester loss suspected to be from cervical incompetence.

Treatment of Cervical Incompetence

The primary treatment for cervical incompetence is a cervical cerclage, or stitch. If a woman has a history of cervical incompetence, or if she is showing clear-cut symptoms of cervical incompetence, the cerclage can be placed in and around the cervix, pulling it into a tightly closed position. This procedure requires some form of anesthesia and a brief hospitalization, usually at the end of the first trimester. There are more risks if the cervical cerclage is placed after eighteen weeks' gestation or once the cervix has opened two to three centimeters. No cerclage is attempted if the cervix has opened four centimeters or more. The cerclage is usually removed in the thirty-seventh week of pregnancy, before labor begins, so it will not tear the cervix as it begins to open.

Success rates for cerclages are difficult to calculate, but some doctors report that using the cervical cerclage prior to dilation on women who have experienced previous cervical incompetence enables 80 percent of them to have full-term pregnancies. Complications of the cerclage include bleeding, leaking of amniotic fluid through ruptured membranes, infection to either the mother or the unborn baby and the onset of labor.

If cervical incompetence is not detected until the cervix has dilated, or if the patient had a cerclage and developed complications in spite of the stitch, bed rest is recommended. Complete bed rest is generally best achieved in the hospital, where the woman can be cared for by professional staff twenty-four hours a day.

Uterine abnormalities that are related to cervical incompetence pose a more difficult problem. Some, such as a uterus divided by a wall of tissue, or septum, can be surgically corrected if necessary; others, specifically the T-shaped uterus common to DES daughters, cannot routinely be repaired through surgery. And surgery has its own risks, such as scarring, which could create additional problems in a subsequent pregnancy.

Causes of Cervical Incompetence

It used to be that poorly done D&C procedures associated with illegal abortions were the primary cause of cervical incompetence, but since the legalization of abortion, these statistics have dropped dramatically. Most cervical incompetence is now traced to uterine or cervical abnormalities a woman is born with, especially a cervix that is unusually short.

One of the primary causes of this type of structural cervical incompetence is exposure to the drug DES while a woman was in her mother's womb. If a woman knows she has been exposed to DES, she may have wondered why her doctor didn't perform a cervical suture as soon as her first pregnancy occurred. Since many women with DES-related cervical defects have normal pregnancies, the risks inherent in performing a cerclage outweigh any potential benefits until an incompetent cervix has definitely been diagnosed.

Some spontaneous cases of cervical incompetence show up in women with no known risk, generally after one or more full-term pregnancies. These cases may have resulted from an undetected tear in the cervix or other cervical damage that occurred during the delivery of a previous child. Cone biopsy, a form of cervical surgery, was once implicated in cervical incompetence, but more recent studies have disputed this correlation.

Emotional Aftermath Following Cervical Incompetence

Even the medical term *incompetent cervix* may give a parent pause. Some believe it implies a degree of ineptness on the part of the mother, who should not be made to feel guilty about a structural cervical problem she did not cause. Ruth, a DES daughter, strongly objected to this language:

> It was a horrible terminology to me because it made me feel as if the medical profession was saying that I wasn't quite good enough to be a mother. My cervix was short and I could visualize that. A short cervix that I couldn't control didn't seem as judgmental to me as an *incompetent cervix*.

If you and your partner experienced a pregnancy loss through cervical incompetence, you should expect to have special medical precautions taken during each subsequent pregnancy. The recurrence of cervical incompetence is relatively high, so future pregnancies are anxious pregnancies; the innocent expectation of a picture-perfect pregnancy can no longer be yours.

The increase in the number of doctor's appointments can be a drain on your time and energy, adding to your tension in a subsequent pregnancy. Laurel, who had lost one baby because of cervical incompetence, described what this medical vigilance was like:

> In my next pregnancy, I saw my doctor weekly from twenty weeks on, at my request. From thirty-two weeks on I was hooked up to a fetal monitor weekly, and at thirty-five weeks I also started having a sonogram every week. All this made me extremely anxious.

You and your partner may be yearning for a way of accepting your sorrow, of integrating it into your life so you can believe your prematurely born infant had not lived, however briefly, in vain. Amelia felt she had established a strong connection with her second baby through weeks of hospitalization, even though his premature birth could not be stopped and he lived only about two hours:

> Ethan became a source of companionship for me while I was hospitalized. I actually talked to him and felt we were allies fighting the battle together. Other people came to visit me when it was convenient for them, but Ethan was always there. Ethan was incredibly loyal.

Marianne, who suffered from cervical incompetence, ultimately felt her losses had a bittersweet meaning:

> My losses helped me; they taught me to learn what was important in life and what wasn't. People who experience tragedy are more sensitive to others. Not that I would wish sorrow on anyone, but if it happens, we might as well try to make it a part of our lives and not deny it. And we should try to grow from it.

KEY POINTS FOR COPING WITH YOUR LOSS IN A CRISIS PREGNANCY

A loss following a crisis-ridden pregnancy poses particular problems. You and your partner had already invested a great deal of time and energy in the pregnancy, perhaps after days or weeks of hospitalization or home bed rest. Such sacrifices probably added to your bitter disappointment and frustration when your pregnancy ended in a loss, compounding your feelings of grief.

Here are some suggestions to help you cope with your loss:

- Many parents feel a sense of relief when a difficult pregnancy has ended. Relief doesn't mean you didn't love your baby.
- Discovering that you have an underlying medical problem can leave you angry, especially if you endured bed rest or other stressful interventions. Try to channel your energy into finding the best medical care during your next pregnancy.
- Try not to berate yourself for making decisions about medical care that seemed to pit the mother's interests against your baby's. Balancing these issues is extremely difficult, especially when the outcome is uncertain.
- If you were hospitalized, allow time to regain your physical strength—about three weeks for each week spent on bed rest—and to reestablish your relationship with your partner and any children at home.

7

Stillbirth and Newborn Death

If your baby was stillborn or died shortly after delivery, you experienced childbirth, but it was a tragedy instead of the happy event you had anticipated. You were committed to the pregnancy, nurtured it and planned for the birth of your child. Instead, you now face unfathomable grief.

Losses beyond the first trimester are less common than early miscarriages. Fourteen percent of all pregnancy losses occur in the second trimester and 6 percent in the third. Yet the causes of both stillbirth and newborn death are numerous. Problems with the structure, positioning or functioning of the placenta or umbilical cord; maternal illness; premature delivery for any reason; birth defects in the baby; and low birth weight have all been implicated in precipitating later losses. While the cause of many newborn deaths can be determined, over 50 percent of all stillbirths remain unexplained.

After having a loss so late in your pregnancy, you may move through intense grief reactions, especially if you saw your baby and said goodbye. If you have no other children, the shock of such a sad outcome to your pregnancy confronts you with an identity confusion in which you may wonder, "Am I really a parent?" You can be left with the painful contradiction of feeling like a childless mother or father.

ISSUES COMMON TO ALL STILLBIRTHS AND NEWBORN DEATHS

Like many parents, you may begin to feel guilty, assuming that you somehow caused or might have prevented this tragedy. If your loss was triggered by environmental or genetic causes, your sense of responsibility for being exposed to dangerous toxins or passing on a defective gene may compound your grief. Even if you know the tragedy was beyond your control, you may still succumb to guilt, since blaming yourself is one way of trying to comprehend an incomprehensible loss.

78

Although Wendy realized that her baby daughter died from a congenital heart defect she could not possibly have caused, she still felt guilty. "I always wanted a girl," she explained, "and in a way I worried that was why she had died—because I preferred to have a girl and was being punished for wanting one sex more than the other."

You may find yourself wishing that you had received different prenatal care, believing you could have saved your baby had you been more vigilant. Even when your doctors have assured you there was no way to prevent your loss, you can still be haunted by a longing to have done more.

Roger, whose first child was stillborn after the placenta stopped functioning properly, continued to wonder if the problem might have been detected if his wife had been classified as a high-risk mother and under more constant medical care. "There was little solace for us in knowing we hadn't caused the loss," he admitted.

If your pregnancy was complicated by medical problems that required bed rest or surgery for the mother, your loss can seem profoundly unjust. "My sense of unfairness was heightened by having been bedridden for so long both times," admitted Amelia after she lost a second premature baby. "It seemed as if my husband and I had suffered enough just trying to hold on to the pregnancies."

Late losses can occur with no warning signs. The mother may have experienced a problem-free pregnancy, which gave her, her partner and her doctor a sense that all would continue to go well. If she was under thirty-five, with no family history of abnormal births, her doctor may have considered her too young to be given prenatal diagnostic tests that could have revealed a problem. Parents' shock and grief at losing a baby who had seemed fine for so many months can be overpowering.

Once you have accepted your loss, you can still feel intense frustration over not having been able to protect your baby from harm. However blameless, you may feel you failed your infant, who was vulnerable and dependent. These feelings may intensify when you return home to face the baby's room, complete with crib and layette. You and your partner may have even moved to a bigger apartment or bought your first house, which is rendered uselessly large and empty by your loss.

It is important to think through and trust your feelings before deciding what to do with the baby's room and layette. Don't rush into a decision that doesn't feel right to you because family or friends are pressuring you, or because you think it's the proper thing to do. Some bereaved parents want the baby things packed up and out of sight before the mother returns from the hospital, so the house doesn't feel like a baby is still expected. Others find the layette a poignant reminder of their love, and they spend quiet moments in the baby's room remembering and grieving, and eventually hoping and planning for another baby.

Irene had gathered a few baby items because she wanted the first days after the birth to be a special, quiet time for her new family. Her baby was due in August, and she didn't want her husband to have to run around shopping in the summer heat. Irene discovered that after her daughter was stillborn, it gave her courage to see the baby's things and that their presence helped confirm her commitment to have another child. "I had made the crib bumpers and sheets myself," she explained, "and when I put them away I said to myself, 'I *will* use these someday.'"

Having this tangible connection to your baby can provide an expression of love and grief in the early stages of mourning, enabling you, your friends and your family to achieve another level of acceptance. This happened for Amelia and Charles, who had prepared a room for their firstborn, a premature daughter who died unexpectedly after being cleared to go home. They discovered that entering their baby's room and being able to see and touch Olivia's pictures, toys and clothing gave reality to her existence, their love for her and, ultimately, their need to say good-bye.

This crystallized for Amelia one afternoon when a friend brought her three-year-old daughter, Sarah, for a visit:

> We were upstairs and Sarah said, "Is that Olivia's room? Can I see it?" We went through Olivia's photo album, too, which was in the room. Sarah's only experience with death had been Olivia's dying, and I wondered if this was going to be okay for her. When we got to the end of the photo album, Sarah didn't seem afraid at all. Actually, going into Olivia's room and looking at the album put all the questions to rest that Sarah had been asking about death, and it helped me enormously, too.

You may find yourself in the awkward position of having to cancel arrangements for child care or other household help that were made in anticipation of a normal birth. Molly had hired a housekeeper to start cleaning on a weekly basis after her baby was due. When her son was stillborn, Molly was so distraught she kept putting off calling the housekeeper to tell her the news. The housekeeper finally called her. "Before I could say anything, she wanted to know if I had the baby yet and was it a boy or a girl," remembered Molly. "All I could do was say the baby died and hang up on her."

Most parents prefer to have a friend or family member call to explain the loss and the change in plans, but again, trust your own inclinations. No matter who makes the call to cancel arrangements, it is best to do it promptly, to avoid the pain and embarrassment of having the sitter or housekeeper call first for news of the baby.

Once parents have managed to absorb their loss and deal with issues and decisions they can control, mothers must still struggle with their body's response to the pregnancy, which is both a physical and emotional reminder of the loss. Even if a woman has injections to prevent lactation, her milk may come in, reminding her how disastrously amiss it is to have her breasts so full of milk with no baby to nurse.

All of these sensations and dilemmas conspire to make you and your partner feel the loss of your roles as parents as well as the loss of your child. Leah, whose newborn lived only a few hours, found this loss of motherhood especially troubling:

> When Mother's Day came around the following month, I just felt awful. Technically I wasn't a mother anymore. It seemed to me that caring for a child was what makes us parents and that not being able to continue caring for a child took that away.

Another mother, however, felt strongly that her stillborn daughter had enabled her and her husband truly to become parents:

> I think Mindy made us parents, because even though we didn't have a baby in the house, we still loved this child. And that's the sadness of pregnancy loss. You have the love for your child that does indeed make you parents; only you don't have the child.

Experiencing a stillbirth or newborn death makes subsequent pregnancies extremely trying, since no point in the pregnancy ever seems safe, even if your chances of delivering a healthy baby are good. "I was convinced my next baby would die the same way," said Molly of the healthy pregnancy that followed her stillbirth, "but I also knew nobody wanted to hear about that, so I had the added burden of keeping the fear inside."

Once you are beyond the initial shock of your loss, you face the hard work of integrating this tragedy into your life. You will never forget the death of your baby, but you can find new richness in your life once you have absorbed your loss and learned to go on. Gayle and her husband had lost three newborns to a rare genetic factor and struggled with the impact that losing the babies had on their lives:

> What I found especially upsetting about the losses was that I was raised to feel if you work hard enough, you will get whatever you want. "It's up to you" was a phrase we heard a lot around our house when I was a kid. But it's not, and pregnancy loss teaches you that. Yet we didn't want to use our bad luck as a crutch to become unhappy. We both wanted to go on with life, to try to have other children. And we did.

Irene and her husband were able to discover a positive legacy amid their sorrow following their daughter's stillbirth:

After Mindy was stillborn, I became more sensitive to other people's feelings. I might even go overboard now. I try to help people and be more sensitive to other people's grief and sorrow. I think it affected my husband, too, in the same way, in being more sensitive. This is our daughter's gift to us.

EXPERIENCING A STILLBIRTH

> I was so excited about the pregnancy. It was our first, and it had gone so well. I worked right up to the eighth month. One night in the ninth month, my husband, Roger, and I were eating in a restaurant and I felt some violent movements in my womb. Three days later, the baby didn't move at all. I went to the doctor's office, but she couldn't find a heartbeat. She tried vaginal stimulations but couldn't get any response. By the next day I had started labor on my own and was admitted to the hospital, where our baby was born dead.
>
> —Sally

Sally and Roger had experienced a stillbirth, a tragedy that befalls over fifteen thousand couples each year in the United States alone. Stillbirth is a contradiction of what we are led to expect in life: death comes before birth, stillness replaces movement, birth becomes an ending instead of a beginning.

Because of this disparity, the symptoms of grief can be exceptionally strong following a stillbirth. Some parents experience aching arms and hear phantom crying for days or even weeks after learning of their baby's death. It is hard to accept that something has gone so drastically wrong after long months of anticipation. Parents feel cheated when their child is stillborn, after investing so much time in the pregnancy and enduring childbirth—all for naught.

Diagnosis and Treatment of a Stillbirth

Symptoms of stillbirth are sometimes difficult to perceive. Even the most active baby can be still for long periods of time in its mother's womb. In the last stages of development before birth, babies rest and often enter a state of deep sleep that can last forty to sixty minutes. Once the baby has grown considerably in the final month of pregnancy and its head is engaged into the pelvis, the baby cannot move as freely in the womb as it once did. The occasional kick and shift of position is about the most movement a full-term baby can manage in the final two to three weeks before birth—and these are often the abrupt movements more closely associated with the baby's sleep state. Many healthy but subtle fetal movements, such as thumb sucking, are not even perceptible to the mother. Some women, such as Sally, experience violent movements prior to a stillbirth, after which the baby becomes uncommonly still. Others may perceive the stillness only after one or two days have passed.

The most immediate means of diagnosing a stillbirth is to listen for the baby's heartbeat. Since fetal heartbeats cannot always be heard through stethoscopes, doctors often use a handheld device called a Doppler instrument. If this is inconclusive, a full sonogram is scheduled. Both fetal movement and a baby's heartbeat can be seen immediately during a full ultrasound exam, and in their absence, a diagnosis of stillbirth is accurately confirmed almost 100 percent of the time.

Until relatively recently, there was little doctors could do to hasten the birth of a baby who had died in utero, and the woman was forced to carry the baby until the onset of natural labor. Waiting for labor poses little medical danger to the mother, unless it is delayed for a month or more after the death. But the psychological impact of carrying a dead baby while looking very pregnant is difficult to handle, especially if labor does not begin for days, or even weeks, following the diagnosis.

Although waiting for the onset of natural labor may be the safest medical course to take, many doctors are willing to induce labor to spare parents the agonizing delay before a futile, spontaneous delivery. The most common induction methods have been in practice for over two decades and include prostaglandin vaginal suppositories, Pitocin, and laminaria sticks. The newest method involves a pill taken either orally or vaginally, but with any form of induction, labor can be full, long and difficult.

Causes of Stillbirth

In about 50 percent of all stillbirths, no specific cause can be determined. Of the remaining half, the primary reasons fall into three basic categories: problems with the structure or functioning of the placenta or umbilical cord; maternal illnesses or conditions that affect the pregnancy; and birth defects in the baby, caused by chromosomal or genetic abnormalities.

One of the more common causes of stillbirth is the premature separation of the placenta from the uterine wall, which is called placental abruption. Normally the placenta does not begin separating from the uterus until after birth has occurred, but if this process begins before or during labor, the baby's lifeline for oxygen and nutrients is cut off at the source—the mother's body. Women who have one early placental separation leading to stillbirth have a 10 percent chance of experiencing a second abruption. If a woman has had two abruptions, her chances of experiencing another in a subsequent pregnancy are greater than 25 percent.

If a pregnancy goes longer than it should, the placenta can stop functioning properly. Structural defects in the placenta and the umbilical cord can also cause stillbirth. Sometimes a kink or knot forms in the cord, cutting down on the flow of blood and oxygen to the baby. A cord can become wrapped around the baby's neck or some other part of its body either before or during birth with the same effect, one that is often accelerated during the stress and pressures of labor. If the cord prolapses, or comes out of the uterus prior to delivery, it can be squeezed, cutting off the baby's blood supply.

Many maternal illnesses can cause stillbirth, primarily because the mother's health affects the functioning and well-being of the placenta. Since the placenta absorbs diseases and drugs from the mother's body, it can be so adversely affected that adequate nutrients and oxygen do not cross over to the baby. Lupus, hypertension, diabetes, preeclampsia and infections such as syphilis, listeriosis and rubella have all been implicated in stillbirths. Smoking cigarettes can inhibit the flow of oxygen through the placenta, and the use of cocaine can cause the placenta to constrict, inhibiting the transport of nutrients to the baby and leading to stillbirth.

Many illnesses implicated in stillbirth can be treated during a subsequent pregnancy, but the sad fact remains that stillbirths often occur to women with no known risk factors.

Chromosomal defects account for 15 to 20 percent of all stillbirths. Down syndrome babies, for example, have a greater than 30 percent chance of being stillborn. Malformations that are not chromosomal in nature, such as urinary tract obstructions and gastrointestinal tract malformations, can also cause stillbirth.

Stillbirth can occasionally occur as a result of an abnormal labor and delivery. The placenta may pull away from the uterine wall during labor, or the umbilical cord might become constricted during delivery. Fetal monitoring is generally so routine in hospitals during labor that such crises can usually be determined, and interventions, such as cesarean deliveries, implemented to prevent the baby's death. However, a woman may arrive at the hospital too late for her baby to be saved if her labor was quick and the damage has already occurred.

Once you have experienced a stillbirth, it is very important to try to determine a cause, especially if you are planning future pregnancies. An autopsy can help ascertain the cause of death, or at least rule out some possible reasons for the stillbirth. A biopsy and genetic testing, or karyotyping, of your baby's tissues should be done immediately after delivery. Even if another, more obvious cause seems readily apparent, such as the cord being wrapped around the baby's neck, these tests ensure that all underlying causes have been considered. The baby might have had Down syndrome or a genetic defect that could have precipitated its death in utero, a risk you may want to examine before planning a subsequent pregnancy.

If the baby was normal in every way but your pregnancy suffered from some random and unpredictable event, such as a cord accident, your chances of having another healthy pregnancy are very good. A subsequent pregnancy would not necessarily be considered high-risk, and your doctor might recommend routine medical care. Tests that evaluate the baby's health while still in the womb, such as nonstress testing, contraction stress testing, fetal movement charts and sonograms, can be reassuring options you may want to discuss with your doctor.

Emotional Aftermath Following a Stillbirth

Like many parents who experience stillbirth, you may have been upset by having to wait for labor to begin naturally. "I knew Sally's doctor felt it was best for our having future children that labor not be induced," explained Roger when he learned his first child would be stillborn, "but it seemed so horrible for Sally to have to carry the baby around and wait."

In some ways, however, waiting may have helped you deal with the loss more effectively. You had time to absorb the tragic news and think about decisions you and your partner would face after delivery, such as holding and naming your baby or having an autopsy and planning a burial. The time delay also may have allowed you to feel somewhat more emotionally prepared for your difficult delivery.

Gloria and her husband preferred to wait for labor to begin once they learned their unborn baby had died, and were pleased to find the hospital staff supported their wishes. "We asked if we could go home until I went into labor spontaneously," she remembered, "and my doctor agreed. We wanted the birth to be as natural as possible, as we had originally planned, with as much privacy as possible."

If you chose to wait, you probably preferred to stay indoors to avoid dealing with people's comments about your pregnancy. "I thought if one more bus driver cheerfully asked me when my baby was due," recalled one mother of the time when she waited for labor with her stillborn child to begin, "I would start screaming and not be able to stop."

Once you delivered your stillborn baby, you may have been able to marvel at the baby's beauty and innocence, no matter what the cause of the stillbirth. Roger remembered how difficult this seemed at first:

> The hardest thing was to hold him in my arms, but I'm glad I did. He had all his little toes. He was a very normal-looking baby. I just rocked him and cried uncontrollably as I looked at his round face and nose—his little ski nose—and his little lips. It was so important to hold him.

Even with the finality of the stillbirth, you may have felt as if your nightmare was just beginning. "Leaving the hospital without the baby was the toughest," admitted Roger, recalling the day after his stillborn son's birth. "It seemed so very wrong." Each event related to the still-birth weighs heavily in your thoughts, and you may find yourself reliving the labor and birth of your baby over and over again.

As time passes, however, you may become more aware of the profound effect your stillborn child has had on your life. "Jason brought my wife and me closer together," Roger remembered. "It is one of his legacies to us."

Molly had turned to friends and relatives for comfort after losing her stillborn son. When she found that many people couldn't handle her and her husband's pain, it seemed to magnify their loss, and she vowed to help others through this difficult time. She trained to be a lay counselor with the pregnancy loss support group that had helped her cope with her stillbirth. Although the work is emotionally demanding, Molly finds that it helps confirm the positive effect her son's brief existence has had on their lives:

> I feel passionately about trying to help others. I try very hard now to reach out to people in the same way that I found helpful. This not only helps them, it is another way of establishing Nathaniel's existence for me. Nathaniel was real. He was our son.

EXPERIENCING A NEWBORN DEATH

> Ashley was born and died on Thanksgiving Day. I went into labor on schedule and was given Pitocin, so it progressed quickly. When Ashley was born, the delivery room got very quiet. The doctors rushed her out of the room and said nothing to us. I was taken to recovery, and all the doctor told my husband, Joel, was that he had to be strong.
>
> Later we learned that our baby was born with severe congenital anomalies. She lived fifty minutes. Joel told me when she died. He brought her in for me to see, wrapped in a pink blanket. That is when it hit me. Joel wouldn't be a father. We wouldn't be taking Ashley home.
>
> —Sylvia

In 1998 close to 3.9 million babies were born in the United States. Approximately 36,000 of those lived less than a month. Learning that your ill newborn did not have a good chance of survival forced you to endure the torment of uncertainty about your baby's health as you watched your child struggle for life, ultimately in vain.

You may have been confused and overwhelmed by the medical choices regarding your baby's care that were suddenly thrust on you. Even if the baby's prognosis was bleak, avoiding medical intervention may have seemed tantamount to abandoning the child you had nurtured and loved during the pregnancy. Leah responded to her newborn son's multiple defects by requesting that everything possible be done for him:

> I remember telling the doctors, "Save him! Save him!" but there were no choices, really. His genetic problems were so severe. There were no decisions to make, so we didn't have to face any. Christopher lived only four hours.

Facing major decisions about surgery, removal of life support systems, and other interventions in an infant's care can cause additional anguish to already overburdened parents. Adam and Lisa's baby daughter was not expected to live because of severe congenital anomalies and was placed in the neonatal intensive care unit until she died. Even knowing that her life would be brief, the couple was not spared a series of medical decisions that eventually created friction between them. Since the baby could not suck on her own, the doctors asked the distraught parents if they wished to have a feeding tube inserted through her nose. "I didn't agree with the feeding and the use of the tube," acknowledged Adam. "I didn't see the need for prolonging her misery and our agony. We knew death was just a few hours away."

Lisa felt differently and asked the doctors to insert the tube:

> I couldn't bear the thought that on top of everything else she was suffering, that she would also be hungry. But when they tried to insert the tube, Lara winced and cringed, and they felt they were hurting her more than helping her, so they left it out. I still have a problem with the whole issue and the antagonism it created between us as parents.

Parents may be perplexed by conflicting information from medical experts. Amelia and Charles's first baby, a premature daughter, had been on a ventilator from birth, and her short life was a roller coaster of hope and fear. One day, after their daughter had been transferred to a more sophisticated neonatal intensive care unit in a different hospital, the physician who headed the unit asked to have a meeting with Amelia. The new doctor suggested that their baby should continue on the ventilator and stay on it for as long as two years:

> I was caught by surprise, since there had been no previous conversation about this topic. In fact, at the hospital where our daughter was born, no goal was more important than getting babies off the ventilator, because eventually it causes its own damage. After two years on a ventilator, our baby probably would not have been able to move well, swallow, cry or even eat normally.

Caught off guard and feeling especially vulnerable because her husband wasn't available at that moment, Amelia found the choices were suddenly clarified. "I looked at all the doctors present at the meeting and said, 'I am speaking for both my husband and myself most emphatically, that we will *never* choose that kind of life for our child,'" she recalled.

Experiences like Amelia's may have left you concerned about how much authority you ultimately had regarding medical interventions in your baby's care. You may have wondered what your legal rights were and worried that a doctor could decide on medical treatment for your child without honoring your wishes.

Perhaps you had access to a second expert medical opinion when faced with these difficult circumstances. Some states have grappled with this issue and now support the concept of letting parents of ill newborns sign a living will, a document that clearly declares and protects parents' wishes concerning treatment and intervention in their baby's care.

If your baby had been very ill, she may have been hooked up to monitors and other medical apparatus, or she may have been placed in an isolette, which prevented you from holding and cuddling her. She may have looked exceptionally fragile and made you afraid that touching her might jostle delicate medical instruments and cause harm. Once your infant died and the tubing and monitors were removed, you may have found it comforting to cradle your baby in your arms as you had longed to do while she was alive.

Amelia recalled one of the nurses recommending a touching ritual immediately after Amelia's premature daughter died:

> It seemed so bizarre at first, but so right after we did it. She suggested that we give Olivia a bath. It was wonderful! It was the first time Olivia wasn't encumbered with any electrodes and tubes. She was still warm and pink, and we put her in one of her little outfits. We stayed a little longer and then went home. The last thing we saw of Olivia that day was her dressed in the little pink and white stretchy suit we had put her in. It was a wonderful memory.

Even if you saw and held your infant, you may have grappled with the distress of having so little time with your baby. You may have wondered if your tiny child could really know how much you loved her. You knew you wanted to cuddle and reassure your baby, but that may have been impossible because of the baby's constant medical care. Amelia recalled being so caught up in the emergency surrounding her second baby's premature birth that she felt she spent more time on the medical crisis than on just loving her son. "There were so many decisions to be made," Amelia said. "I know I was protecting our baby's rights, but I spent so much time talking to the neonatologist and I wish I had spent it talking to Ethan instead."

If you were the mother of a critically ill newborn who was transferred to a different hospital for special medical care before dying, the separation from your baby was especially wrenching. Your doctor may have discharged you early so you could spend precious time with your child. Rose, whose baby lived only twenty-three hours, explained what this shared time meant to her: "I knew he was dying," she said. "But it made me feel better to be with him, to know at least I had done that for him."

If you could not leave the hospital and your baby had to be transferred, you faced an unavoidable separation from your infant, which may have made you feel you had literally abandoned your baby. Dr. Gary Benfield, of the Children's Hospital Medical Center of Akron, Ohio, suggests a number of practical measures that can help in this situation. After the baby's urgent medical problems have been attended to, he recommends the mother see and touch her infant before the transfer and suggests she keep a photograph of the baby with her. He advises the nursery staff to give her the name of a contact person she can call at any time for information about the baby's condition. Some special-care nurseries even have a toll-free number, to make them as accessible as possible. Dr. Benfield encourages the baby's father and grandparents to visit the baby as frequently as they wish and to describe the infant's condition to the mother. These measures allow the mother to feel connected to her baby in spite of their separation.

Other problems may have compounded your distress during your baby's illness. You may have been alarmed by the staggering hospital bills for your newborn's care and then felt guilty that you dared to worry about finances when your baby's life was in jeopardy. When Lisa was told her infant had fatal malformations two weeks before her due date, she struggled with her initial reaction:

> I knew our baby was not supposed to live, but I kept thinking over and over, "What are we going to do?" and "How do we raise this baby?" I knew about infant nursing homes and what they cost. Thinking about how we could afford all this seemed so selfish.

Medical care of sick newborns is indeed critical, constant and enormously expensive. An isolette in the neonatal intensive care unit is the single most expensive bed in the hospital and can run well over a thousand dollars a day, not including medications, supplies and special procedures.

One father found that his feeling of being overwhelmed by the staggering costs actually diminished as the bills for his ill newborn son's treatment mounted. "If you have reasonably good insurance coverage," he admitted, "the thought eventually occurs to you that they will pay it." When the bills started reaching tens of thousands of dollars, he felt that "it was kind of like thinking about the national debt. It moved out of the realm of reality, and I stopped worrying about it."

Even if you feel confident that your insurance company will cover the bills, keeping up with the paperwork is an enormous task. "And heaven help you if you get into an appeal situation with your insurance company, which happened to us," explained Amelia. "You have to get letters and documents to mount an entire campaign."

It is especially distressing if bills continue to arrive and insurance forms have to be completed after your baby has died. As one mother bitterly recalled:

> It seemed like an enormous indignity to have to maintain the effort of appealing nonpayment of claims and keeping up with all the insurance paperwork after our baby died.

You may be able to solve some of these problems by meeting in person with a supervisor in the hospital billing office, but when your baby has just died, it is still the last thing you want to do.

Because of the emotional, physical and financial strains of caring for a critically ill newborn, you may have struggled with a feeling of relief when your baby died. Although this is a normal response under the circumstances, it can be troubling. Try to share this difficult emotion with your partner or with other understanding adults so you can gain the perspective you need to forgive yourself and move on with your life.

Causes of Newborn Death

Premature delivery and low birth weight are the primary causes of newborn death, although with medical advances, the survival rate is always improving. Birth defects such as heart and kidney problems are frequently implicated in the death of a newborn infant. Maternal conditions or illnesses such as that caused by the group B streptococcus microorganism can also precipitate newborn death.

Complicated labor and deliveries used to be more frequently cited as factors in newborn death; however, with the advances in technology used in prenatal care and labor monitoring, such deaths are now rarer. If a newborn death occurs during delivery, it is usually because the baby or the mother was sick during the pregnancy or because the oxygen supply was inhibited by a rare complication during labor.

Once you and your partner have suffered the death of your newborn baby, it is important that you try to discover the cause. Your doctor should check for any maternal condition if the birth was premature and, if possible, correct it. If your baby showed signs of chromosomal or genetic abnormalities, you may want to request a full autopsy and analysis of the baby's tissues. You may also wish to consult a genetic specialist before embarking on another pregnancy.

If your baby died from asphyxia, or lack of oxygen, during labor and delivery, or if your baby was carried past the due date, you should inquire about monitoring the baby's growth and health during your next pregnancy. Procedures such as sonograms, maternal blood tests, a nonstress test, or a contraction stress test can pick up signs of potential problems. However, these causes of newborn death are far less likely to be repeated in a subsequent pregnancy than other causes related to maternal health or genetic problems.

Emotional Aftermath of Newborn Death

As angry and cheated as you feel following your newborn's death, you probably cherish the brief memories you have of your child, discovering solace in having known your baby, even for a short time. "In my darkest hours," admitted Wendy, "I was still grateful for the fact that at least I had two weeks with my daughter."

You may be able to focus on some aspect of your baby's life that is positive and meaningful to you. Lisa's anencephalic daughter, who was expected to die within a few minutes following delivery, eventually lived for several hours. "I think about my daughter," marveled Lisa, "and how much she wanted to live—eight full hours! She was a real fighter! I loved her for that." Her husband, Adam, felt that even in their daughter's short life, she must have known how much her parents really cared for her, loved her and wanted her. "That knowledge gave us something to cling to," he admitted. "The fact that she knew we held her and tried to comfort her as best we could gave us great comfort, too."

You may worry about losing memories of your baby because they are so fleeting and fragile. Holding on to some tangible keepsakes—a journal, a crib blanket, or a toy—can be important. If you have photographs, you might put them in an album or a special picture frame.

Amelia put one of her baby's photographs in a magnetic frame on her refrigerator, where she could look at it whenever she was in the kitchen. "I loved having her there," said Amelia, "and I loved having people ask about her picture. It helped break the ice a lot after she died when people came to visit and weren't sure of what to say."

You may struggle to find some meaning to your sorrow in an attempt to give your baby's brief life purpose and dignity. After Amelia's first two babies died from prematurity, she gave birth to Jacob, who lived. Her suffering prompted her to reflect on the legacy of all her children:

I keep asking myself why negative learnings are always so powerful. I think our losses have made me and my husband different people. I think and hope that we respond more kindly to others in crisis situations. We no longer take anything for granted. Last summer there was a beautiful warm night, and the three of us—Charles, Jacob in his stroller, and I—went out for a walk after dinner. For us that walk together in the warmth of the evening was more pleasurable than if we had spent thousands of dollars on some big-deal vacation. We have started placing more value on things that to others might be considered pretty mundane.

Wendy strongly believed that her daughter had been born for some positive purpose, even though her life had been so brief:

If I felt Samantha served the purpose of only bringing hatred and anger into my life, I couldn't take it. I am more compassionate to people who suffer losses now that I have had my own. If I felt too sorry for myself, I couldn't do this for others. Samantha came to bring good into our lives, not bad. I do believe that.

KEY POINTS FOR COPING WITH YOUR STILLBIRTH OR NEWBORN DEATH

Stillbirth and newborn death create particular grieving difficulties. You had committed a great deal of time to the pregnancy and may have been totally unprepared for this tragic outcome. The birth became a sad ending instead of a happy beginning.

Here are some suggestions to help you begin to grieve your loss:
- Find out as much as possible about what might have caused your baby's death. The more information you have, the better able you will be to grasp what has happened and plan for a future pregnancy.
- If you gave birth to an ill newborn, try to understand and accept any feelings of relief—and consequent guilt—you might experience after your infant's death. These are natural reactions to your loss and should lessen with time.
- Try to accept medical decisions you may have been forced to make quickly. Focus on the fact that you cared for your baby and wanted the best for your child with every choice you faced. Try to let go of this guilt; your sorrow is great enough without the burden of self-blame.
- Make the decisions that feel right for you, even if friends and family attempt to change your mind. This is your baby and your grief.

8

Prenatal Diagnosis and the Burden of Choice

Our family was ready to go out for dinner when the genetic counselor called. I could hear in her voice that she had bad news. I felt like I was in a tunnel; it was like a bad dream. I started screaming, right there in front of my husband and the kids. I had to wait two weeks before I had the procedure. The baby was kicking. I thought I would lose my mind.

—Elaine

W hen prenatal diagnosis reveals that your unborn baby is impaired, this devastating discovery creates a crisis for you and your partner. If you had never resolved what you would do in this situation, you have to decide quickly. Even if you had previously agreed to end an impaired pregnancy, you still must review and reconfirm this choice. Like many women, you may find that your partner defers the decision to you, which makes you feel even more alone with the burden of choice. You may not know what to do and may not have reached a mutual decision with your partner. You may turn to your health care providers—a genetic counselor, obstetrician or pediatrician—for information, guidance and help in your tragic and bewildering circumstances.

Many couples feel sure of their decision to end an impaired pregnancy. They know genetic testing poses certain risks and are willing to undergo the procedure only because they would definitely choose to end their pregnancy if abnormalities are found. "This pregnancy was not meant to be," one woman said. "Ending an impaired pregnancy is helping nature take its course."

Some parents prefer to end an impaired pregnancy due to the stigma and hardships both the disabled child and the family would endure in our culture. There are couples who have a clear sense of their personal limitations. Some parents are deeply concerned that their marriage would not be able to survive the care of a handicapped child; others worry about the burden placed on their healthy children as the couple ages.

But for many parents, it is dreadful to choose between ending a wanted but defective pregnancy or giving birth to an impaired child. Ever since advances in medical technology created this dilemma, philosophers, religious leaders, lawmakers and medical ethicists have been grappling with the consequences. And even these experts have been unable to produce any uniform laws or reasonable guidelines. It is understandable if parents feel the best course of action is unclear and worry that they will be saddened by either decision they make.

Your choice may be further complicated by the fact that sometimes tests can diagnose an impairment but cannot indicate its severity. This is true of Down syndrome, the disorder most commonly tested for and diagnosed. A child with this condition might be mildly retarded, with minor physical problems, or severely retarded, with serious ailments including leukemia or heart, digestive and respiratory anomalies. You may feel able to raise a mildly impaired child but not a child who would need frequent hospitalizations or invasive surgeries.

Parents who discover through prenatal testing that one baby in a multiple pregnancy suffers from a severe disorder face an additional quandary. Although selective pregnancy reduction can eliminate the impaired baby, the procedure carries potential risks, such as infection and preterm labor, which can endanger the entire pregnancy. If you need specific help with this issue, please check the index under the topics "multiple gestation" and "pregnancy reduction."

If you have to make a decision based on imprecise medical information, you are forced to gamble when the stakes are your unborn child and the quality of your family's future. Understandably, you may find the mourning period that follows especially difficult.

Parents tend to adjust better following their decision, with less self-reproach, if they have experienced firsthand the impairment that was diagnosed. Some adults who grew up with an impaired family member may not want to put themselves through the same suffering again, nor want to inflict it on their child. They may also not want their other children to be burdened later in life by having to care for a handicapped sibling.

Dr. Bruce Blumberg and a group of colleagues at the University of California School of Medicine in San Francisco surveyed parents who ended impaired pregnancies. In his study, Dr. Blumberg described a couple who had watched their first baby deteriorate and die from Gaucher disease, a progressive neurological disorder. When the couple's next baby was found to have the same condition before it was born, the father remarked:

After seeing what the first baby went through, there was nothing to think about in deciding to end this pregnancy. It is hard to feel guilt after seeing our first baby suffer.

PREPARING FOR PRENATAL TESTING AND RECEIVING THE RESULTS

Like many couples who receive an abnormal prenatal diagnosis, your tests may have been given without any counseling. You may not have seriously considered the possibility of a problem being detected, so you may not have weighed your options before receiving the diagnosis. "I looked around the waiting room before my amniocentesis, wondering what poor soul was going to get bad news," recalled Elaine, who received a diagnosis of Down syndrome. "I never dreamed it would be me."

Audrey Heimler, who was for many years the senior genetic counselor at Long Island Jewish Medical Center, considers genetic counseling prior to prenatal diagnosis an essential patient service. She feels strongly that genetic counselors can help expectant parents carefully consider the implications of having or not having the tests. Parents should be informed about problems that may be detected and encouraged to think about what course of action they would take if abnormalities are diagnosed. The genetic counselor can arrange in advance the time and place to notify the couple in the event a problem is found— for example, at home in the evening when they are together, rather than at work.

Parents may prefer to schedule an appointment in advance so that they receive either positive or negative test results in person. This prevents them from worrying that each time the phone rings, it could be the news they dread. If a problem is found and the parents do receive the news by phone, a meeting should be scheduled immediately in recognition of the urgency of the situation. If the genetic counselor delays scheduling an appointment, the couple should call a patient representative or the chairman of the hospital genetics department.

During the session, a helpful genetic counselor conveys respect for the couple's personal values and religious beliefs and has referral information for other resources at hand. Should the parents decide to end their pregnancy, the genetic counselor can make the appointment for them and call a few weeks later to see how they are doing.

Parents need help in thinking about living with the consequences of either choice. Aaron found his discussion with a medical geneticist about his unborn baby's Down syndrome very helpful:

She explained the condition and the range of disability we might find. She told us about all our options and was really impartial. She said some people keep babies with Down syndrome. She told us about a special school for these kids we could visit. She said we could also place the child for adoption.

She asked another very significant question. She knew we were feeling upset and guilty, but wondered what it would have been like for us had we not had the testing and had learned of the baby's problems at birth. We knew we would have been devastated, and that painful as the test results were, they allowed us an important choice.

Aaron and his wife found that this approach to counseling enabled them to learn the facts and hear each other's feelings and opinions. They discovered they were in agreement about ending the pregnancy and supported each other's decision. The careful review of the known facts, the unknown variables and the options available to them enabled them to make what they felt was an informed choice.

Unfortunately, many couples do not have access to a trained genetic counselor, medical geneticist or physician knowledgeable in this specialized counseling process to help them sort through the facts of the diagnosis and the difficult choices they face. Many doctors recommend prenatal testing, but some fail to offer compassionate help when a problem is diagnosed.

Kara and Lewis had suffered from infertility and were elated when they finally conceived, only to learn from prenatal testing that their unborn baby had Down syndrome. While in agreement about ending the pregnancy, they were still distraught by the news. Kara felt their doctor's response only added to their trauma:

I called the center that had done the amniocentesis and was told my doctor already had the results. I knew there was a problem, since they wouldn't tell me the outcome. I called my doctor's office right away, from work. Evidently, the least senior doctor in the practice had been told to speak with me. He told me the results over the phone, and I had to drive to his office and meet my husband there. It's a wonder I didn't get in a car crash on the way over!

First he kept us waiting for twenty-five minutes, with all these other pregnant women. Then, when he met with us, he was very clinical and cold. He told us about all the possible anomalies a baby with Down syndrome might have, in addition to the mental retardation. My husband tried to tell him we had decided to end the pregnancy, but he just kept on talking. He told us it was a boy, and we really didn't want to know the sex.

The worst part was when he told us he wasn't sure he agreed with people having an abortion. At this point I really blew up! My own doctor had strongly recommended the amniocentesis. I asked this other doctor why he was in a practice where people have this test if he was going to tell us not to end the pregnancy! He admitted he had not personally come to grips with this.

When we asked how to arrange for the procedure, he said, "We don't handle that here," and gave us a piece of paper with a phone number. Here he
had just given us about the worst news you can tell an expectant couple and
he wouldn't even pick up the phone!

The crisis that began when you received the test results continued
while you grappled with your decision, especially if the diagnosis was
made after you could feel the baby's movements. "Once you get the
results," one woman professed, "every day your baby moves, you are
dying inside."

CONTINUING YOUR PREGNANCY WHEN YOUR BABY IS NOT EXPECTED TO LIVE

Some parents decide to bring their impaired pregnancy to term, even
when it means their baby will die at birth or shortly thereafter. The true
concept of choice means that parents should be able to choose what is
best for them and their baby without pressure from professionals who
may disagree with their decision. As one mother who carried her anencephalic baby to term said:

It seemed to me that it was the only life our daughter was going to have. It
was the least I could do for her, giving her those nine months of life, even
though she only lived a couple of hours after she was born.

Continuing with a pregnancy of a severely impaired baby can give
parents more time to cherish their baby, however briefly, and to plan a
comforting ritual for their baby's religious blessing and burial. Some
parents simply wish to experience every aspect of their pregnancy,
including spontaneous labor. "I wanted to feel what it was like to give
birth, even though the outcome was so sad," said one mother. "My husband and I also wanted the chance to hold our son and say good-bye
and let him know how much we loved him."

If your child is not expected to live following birth and you decide to
continue with your pregnancy, be sure to check on the hospital's policies concerning living wills for babies. Going to full term and experiencing childbirth may inadvertently expose your baby to medical
procedures you neither wanted nor anticipated. Speaking with a
patient advocate or a sympathetic member of the social work or chaplaincy staff may help guide you during this difficult time so that you can
accomplish what you believe is right for you and your baby. Being an
advocate for your baby under any circumstances, including death, is an
important part of being a loving parent.

Since you will experience the birth of your baby, the information in Chapter 7, "Stillbirth and Newborn Death," will probably be especially comforting. You may also find helpful the key points at the end of that chapter.

YOUR HOSPITAL STAY WHEN YOU END A PREGNANCY

However certain you and your partner might have felt in your decision to end an impaired pregnancy, you may have been unprepared for the physical and emotional ordeal of the procedure. If you received abnormal results in the first trimester from the prenatal genetic test chorionic villus sampling (CVS), your doctor probably used the standard dilatation and curettage (D&C) procedure to end the pregnancy. If you had the more common amniocentesis test performed in the second trimester, your doctor ended the pregnancy either by dilatation and evacuation (D&E) or by inducing labor.

Sometimes couples are given the choice of which procedure to have, but often other factors determine the method. These include how far advanced the pregnancy is, what medical facilities are available and whether the parents want to have their infant tested for a genetic disorder.

Couples who want to see and hold their baby, and who have a choice of procedure, need to have labor induced so that the baby will be born intact. Regardless of the procedure used—D&C, D&E or induction of labor—parents may choose to have a funeral and burial for their baby. Couples need to notify the hospital of their wishes and may need to work with an accommodating funeral home. A hospital social worker or patient representative can help.

If the couple chooses induction to end the pregnancy, the mother will go through full labor. This can be painful and emotionally exhausting, even with medication, and can last from several hours to a few days. The less arduous and time-consuming D&E and D&C procedures can also be very stressful. Whatever procedure the couple chooses, it is vital for the mother to have the baby's father or another support person accompany her to the medical facility and remain available through her discharge.

Now that more states are enacting restrictive antiabortion laws, legal factors may also play a role in the choice of procedure. Appendix A includes more information on medical procedures used for ending a pregnancy following an abnormal prenatal diagnosis. Appendix D suggests resources for help in finding out about the state laws that may be applicable in your community.

Many parents faced with the ordeal of ending a wanted but impaired pregnancy find it upsetting to have the procedure at a facility that is primarily used for ending healthy but unwanted pregnancies. There

are good reasons to use such a facility, such as readily available oper-
ating rooms and lower costs, but couples need to know in advance if
they are being sent to an abortion clinic. Aaron and his wife had no
such preparation:

> When I walked into the clinic with my wife, my first impulse was to turn
> around and walk out. The waiting room was full of teenage girls who were
> presumably there to end unplanned and unwanted pregnancies. And there we
> were, ending a pregnancy we had wanted so badly. We were in that waiting
> room for several hours. It was dreadful.

A couple's experience of the birth may vary widely, depending on
the clinic or hospital staff. At some medical facilities the baby is
removed without being seen by either parent. At others, staff give the
couple the choice of seeing and holding the baby, and discuss plans for
a funeral or burial with them. Most parents choose at least one of these
options when they are offered. If you were not given a choice and wish
you had said good-bye to your baby, try to remember that it was the
staff's responsibility to offer you this opportunity, not yours to ask.

Hospital staff sometimes encourage the couple to make decisions
prior to the procedure about seeing the baby or having a burial,
painful though that may be. The alternative is to make these important
choices right after the procedure, when both parents are distraught
and the mother may be in a haze of medication.

Although hospital staff are sometimes reluctant to show parents a
malformed baby, Carol Goldman, for many years an obstetrical social
worker at Mount Sinai Medical Center in New York City and at Thomas
Jefferson Hospital in Philadelphia, believes it is important for a couple
to see their child. She recommends that a caregiver prepare the parents beforehand by describing any visible abnormalities and reassuring
them they did nothing to cause the condition. Ms. Goldman finds that
parents can be fearful of their baby's appearance and are relieved if the
infant looks normal because the impairments are internal or mental.
On the other hand, seeing visible defects can help validate a parent's
decision to end the pregnancy.

HOW TO DISCUSS ENDING YOUR PREGNANCY WITH YOUR CHILDREN

Be sure to discuss the loss with your children at home, even though this
will be a difficult conversation. Many parents struggle to explain ending a pregnancy to children old enough to know their mother was
pregnant but too young to grasp the issues involved. Most children
react to this kind of loss as they would to a spontaneous loss. They may
feel angry and disappointed that the expected baby is not coming

home and can worry that roughhousing with their mother, or harboring feelings of jealousy, caused the loss.

With children from the age of three to about ten, it is best to give a partial explanation without telling them that ending the pregnancy was your decision. Instead, you may want to say the baby didn't grow properly from the very beginning or that the pregnancy miscarried. Telling a small child you ended a pregnancy because the baby was abnormal or sick could make your youngster worry that if *he* gets sick or has something wrong with *him*, you might get rid of him, too.

As you prepare to explain this loss to your children, keep in mind that as they grow older they will probably question you about it again. You may find it helpful initially to include known facts about the baby's abnormalities, such as chromosomal defects, so you have a foundation for a more complete discussion in the future.

With preteens and teenagers, you face another difficulty. It is hard to tell an adolescent who is inevitably struggling with his own imperfections that you ended a pregnancy of a "less-than-perfect" child. You may find it helpful to share with your adolescent children your own fears about the suffering of the baby or the sacrifices required by the family when a handicapped child is born. You might acknowledge that this was a difficult decision for you, with no easy answer, and then be guided by your adolescent's questions.

If you have small children, or if you have other children later, it will probably be important to tell them at some time about the prenatal diagnosis and your decision to end the pregnancy. This may be necessary when young children reach adolescence or when grown children need information about the family's medical history.

Chapter 12, "Helping Your Children at Home," includes a complete discussion of ways you can talk with your children about the loss, to help you understand their worries and to help them cope with their own sadness.

YOUR EMOTIONAL RECOVERY AFTER ENDING YOUR PREGNANCY

Your choice to end an impaired pregnancy can have a painful emotional aftermath, as it entails losses on many levels. You are mourning the ended pregnancy and you are also grieving for the wished-for, healthy child you did not conceive. The sorrow may be intensified because your loss was in part by choice and not only by chance. Although you may have ended the pregnancy to spare your child incapacity, illness and anguish, your decision can cloud your identity as a loving, nurturing parent. "It's a double taboo," commented one father. "First, people think something is wrong with you because your baby was defective. Then they look down on you for having an abortion."

Even if you feel certain you made the right decision, you may occasionally wonder what your life would have been like if you had made the other choice. The burden of this decision and its accompanying guilt contribute to the suffering that follows this loss. As one father put it, "Everybody feels bad for you and says you made the right decision. But *you* made the decision—and *you* have to live with it."

Dr. Paul Donnai and a group of colleagues in Manchester, England, have conducted studies indicating that both women and men are more depressed after they choose to end an impaired pregnancy than after having a spontaneous loss or ending a normal but unwanted pregnancy. Like Dr. Donnai's patients, you may feel singled out and stigmatized, especially if you do not know anyone else who has experienced this kind of loss. You may fear criticism and inform your friends and colleagues only that you had a loss, without saying the baby was defective or that you were forced to make an agonizing choice.

One mother told friends she suffered a spontaneous loss, and a friend remarked that the loss "was God's will." "Well, yes," the mother thought, "the first part, the disability, was. The second part was my decision." The isolation you may feel, and the inability to speak freely of your ordeal, can lead to depression.

Parents, especially mothers, faced with this type of loss often show intense emotional symptoms that may persist from a few months to a year or more. "I had nightmares, terrible headaches and no energy for anything," Lily recalled. "I dreamed that my children were drowning in front of me and I couldn't save them." Elaine admitted that she was irritable and tearful for months. "I started feeling better," she recalled, "then it got worse again as the anniversary approached." She noted that she had been unable to lose the extra weight from her pregnancy in reaction to her psychological trauma. "I'm punishing myself for having time for myself," she explained, "instead of caring for a sick baby."

It is important for medical staff and relatives to include fathers in expressions of care and concern. As with most types of pregnancy loss, the mother often receives more attention, but fathers mourn the loss of their babies, too. When Dr. Bruce Blumberg conducted his survey of parents who had ended impaired pregnancies, he found that men as well as women suffer from depression after this kind of loss. One father was left particularly bitter, feeling that the basic goals for which one strives in life, such as raising a healthy family, were unattainable. Another man who had been through years of infertility before ending a pregnancy with a Down syndrome baby was deeply shaken. He found it difficult to be around children and gave up some friends and favorite recreational activities because he knew children would be present.

Dr. Blumberg also found a high incidence of marital separation among couples during the stressful aftermath of ending an impaired pregnancy. The fact that men and women grieve differently, just as they do following a spontaneous loss, contributes to the couple's distress. Although marital stress often persists for many months, follow-up studies have shown that most couples eventually reunite.

You may, however, find that a stronger bond is forged between you. When Lewis and Kara ended a pregnancy because of a Down syndrome diagnosis, the devotion her husband demonstrated throughout their ordeal made a lasting impression on Kara:

> We are closer as a result of the loss. I never realized how much I meant to my husband or how dependable he was. I didn't know the extent of how good he was to me until all this happened.

Many factors can affect how you manage in the early weeks and months after you end an impaired pregnancy, including your personality, the strength of your primary relationship and the availability of other sources of support and comfort. Both you and your partner will need patient, understanding family and friends, and possibly professional guidance as well.

FINDING THE SUPPORT YOU NEED AFTER ENDING YOUR PREGNANCY

You may find that reaching out to others is key to your recovery. You must choose your listeners with care, however, because while some people may welcome the opportunity to be supportive, others may not be sympathetic. Please see Chapter 11, "The Response of Your Family and Friends," for guidance on how to handle insensitive questions and remarks. If you tell compassionate family and friends what the loss meant to you, describing the grief and turmoil you are going through, you may receive genuine concern in return.

This was true for Lily, who had one healthy child and then ended two pregnancies because of severe genetic problems. She was deeply depressed after both procedures and wondered what to tell her friends. "In the end I just told them the truth," she admitted. "I had no energy to lie, or hide it, or say it was a miscarriage. And people were wonderful."

Elaine reached out to friends when she conceived a baby with Down syndrome. She felt upset, guilty and depressed when she and her husband decided to end the pregnancy, emotions that only intensified when her husband didn't want to talk about the loss. Elaine found that she needed the outlet of friends to whom she could say, "I'm going nuts today!" As she explained, "It really helped to know my friends were there for me."

You may come to terms with the decision you made by honestly facing your personal, psychological and family limitations. Accepting how difficult raising an impaired child might have been for you and your partner can help alleviate your guilt.

Rebecca's prenatal diagnosis had revealed a rare chromosomal disorder that probably would have caused mental retardation and mental illness. Her husband could not cope with the prospect of a mentally impaired child, and Rebecca realized she felt the same way:

> I had to face the fact that someone else in the same situation would have chosen to have the baby. There are some things I don't totally like about myself. I have limitations. But this is who I am.

Both you and your partner may find a peer support group or psychotherapy helpful, either together or individually, so you can unburden yourselves without worrying about bringing up a subject friends and relatives may treat as taboo. The opportunity to talk with other parents or an understanding professional can lessen your distress during the difficult aftermath of your loss.

Perhaps because of the unique psychological and moral dilemmas involved in ending an impaired pregnancy, there are few pregnancy loss support groups geared specifically for this circumstance. Parents who do have access to a support group for this loss describe it as enormously beneficial. Hilary attended such a group after enduring years of infertility and then ending a much-wanted but impaired pregnancy. Although she was clear about her decision, the diagnosis seemed particularly cruel after waiting so long for her "miracle baby." Hilary was surprised at how much the group helped her:

> Before I went into the group, I thought no one in the world could be as badly off. Then we learned that another couple in the group had also been through years of infertility before their loss. Even people in the group with healthy children at home were just as devastated.
>
> The group helped us to get out the things we were not willing to face. We chose to end the pregnancy because I know Down syndrome children can be born with physical as well as mental handicaps and that they can suffer greatly. And we had to look at how we would care for a handicapped child when we were sixty. But I didn't want to accept that part of my decision was selfish, that I didn't want a less-than-perfect child.
>
> Then other couples said they blamed themselves for not being strong enough to deal with an abnormal child. When they said this, it was like a dagger through my heart, because I knew it was true for me, too. I cried for two solid days, but I had to face my guilt. Those feelings are there, and if you don't get them out, they eat away at you.

> I would recommend this group for anyone, even for a very shy person. I
> don't usually see myself as a group person, but it was highly therapeutic.

If a support group does not exist in your area, consider asking your physician or genetic counselor to put you in touch with parents who have been through a similar loss. Couples who have endured this difficult choice are often willing to talk with others in the same situation.

Some parents find that creating a ritual helps express their love and grief for their baby. If allowing yourself to say good-bye might provide you comfort, please see Chapter 10, "Finding Solace in Your Religion," and Appendix B for help in designing a meaningful ceremony.

Like many couples, you may feel that your hurt is healed only after a subsequent, healthy child is welcomed into your family or after you learn to accept your life as it is. You may discover that you are more open to experiences that give you perspective on your tragedy. Hilary, a physical therapist, said her work with accident victims helped her cope with her own loss. As she explained, "I know from my job that life isn't fair to any of us and that there are others a lot worse off than me."

You may find that ending an impaired pregnancy has changed you and that it takes time and understanding to integrate your loss into your life. "I think about it every day, even just for a second," one woman remarked. "But life has to go on." Grieving your loss, and the normal baby who never was, will help you eventually shift your focus to other, positive aspects of your life.

As time passes and you gain some distance from your loss, you may feel more strongly that your decision was right for you and your family. However, you might still deeply regret that you were forced to choose. "I don't feel bad about the decision," one woman reasoned. "I'm just sorry that I was put in that spot."

KEY POINTS TO HELP YOU COPE WITH AN IMPAIRED PREGNANCY

You may find the process of emotional recovery after enduring an impaired pregnancy to be a long one. Although in no way at fault for the abnormality, you may feel you have failed as a parent, for having produced an impaired child and for ending the pregnancy or having your newborn die. Your memory of the procedure or the birth and of being forced into an active decision can affect you deeply.

You also carry the burden of having to decide how much to tell relatives and friends about your loss. If you keep your decision private, you may feel even more depressed as you find yourself cut off from potential sources of support.

Here are some suggestions to help you cope with the special difficulties associated with your loss:

- Be sure both you and your partner are there together, or arrange for another support person to stay with you, during the procedure or the birth. Be well informed about any choices of procedure you may have.
- Don't blame yourself if medical staff did not give you the opportunity to see and hold your baby. Work through your regret with the help of a peer group, in psychotherapy or through the comfort of rituals.
- If you feel the need for a ritual following your loss, see Chapter 10, "Finding Solace in Your Religion," and Appendix B about creating a service that is comforting to you.
- Decide with your partner how you will discuss the loss with other children at home. If you have questions about this, a hospital social worker or qualified psychotherapist can advise you. See also Chapter 12, "Helping Your Children at Home."
- Find caring people to help you through the initial grieving period. Peer support and psychotherapy can be vital, especially if family and friends lack understanding. For a complete discussion of this issue, please see Chapter 11, "The Response of Your Family and Friends."

Section III

The Response of Others

Although your pregnancy loss is highly personal, your capacity to cope depends greatly on how those around you react to your sorrow. Some medical staff and loved ones may console you with the right words; others may inadvertently make hurtful comments or offer unhelpful advice, wounding you deeply.

The chapters in this section can help you manage your sorrow and your anger when you feel you have not been treated compassionately or fairly. You will also read about how to help your children at home deal with your loss and how grandparents can learn to cope when their adult child loses a baby.

9

Medical Care when You Lose
Your Pregnancy

In the aftermath of your pregnancy loss, you may realize that the medical care you received continues to have an impact on your emotional recovery. The ability of medical staff to go beyond concern for your physical well-being and to acknowledge your grief likely affected your expression of sorrow at the time of your loss and your capacity to grieve later. If the medical staff was properly trained in bereavement counseling, they understood your sorrow and helped prepare you for your vulnerable emotional state in the weeks and months following your loss.

If your loss was mismanaged by a medical professional—whether a hospital nurse, your obstetrician, a sonographer or a childbirth educator—you may have been further traumatized and your mourning impeded.

LEARNING ABOUT YOUR LOSS

You will probably remember forever the way you learned about your pregnancy loss. At this personal and tragic moment, you deserved to be told the truth directly by a compassionate medical caregiver who acknowledged your loss. If you received thoughtful treatment, you were probably better able to focus on the reality of your tragedy and to begin a healthy grieving process.

Gloria recalled how important it was for her to have her doctor and midwife present when her baby's death in utero was confirmed. "My doctor got teary-eyed when she saw the ultrasound, and the midwife was visibly moved, too," Gloria recalled. "It meant a lot to me for them to be there and to show that kind of feeling."

If your doctor was sensitive to your situation, he probably told you of the loss when both you and your partner were present. The doctor respected your need to absorb the news and to ask questions as well as to have private time with your partner. However, you may have learned of your loss in a way that added to your distress. This is more likely to have occurred if you were cared for by medical personnel you did not know, such as a partner in your doctor's practice, a clinic physician or emergency room staff.

Carmen went to the emergency room after her midwife detected a problem when she was thirty-one weeks pregnant:

> No one talked to me or looked at me. The doctors talked among themselves, saying they could not find a heartbeat. Nobody told me the baby was dead; no one actually said the word. I suppose they thought I would guess. Then they left me in the hall in a wheelchair, crying.

If you experienced an early pregnancy loss, your doctor may have unintentionally minimized your sorrow. Many physicians have the medical perspective that a miscarriage is a normal part of a woman's overall reproductive experience and is often followed by a healthy baby. This view, as well as your doctor's wish to protect you and himself from sadness, can also make him downplay your genuine grief.

Annette had a miscarriage that her doctor presumed was due to a blighted ovum, but his medical reassurances did not diminish the sadness she felt at losing her baby:

> He told me that it happened for the best, that it wasn't a healthy pregnancy anyway. But I wasn't comforted by those comments at all. I was nurturing and carrying a baby I loved, even if it was only for a short time. Then to be told my loss was for the best because the baby wasn't healthy, good or perfect seemed to be an excuse to tell me I shouldn't be sad.

Your unborn baby's death may have been confirmed by a technician or physician you had never met before. Perhaps you had one of those sonographers who would not tell you the outcome but left you guessing and frantic while he conveyed the results to your doctor, who then told you the news in person or by phone. You may have preferred to hear the news directly from the sonographer without having to wait.

At such a difficult time, even small gestures of concern are remembered and appreciated. When Ellen's sonogram confirmed her third miscarriage, she left the examining room visibly upset. "The ultrasound technician followed me out and asked if I was all right," Ellen recalled. "I wasn't all right, and there was nothing she could really do, but it meant a lot to me that she asked."

In your sorrow, you may believe that your shock would have been lessened if your doctor had provided more information about pregnancy loss before your problem developed. If your loss occurred after you began childbirth classes, you may feel angry that your instructor never even alluded to such possibilities. Perhaps you assumed your pregnancy was safe as long as you kept your medical appointments, took good care of your health, and prepared properly for the birth.

Doctors and childbirth educators can feel in a bind because pregnant women and their partners generally do not want to hear about losses, nor do medical professionals want to cause needless worry. And there is probably nothing a caregiver could have said in way of preparation that would have diminished your sadness.

Some obstetricians do explain which symptoms might jeopardize a pregnancy or be warning signs of an impending loss and warrant immediate medical attention, such as a high fever, vaginal bleeding or loss of amniotic fluid. Pregnant women who are given this kind of matter-of-fact information are more likely to become informed participants in all aspects of their prenatal care. While most do not imagine *their* pregnancy could end in loss, they know problems in pregnancy can occur, so that if they experience a loss, they perceive it as a tragic event but not a bizarre one.

YOUR HOSPITAL CARE

> All around I felt I was given the lowest priority because the baby had died. I told them I wanted pain medication for the delivery, but the doctor arrived too late. The staff avoided me. They didn't seem to know what to do with me. I had to pester them to get shots to stop my milk before I went home.
>
> —Carmen

> I'll never forget when I went into the special-care nursery where our daughter had been placed to live out her short life. The nurse asked me, "How are you doing, Mommy?" Tears streamed down my face. That meant so much to me. Nobody else at the hospital ever acknowledged the fact that I was a mommy.
>
> —Lisa

Although one in four pregnancies ends in a first-trimester miscarriage and about 1 percent of deliveries results in a stillbirth or newborn death, many hospital obstetrical departments still lack bereavement services for parents who suffer a loss.

The field of obstetrics is geared toward bringing new life into the world. When death occurs where new life is expected, unprepared obstetrical staff may react with anxiety and helplessness, making it difficult for them to assist bereaved families. Staff members untrained in bereavement may respond to a pregnancy loss by avoiding the grieving

parents because they don't know what to say, or because they are afraid
the parents will only cry and become more upset, not realizing this is
just what bereaved parents need permission to do.

The American Academy of Pediatrics and the American College of
Obstetricians and Gynecologists have jointly issued hospital guidelines,
called a bereavement protocol, for helping parents who suffer a pregnancy loss or infant death. They suggest that parents need help from
hospital staff to express their love and say good-bye to their baby. If the
loss occurs after the first trimester, parents may want mementos such as
a picture, footprints or a lock of hair. They should also be given the
chance to see and hold their child. With any pregnancy loss, bereaved
parents should have access to grief counseling, pastoral care and
options for rituals, as well as guidance on how to obtain relevant medical information following their tragedy. Please see the bereavement
protocol checklist at the end of this chapter.

Like many bereaved parents, you may fault yourself for not having
requested these services. Given your emotional state after your loss,
you could not have taken the initiative in requesting appropriate care.
Clinical studies have repeatedly shown that when hospital staff do not
offer bereavement services, most parents do not ask for the care they
need and, therefore, do not receive it. It is the hospital's responsibility
to train staff in a bereavement protocol so patients are provided with
this important service.

If you are a mother whose loss posed a danger to your life, you may
have found that hospital staff ignored your emotional response to your
loss. The medical emergency necessarily shifted the focus of concern
from the pregnancy to you.

Tracy felt that the grief she experienced following emergency
surgery for an ectopic pregnancy was completely overlooked:

> I think the medical staff should be more sensitive to the woman's need to
> mourn. They should acknowledge that there was indeed a loss, even if they
> feel she should be grateful simply to be alive. I *was* grateful, of course, but I
> was also tremendously sad because I was mourning the loss of a baby I
> wanted so badly.

As a bereaved mother, you may have borne the stressful aspects of
your medical care alone. The location where you were placed in the
hospital for your care probably had a profound effect on you. If you
were cared for in the labor and delivery unit, you likely heard other
mothers giving birth to healthy babies, which was undoubtedly distressing. However, if you went through labor on a surgical floor, with other
postoperative patients, you may have found yourself to be the nurses'
lowest priority. You may have been virtually uncared for during your

labor, and your need to be comforted after your loss was probably completely overlooked.

Martha was two months pregnant when she started bleeding profusely. Her doctor sent her to the hospital, where she was put in a room on a surgical floor:

> I was left unattended for hours. No one came in to check on me, or hand me a bedpan. At 4:00 a.m. I passed the fetus. A nurse took it and was going to throw it away until I told her I wanted my doctor to examine it. She got a jar and put it on my nightstand. That was upsetting, too.
>
> During my two-day hospital stay, I cried constantly. Someone could have said, "Do you want to talk?" or "Is there anything you need?" I got nothing.

Some hospitals avoid this problem by treating women who are showing signs of pregnancy loss on the obstetrical floor, where nurses may be more aware of their physical and emotional needs. But when an unborn baby is known to have died already, the mother may be left unattended here as well. "In part this is because the nurses don't have the health of the baby to worry about," one nursing supervisor in a major medical center pointed out, "and in part it's because they don't know what to say."

If the medical staff were trained to care for your special needs, you probably felt emotionally protected as well. After Carla suffered a pregnancy loss at twenty-six weeks in the delivery room, she was transferred to the gynecology floor, where she found the nursing care to be extremely helpful:

> The nurses held my hand and were sympathetic. A couple of them gave me and my husband their phone numbers and told us to call anytime we wanted someone to talk to. One nurse gave me something to read on pregnancy loss. She said, "I know you can't look at it now. Take it; it will help you later." The social worker was wonderful as well. She came to see me twice and gave me information about support groups.

If your hospital had private rooms and you could afford one, your recovery in the postpartum unit could have been away from newborn babies while still close to specialized nursing care. "I was put on the postpartum floor, but far from the nursery, right next to the nursing station," recalled Sylvia after her newborn baby died. "My husband spent the night with me. The staff were very good about that."

Judy Kirsh, an obstetrical social worker at New York University Hospital, finds that sometimes women with several children at home prefer to recover in the postpartum unit. "They will be going back to a house and probably a community where there are lots of kids," she points out, "and they don't see the point in being removed from mothers and babies in the hospital."

If you required a D&C following an early miscarriage, your doctor may have recommended that you go to an outpatient clinic rather than the hospital. Clinics are less expensive than hospitals and can schedule the procedure more quickly. But you may not have realized that these facilities are primarily abortion clinics, whose staff is unlikely to acknowledge your grief.

"My doctor should have alerted us," recalled Karen, who was sent to a clinic for a D&C after one of her miscarriages. "Until we walked in, my husband and I didn't realize it was really an abortion clinic, and our first impulse was to turn around and walk out again."

The value of the medical staff's having bereavement training and established procedures for handling pregnancy loss becomes painfully clear in its absence. Without guidelines, details are bound to be forgotten.

Laurel went into labor when only twenty-three weeks pregnant and knew her baby could not survive. She delivered on the gynecology floor without seeing her baby, whom the nurse quickly removed. The next morning her doctor came to see Laurel and her husband. He was compassionate, and gently but firmly encouraged the couple to see their infant, but he neglected to swaddle the tiny baby, as a bereavement protocol would have indicated:

> He brought her into my room and with gloved hands, removed her from the surgical container she had been in. He held her little body for us to see.
>
> I cried, realizing that she was so perfect. I cried realizing that her death was so final and I understood none of it. Later, months later, I would cry at this thoughtlessness—seeing our daughter lifted like a laboratory specimen, dripping wet, from a container filled with saline solution.

Your need for special emotional care from staff continued after your loss. Contact with an understanding nurse, social worker or obstetrician, who allowed time for you to review your loss in detail, undoubtedly helped you begin to heal both physically and emotionally. "I wanted the medical staff not to just take care *of* me," said one bereaved mother, "but to care *about* me as well."

SPECIAL CONSIDERATIONS WITH STILLBIRTH AND NEWBORN DEATH

Our baby was born very prematurely when I was five months pregnant. We knew she wouldn't survive. I didn't see her, and I didn' t know if it was okay to ask to see her. I finally asked if it was a boy or a girl. I never asked if she was alive, and I never asked to hold her. I was haunted by this long afterward.

—Ruth

I stayed up the entire time Michelle lived. I couldn't bear the thought of going to sleep during any of her life because it was going to be so short. I didn't want to miss a single moment. The staff were wonderful. They had a room right off the neonatal ward where my husband and I could stay with Michelle. She died in our arms.

—Gayle

As a mother, you confronted many crucial decisions once you were hospitalized. If you labored with a baby who was stillborn or not expected to live, you had to choose whether to take pain medication during delivery. You may have been torn by the desire to experience the entire process of giving birth and the wish to be free from the physical pain of a hard, fruitless labor. "Even knowing our daughter was going to die," admitted Ruth, "I still didn't want to have drugs and not be there for her. However brief her life was to be, I wanted to be her mommy every minute."

If you remain troubled about your decision to take or avoid pain medication during delivery, try to accept that you made your best choice under severe stress or that your doctor took the decision out of your hands. You could not be expected to make reasoned decisions under these circumstances.

If your baby was stillborn or born gravely ill, staff may have encouraged you and your partner to see and hold your infant. Holding the baby and saying good-bye may have helped you express your love and begin to grieve, while missing this opportunity could have left a legacy of regret.

Medical staff trained in bereavement should have taken the initiative in helping you see your baby. Your first impulse may have been *not* to see your child because you were still in emotional shock, afraid of the baby's appearance or angry at the baby for dying.

When Hilary's premature twins died at birth, she relied on the hospital nurse for these unexpected decisions:

We had a great nurse who realized our emotional state. She knew we wouldn't ask for a picture or to hold the babies. She brought the babies to us and encouraged us to hold them. Afterward we were both really grateful we did.

Part of the bereavement staff's role would have been to prepare you for your baby's appearance, including the infant's size, coloring and other features, depending on the gestational age and the cause of your loss. Even if your child had visible malformations, as long as you knew what to expect, you probably focused on the positive aspects of your infant's appearance.

Before the nurse brought Lisa's anencephalic baby to her, she explained that a little knit cap would be placed over the baby's improperly developed skull. She also gently told Lisa that the baby's eyes looked vacant. Seeing and holding her baby left an indelible yet positive impression on Lisa once she was properly prepared:

> I was able to tell my mother that her granddaughter was beautiful. She had beautiful long legs and arms, and she had my mouth and nose. Only her eyes had that empty look. She was very small, but I was struck by her beauty.

The death of your baby was a loss for the entire family, not just for you and your partner. Your parents, siblings and other children at home were all affected. If your hospital had an enlightened policy, relatives and close friends may have been allowed to share with you in seeing and holding your baby.

Hospital staff may also have offered you the option of naming your child. Many parents do not know this is possible; yet when told they may name their babies, most do so. If you named your baby, this acknowledged the importance of the infant and can help you and loved ones to talk about the baby and grieve your loss.

You may have wished to keep mementos such as a baby blanket, crib card, identification bracelet or lock of hair. Perhaps the medical staff offered these keepsakes in a way that helped you feel at ease about accepting them and did not make you wonder if you were morbid for wanting evidence of your baby's existence and identity.

You may also have wanted a photograph of your infant, especially if you were not able to bring your own camera to the delivery room. Hospitals usually use instant cameras so they can give parents their pictures immediately and can take additional photographs if necessary. Either Polaroid or a qualified film reproduction lab can make copies from the original photograph, even without a negative.

If your picture was taken by a staff member trained in bereavement, the baby was carefully cleaned and wrapped in a blanket. Carol Goldman, an obstetrical social worker at Mount Sinai Medical Center in New York City, suggests that a second picture, of the uncovered baby, also be taken, especially if the mother was sedated during delivery. This second picture can remind you of details about your baby's appearance you may not recall from the delivery room.

If a photograph was taken and you did not want to bring it home, it was probably placed in your medical record. You can request it later, even weeks or months after your infant's death, when you may need it to help you remember and grieve the baby who never came home.

If you suffered a stillbirth or newborn death, you were probably asked whether you wanted to have an autopsy performed. Some parents do not believe this procedure will yield significant information and choose not to have an autopsy; other parents may forbid an autopsy for religious reasons.

Many parents want an autopsy performed to clarify the diagnosis or the risk of a similar loss occurring in future pregnancies. But having to decide about an autopsy may have shocked you, as it brought home the finality of your baby's death.

An autopsy is a detailed examination of the baby in which some surgery is necessary to remove tissues from internal organs for microscopic inspection. You can still have an open casket at a funeral if the autopsy is performed with this in mind. Some hospitals charge for an autopsy. You will usually receive preliminary results within a couple of weeks; however, you may have to wait up to three months for a complete, written report.

An autopsy can be helpful for several reasons. You may question whether you did anything to contribute to the baby's death, a fear an autopsy can often dispel. In some cases an autopsy determines a specific cause of death, which gives you information about future risks and medical care. If the death was due to a cord accident or a problem with the placenta but the baby's physical development was normal, you may be comforted, since the likelihood of a recurrence is quite low. You may also have consented to an autopsy in the hope that the information it yielded would help medical science and other babies in the future, allowing some good to come out of your tragedy.

You were probably faced with unexpected decisions about your baby, including burial, cremation or a religious service. A hospital social worker, nurse or chaplain may have helped you review your options and make choices, or you may have received no assistance at all. Some parents are guided by religious laws, but you, like many others, may have made a rapid decision to have the hospital take care of cremation or burial and only later wished you had done more for your baby.

While you cannot undo some missed opportunities, such as not seeing your baby or having a burial, there are some choices you *can* alter, even after the fact. Regrets can add to your grief, so talking about them with an understanding person is a vital first step. If you did not have a ritual when the loss occurred, you can still name your baby and hold a memorial service to honor your child. Suggestions for rituals are discussed in Chapter 10, "Finding Solace in Your Religion," and in Appendix B.

COMMUNICATION AMONG MEDICAL STAFF

All medical staff who came in contact with you and your partner should have been informed of your loss. If communication was lacking, staff may have made small mistakes that were nevertheless devastating, such as asking the mother of a stillborn baby if she was breast- or bottle-feeding.

Poor communication among medical staff may have had an equally harmful effect if you and your partner experienced an early loss. You may have received phone calls confirming an amniocentesis appointment or hospital insurance coverage for your delivery weeks after you lost the pregnancy.

If you had undergone prenatal tests before your loss occurred, the laboratory may have sent the results directly to you, with upsetting consequences. "The day I came home from the hospital after losing my baby in the fifth month," remembered Ruth, "I got a call from the lab saying the results of the amniocentesis were fine, that I was carrying a healthy baby girl." If you had this experience, consider alerting your doctor so he can arrange for the laboratory to check with him before contacting patients in the future.

You and your partner may have been needlessly distressed if the mother was referred to specialized services, such as radiology, where doctors and technicians were unaware of your situation. Two weeks before her due date, Lisa learned her baby had a lethal malformation. She was referred for an X ray to check on the baby's position for inducing labor, but the technician had not been informed of the diagnosis:

> She gave me a terrible time. She wouldn't do the X ray because I was pregnant! She wanted me to sign something to release her of responsibility for the X ray. I was so upset that the baby would not live, and having to fight with a staff person was so cruel.

Some medical facilities address the issue of staff communication in bereavement training and use color codes or symbols on charts and hospital rooms to designate a loss. A checklist of services for bereaved parents can be included in the patient's chart, to ensure that all available services are offered. A sample bereavement protocol is included at the end of this chapter.

If you need to alert a lab or the hospital about your loss, you may want to ask a relative or friend to call for you to avoid being telephoned or having to make these difficult calls yourself. If hospital staff involved in your care were unaware of your loss, you may want to let the hospital know about this problem so that they can correct their procedures for future patients. Suggestions for taking this kind of action are discussed later in this chapter.

YOUR HOSPITAL DISCHARGE AND FOLLOW-UP CARE

> *Before I left the hospital, no one said I might be depressed after a miscarriage. My hormones were going wild, my breasts hurt. I thought I was going nuts when the doctor pinched my cheek and said, "You'll be fine." I thought I wasn't supposed to be having these other feelings. I left the hospital so depressed, so empty, so hurt, I'm surprised I didn't have a nervous breakdown on the way home.*
>
> —Martha

In addition to needing sensitive bereavement counseling while the mother was in the hospital, you and your partner deserved preparation for the stresses you faced when you returned home. If your caregivers were trained in bereavement, they may have assured you that your grief was normal and forewarned you that it might improve only gradually, over several weeks or months. They may have explained that men and women can grieve quite differently. The staff may also have guided you on how to discuss the loss with other children at home, to minimize the youngsters' anxiety and allow them to grieve as well.

Bereavement services may have included written information about pregnancy loss and grief, as well as a list of psychotherapy resources and bereavement support programs in your community. If you did not receive this information before going home, you may be able to obtain it through your hospital's nursing or social work department. You might not be ready for this material right away, but it can be a lifeline in the difficult weeks and months to come.

Because no one can absorb information well right after a loss, follow-up contact is especially needed. If your baby was in an intensive care unit before she died, neonatal staff you know personally may have given you the name of a physician or nurse in the department to call if you wanted to talk or if you had questions after your baby's death.

Rose's full-term baby died of congenital defects the day after birth. Both the intensive care pediatrician and the surgeon who operated on her daughter gave Rose their phone numbers and made themselves available:

> We did call back a couple of times in the weeks after the death, with different questions. Once my husband called because he had given blood when the baby needed a transfusion. He had drunk a glass of wine beforehand and wondered if the wine in his system had harmed the baby. The doctor assured him this was not so.

This kind of follow-up, however, is unusual for departments other than the neonatal nursery. Few private obstetricians routinely phone their patients after a pregnancy loss. You may be upset by this lack of contact, especially if your loss occurred late in the pregnancy. After months of regular appointments, you want to know that your welfare remains important to your physician, even though your baby died. Bess, who suffered a stillbirth shortly before her due date, felt her doctor should have remained involved after her loss:

> My doctor never called after my stillbirth. Someone called me from his office about my bill; they didn't even mention the loss.
>
> It would have been a kind thing to do, to call one or two months later to see how I was managing. I had seen the doctor regularly for eight months. I felt he owed me a phone call.

Like most bereaved parents, you probably had limited contact with your doctor and hospital, perhaps for your follow-up exam or a meeting to review laboratory reports or autopsy results. Your doctor may have seen you promptly so as to minimize your wait in the company of pregnant women and new mothers.

Bereaved parents can need a number of special services from their doctor, including referrals for genetic counseling or a high-risk practice. A caring doctor will ask how the woman and her family are managing emotionally and may offer referral information on psychotherapy or support groups. A couple can feel that the physician who fails to offer this information has done them a real disservice.

It took Leonard several phone calls to locate a support group in his area:

> It is criminal for doctors not to have in their office information about support groups, the name of a therapist and of counseling facilities. Patients should not have to go searching for this—they are dealing with enough as it is.

Unfortunately, many doctors do not ask how you are doing emotionally during the follow-up exam. Some do not mention the loss at all, or—even worse—do not remember it. Dr. Stanford Bourne, a British obstetrician, conducted a study of physicians' reactions to mothers who had a stillbirth and found their doctors tended not "to know, notice, or remember anything about the patient who has had a stillbirth." If this happened to you, it probably felt like the ultimate negation of your tragedy.

Carla went in for a postpartum checkup six weeks after her premature baby died. While she was being examined, the doctor asked her, "How's the baby?" Carla, incredulous, said, "Excuse me?" "Oh, how is everything?" corrected her doctor. "You're looking good, you look like you're recovering." Carla changed doctors.

Some physicians shy away from discussing a loss with bereaved parents for fear of courting a lawsuit. But Karren Kowalski, an expert in clinical obstetrics, writes that the opposite is true, that "more suits seem to result from poor interpersonal relations than from actual medical malpractice." You and your partner were probably quick to pick up on your doctor's reluctance to acknowledge your loss or to give you information frankly. This may have felt like a breach in the doctor-patient relationship and left you disillusioned with your care.

HOW YOU CAN IMPROVE HOSPITAL BEREAVEMENT SERVICES

> [A]t the time of [an infant's] death, the role of the doctor is not obviated, but rather becomes infinitely more important.
>
> —Lawrence R. Berger, M.D.

Although an increasing number of hospitals are adopting bereavement services to provide parents with practical and emotional help after a pregnancy loss, many hospitals still lack suitable protocols.

Obstetricians, pediatricians and hospital staff work under constant time pressures while juggling demands in both their training and their work. It is not surprising that they do not routinely learn the special skills required to help a family after a pregnancy loss has occurred, when their medical knowledge is no longer pertinent.

Yet obstetrical, pediatric and nursing departments have compelling reasons to undertake such an investment in time and training. Helpful management of a pregnancy loss or newborn death has a profound and positive long-term effect on the family's emotional recovery and well-being. If you received skilled assistance in the hospital, you were better able to grieve and move past your untimely loss. Grieving properly helps to restore your healthy capacity for parenting a future child, which can otherwise be hindered.

Bereavement intervention skills give doctors and hospital staff a practical means of helping parents in distress, when health care practitioners would otherwise feel ill-equipped to respond to the loss. This training helps staff respect and manage their own sadness and anxiety as well.

Maryse Bilodeau, a registered nurse at the Royal Victoria Hospital in Montreal, found that bereavement training improved her ability to help patients who suffered a pregnancy loss. Before being trained, she had a typical staff response to a stillbirth she had witnessed. "I was very upset," she recalled. "I was afraid that I couldn't help the patient because I was so emotional myself. I felt totally helpless."

After attending a two-day training program that included grief theory, small discussion groups and role playing, Ms. Bilodeau found she had learned to respect her own response to pregnancy loss:

I feel I can be more present and more emotionally available to the patient as a
result. I know there are some things I can do for her, like show her the baby
and let her talk and cry. These are small things, but they are important. I feel I
have something to offer that will help.

When doctors and nurses begin to utilize bereavement interventions,
they learn to tolerate patients' intense emotions and their own proxim-
ity to death. The lasting gratitude of bereaved parents usually convinces
hospital staff that their training is effective and worthwhile. "The time
and effort involved are less than might be expected," explains Dr.
Kenneth Kellner. "And in supporting families who are presented with
one of life's greatest tragedies, no time and effort could be better spent."

If hospital staff were sensitive to your grief and provided specialized
bereavement services in response to your loss, you may want to send a
note to let them know how grateful you are. Communication from
patients is taken seriously and encourages a commitment to ongoing
staff bereavement training.

If you feel your needs were neglected during your hospital stay, you
may wish to tell the hospital what could be done to help other parents
in the future. You may get the best response through a patient representative, the social work department, the director of obstetrical nursing or the hospital chaplain. One effective method is to write a letter to
the person or department of your choice, with a copy to the chairman
of the board of trustees, requesting a follow-up meeting to discuss your
experiences. The results of these efforts can be gratifying.

Laurel felt the care surrounding her second-trimester pregnancy
loss at a large metropolitan hospital had been poorly handled, both
medically and emotionally. Among other problems, she did not see or
hold her baby girl when she was born, and she was initially told the hospital would not release the baby for burial because it weighed under
five hundred grams. When her letter to the hospital's director and the
board of trustees went unanswered, Laurel asked to meet with the
obstetrical nursing supervisor. The nurse listened to her story and veri-
fied it by checking the hospital records. She agreed Laurel's experience had been unsatisfactory. The nursing supervisor took up the
matter with the chairman of obstetrics and the hospital board of
trustees. Laurel was encouraged by the results:

Many changes occurred almost immediately. A camera was purchased, pictures and footprints are now kept on record, and a social worker is called in
when a loss occurs. Parents are encouraged to see their babies, and private
burial is offered as an option.

Not all hospitals respond so well to suggestions for improvement of
their bereavement services, but when they do take patients' criticisms

seriously, they allow bereaved parents to leave a legacy of compassion to others who suffer pregnancy losses after them.

If you act on your desire for change, you may discover your effort takes on special meaning, as it can become a way to honor your baby's memory. As Laurel explained:

> My work on the hospital bereavement policies gave meaning to a life that never had a chance. It changed my grief and anger into positive action. It was a very, very good feeling to be productive in our baby's name.

KEY POINTS TO HELP YOU OBTAIN COMPASSIONATE MEDICAL CARE

The emotional care and understanding your medical caregivers provided probably had a profound impact on you and your ability to grieve. If you were supported by staff trained in pregnancy loss and bereavement, your baby's importance and your sorrow were both recognized.

However, if the medical staff did not have specialized training, you likely did not receive consistently sensitive care following your loss, and you may suffer lasting regret. Weeks or months afterward, your mourning might be compounded by memories of upsetting incidents that occurred in your doctor's office or the hospital.

Some experiences you and your partner had in the hospital, and decisions you made about the baby, cannot be changed. You may, however, be able to repair some of the hurt afterward.

Here are some suggestions:

- If you didn't request special care in the hospital and now have regrets, try to forgive yourself, as you could not have known what you needed in the midst of your crisis. It is the hospital's responsibility to train staff who can provide this specialized care.
- If you feel your emotional care was mismanaged by your medical caregivers, it is important that you acknowledge and repair the hurt by talking about the incidents with someone you trust. If you continue to feel distressed, psychotherapy can help.
- If you experienced a late loss or newborn death, and the hospital failed to provide mementos of your baby, check with the nursing department. There is a possibility that footprints, a photograph or other items may be on file and available to you.
- When you schedule your follow-up appointment with your doctor, ask for the first appointment of the morning or afternoon and remind her to take you on time so that you can avoid waiting surrounded by pregnant women and new mothers.

- If you want to try to change the care provided by your doctor or your hospital, by all means write to each of them explaining your experience, what it meant to you and what alternative care would have helped.
- Bereavement Services, Inc., offers regional and national bereavement training for hospital staff. For information on Bereavement Services, Inc., see the resources in Appendix D.

BEREAVEMENT PROTOCOL

If you were dissatisfied with your hospital's bereavement services and want to recommend improvements to the hospital administrators, tell them a bereavement protocol would be helpful. Following is a checklist of hospital services compiled from several sources, including the American Academy of Pediatrics and the American College of Obstetricians and Gynecologists.

As a bereaved parent, you should have the opportunity:

- To contact your partner or support person
- To touch or hold your baby, before or after death; this may include you, your partner, your other children and other relatives or close friends
- To be transferred from the maternity floor
- To receive pastoral care
- To name your baby
- To take a photograph of your baby to take home or for the hospital to keep on file
- To receive a memory packet, including hospital birth certificate, footprints, baby's blanket, lock of hair or identity bracelet
- To receive information on autopsy, burial, funeral or memorial services
- To have the grieving process explained and to be provided with written information on bereavement
- To receive guidance on how to help your children at home cope with the loss
- To have the phone number of a staff person to call in case medical questions arise, or if you need emotional support or require referral information
- To receive follow-up appointments for medical tests and genetic counseling or to review laboratory and autopsy reports

10

Finding Solace in Your Religion

I wanted my religion to recognize that my stillborn daughter had existed, that she had been loved by us and by God.

—Connie

W hen you suffer a pregnancy loss, you may turn toward and against your religion in the same moment. No matter when your loss occurred in the pregnancy, you deserve the comfort of knowing that your God has not forsaken you and that your baby has not gone from this world unnoticed or unblessed. Yet you may feel troubled that God failed to safeguard your innocent child's life.

Few events shake religious faith more than losing a pregnancy. "Experiences like ours make you doubt that things are well organized up there," confessed Amelia after enduring two newborn deaths and a miscarriage. "It makes you question the notion of any kind of cosmic justice." Your grief may be so unmitigated that you begin to question your faith.

You may find yourself bargaining with God after your loss, offering a new commitment to religion, to a more thoughtful life—to anything, if only your next pregnancy will produce a healthy baby. If additional losses or infertility occur, you may begin to feel truly abandoned by God.

A well-trained and compassionate member of the clergy can help you find an effective way to address your doubts and anger. When you give expression to your sorrow in a spiritually meaningful way, you may once again find solace in your religion. If, however, the member of the clergy you turn to for help does not comfort you or offer you ritual acknowledgment of your grief, your frustration and anger toward your religion—and even God—can become overpowering.

Birth and death remain the ultimate mysteries of life, and the death of a baby during or shortly after pregnancy is especially troubling.

People, including the clergy, are so unsettled by pregnancy loss and infant death that they tend to offer platitudes such as "It was God's will" or "It happened for the best." As one father argued, "If things always happened for the best, there would be no pregnancy loss in the world to begin with."

The doubt you may be experiencing after your loss does not necessarily mark the end of your faith. "It may even be a new beginning," maintains Matthew Ripley-Moffitt, an ordained Protestant minister. "Your crisis may cause you to go through a transition of faith development, rather than destruction."

For some parents, the trial of sorrow deepens their spiritual life and enriches their relationships with family, friends and congregants at their house of worship. These parents gain a new respect for the preciousness of life, which they may interpret as a parting gift from their baby or a lesson taught by God.

If you are struggling to find solace in your religion, do not be surprised, however, if your faith is shaken to the core. There is still hope for you to achieve the consolation you need and deserve.

WHEN YOUR LOSS FEELS LIKE RETRIBUTION

Like many parents, you probably wonder why this misfortune befell you and your baby. Up until this point, your life may have seemed like a series of challenges followed by rewards for each success. Faced with your loss, you may search for some explanation to help you grasp the ungraspable. Since most major religions espouse concepts of sin and retribution, you may feel anger and guilt mixed in with your sorrow. "If bad things only happen to bad people," one woman wondered, "what did I do to deserve this punishment? And my child was so innocent. How could God have done this to my baby?"

You may feel guilty for not having planned the pregnancy you lost, for ending a previous pregnancy or for feeling ambivalent about becoming a parent. Martha found it particularly difficult to be Catholic and single when she suffered her first-trimester miscarriage. "A lot of the nurses in the hospital were nuns, and I felt they were judging me," she admitted. "Even when I asked to speak to my own priest, I felt more guilty than comforted. I felt I was suffering from having sinned rather than from having been the victim of a loss." It is no wonder that you may find yourself doubting your faith. "If my religion can't comfort me at a time like this," professed one mother, "what good is it?"

WHEN YOU TURN TO THE CLERGY

Parents ask me, "How can I believe in God when my baby dies?" And priests in turn must ask themselves the question, "How do I affirm life

when its greatest symbol, a little baby, is taken away?"
—The Reverend Dr. Vienna Cobb Anderson, Episcopal priest

Your clergyperson's response to your sorrow can greatly effect the degree of solace you obtain from your faith. If your rabbi, priest, imam or minister listens to your concerns and offers relevant rituals, even your negative emotions, such as anger or guilt, can be released, allowing healthy grieving to begin. On the other hand, if the cleric you turn to has not been trained in bereavement counseling and offers only platitudes or denies you meaningful ceremonies, your anger may be unleashed at your religion and at God.

When the Clergy Console You

Members of the clergy who show their human side, who are able to grieve with your family, who listen more than they speak and who do not dismiss your desire for ritual can be enormously effective following a loss.

Amelia's minister reached out to her and her husband throughout their difficult reproductive history, offering prayers, baptism and a memorial service for each loss. "But what I remember most about my minister, what affected me the most," explained Amelia, "was that at our first baby's memorial service she was constantly wiping her eyes and blowing her nose. She was so human."

If you feel the clergyperson you have contacted is too constrained by tradition, try to find another person whose training and creativity are more appealing to you. The hospital social worker or chaplain may be able to help.

Connie called her parish priest after her stillbirth because she wanted a ceremony but didn't know what would be appropriate. He told her that the Catholic Church felt a stillborn baby's soul went straight to heaven and that it wasn't necessary to name her baby or have a burial service for her.

Connie was not satisfied with her priest's response, so she called the hospital and asked to speak with their Catholic chaplain, even though she had already been discharged. He helped her make arrangements with a compassionate mortician so her daughter could have a simple burial—the kind she and her husband wanted. "The hospital chaplain also gave me a candle to light at home," recalled Connie, "a small gesture, but one that meant a great deal to me because it was so tangible."

Mothers in particular view the influx of women into the clergy as a sign that their religions can change and adapt to the need for comfort and ritual around pregnancy loss. "Let's face it," said one devout Catholic woman, "Catholic priests are celibate males. What do they know in their hearts and guts about the experience of having or losing a baby?"

Rabbi Nina Beth Cardin sees a similar influence on Judaism. "All new rituals are developed because congregants want something specific to do and have found rabbis who have responded to these needs," she explains. "Women rabbis, especially those who have created rituals following their own losses, will eventually have an enduring impact."

If the member of the clergy you turn to for help comforts you, writing a note of thanks can be a wonderful gesture. Often the clergy themselves are not certain if they have said or done the right thing. Having the expressed gratitude of a parent can help them realize that their long hours and sincere attempts to serve God and humanity are worthwhile.

When Religion May Disappoint You

You may feel disheartened if your desire for religious solace is thwarted after your loss. This could be the first time you have turned to the clergy for guidance, and you may expect them to know just how to help you.

Spiritual leaders, however, have to wrestle with theology, questions of faith and their congregants' grief, all while considering their own sadness and mortality. Like other people, members of the clergy often feel especially helpless when trying to explain infant death or pregnancy loss. Sister Mary Donohue, a hospital chaplain, asks, "What can you say that makes sense of death and sorrow when you are anticipating life and joy?"

Some priests, ministers, imams and rabbis compound the situation by setting themselves above grief and tears, either as an example of fortitude or for self-protection. A greater problem is that most members of the clergy receive little training in bereavement counseling during their formal education. Divinity students who wish to become hospital chaplains are the most likely to have bereavement training, but their exposure to pregnancy loss and infant death may still be minimal. This lack of preparation can leave members of the clergy so out of touch with the needs of bereaved parents that they may make errors of judgment and taste.

Adam was dismayed when a member of the clergy, whom he had driven to his baby's grave site for a service, brought up the payment of his fee on the way home. Adam was grateful for the tenderness the pastor had put into the brief service, so he was astonished by the sudden discussion of remuneration. "I felt he should have mentioned his fee during our initial conversation when we planned the service," admitted Adam. "It left us with an unhappy feeling about him and our religion."

If you are planning a service for your baby, try to keep several issues in mind. Be sure the clergyperson conducting the ritual knows your infant's name, because having it omitted or mispronounced can be upsetting. You may want to inquire if your imam, rabbi, priest or minister maintains a calendar system to keep track of congregants' anniversaries, so that you will be contacted a year later, when you might be feeling particularly sad. If your cleric does not have a system, you may want to let her know you would appreciate a follow-up call. This is one way you can help your clergyperson understand pregnancy loss; at the same time, you may leave a legacy of improved pastoral care in your congregation.

If you suffered a midterm or late loss, you may have contacted a funeral director, whose training and compassion are important when you are so vulnerable. Unfortunately, some funeral directors are more concerned with making a sale than attending to your needs. "He told me that the casket was all I was ever going to give my child," one mother recalled of the funeral director she had turned to for help. "He said I should spend eight hundred dollars and get her a really nice one instead of the two-hundred-dollar casket I had picked out."

Irene was equally disturbed when, immediately after the conclusion of the graveside ceremony for her stillborn daughter, she heard the sound of a loud motor revving and turned to see a backhoe lumbering over to fill her baby's grave. "It was rude," Irene complained. "They should have waited a while, at least until the family had left."

If you are a member of a denomination that encourages large families, you may begin to feel as if you had failed not only yourself but also your faith by experiencing a pregnancy loss. After several miscarriages, Jody found it uncomfortable to worship every Sabbath surrounded by the many pregnant women and large families in her congregation. She became additionally upset when one pregnant congregant informed her, "When God wants you to have a baby, you'll have a baby." Jody felt differently. "Maybe God has provided doctors with the knowledge to help me achieve a family," she surmised. "Isn't that a gift from God, too? I couldn't believe that God was failing me any more than I was failing God."

If you receive thoughtless treatment from a member of the clergy, a funeral director, cemetery staff or someone in your congregation, try to vent your anger by expressing your displeasure. If you do not want to bring up your concerns in person, consider writing a letter. Professionals may not realize how offensive their lack of training can be unless bereaved parents take the time to tell them. Remember, however, that it is equally important to write a letter if you have received compassionate care.

THE RELEVANCE OF RITUALS

Rituals can help you say good-bye to your baby and begin a healthy grieving response. They also serve as a signal to the larger community that you deserve special attention and care following your loss.

Like many parents, this may be the first time you have had to say good-bye to a loved one or make burial arrangements. You may have no idea what is considered correct or suitable, and you may be unprepared for the impact these decisions have on you and your partner. Irene remembered the difficulty she and her husband had deciding where their stillborn daughter should be buried. "We had to discuss our own mortality," she recalled, "and how and where we wanted to be buried ourselves."

The clergy may inadvertently confuse you by not giving you clear information about your options, suggesting that you do "whatever you want" when you have no idea what you want. Some parents find these concerns so painful that they shy away from planning a ritual good-bye for their baby. They hope their sorrow will fade with time if they avoid a ceremony.

Although it is difficult for many parents to think about expressing their grief in front of others, even loved ones, rituals provide a cathartic moment to release the pain, to acknowledge the loss and to start to grieve. Amelia and her husband knew they wanted a memorial service in the hospital where their first premature baby had lived her short life:

It seems to me that by acknowledging our baby's death with a ritual, we were acknowledging that our baby lived and that she had made a difference in a lot of people's lives, even though hers was so short. If we hadn't done something, it would have been like sweeping her ashes out into the street.

For Laurel, planning a ritual good-bye for her baby became a way of turning an unbearable shock into a comprehensible sorrow. Although her rabbi tried to dissuade her from attending the funeral, Laurel believed that being there was the only way the loss could ever become real to her. "I instinctively knew I needed to go to the funeral," she admitted. "It was the only normal thing that happened through the whole ordeal."

Sometimes the mother can't attend a planned ritual because she is still hospitalized and the funeral can't be postponed. If this happens, keep the burial as scheduled but arrange a memorial service later, when the mother can attend. Another solution is to make a video or audiotape of the ceremony. It is also helpful if the hospitalized mother is allowed to plan as much of the service as possible and if a relative, friend or member of the clergy stays with her during the ceremony.

Many hospitals offer an ecumenical memorial service for all pregnancy losses and infant deaths once a year, usually around the winter holidays. Parents who have been unable to attend the burial of their baby or who had a first-trimester loss may find this annual ritual comforting.

Some parents prefer the option of cremation. Ashes can be interred at any point following the loss, so cremation may provide a sensitive, accommodating alternative.

Naming Your Baby

> *The moment we knew it was a daughter we named her Melanie, and she has been Melanie ever since. By naming her, I have acknowledged that she was very real to me, and I can refer to her in a very real way. And it is a name I can never use again. I had a daughter named Melanie.*
>
> —Ruth

Naming your baby allows you to refer to your child personally with love and honor, lending reality to both the baby and your loss. "It seems to me the ultimate nonidentity is to refer to a baby as 'it,'" said Amelia, who named both of her premature babies, who died shortly after birth. "It would have been hard always to refer to Ethan, for example, only as 'the boy baby who died.'"

Few rituals give more concreteness to a loss than naming the child. And few rites could be simpler. Although many parents may not wish to acknowledge an early loss in this way, some do, and they should be allowed this comfort. Most members of the clergy encourage naming infants as a way of affirming the unique identity of the baby and the baby's place in the family.

Some parents are afraid they'll never find another name they love, so they "save" the name for later and give the child one they don't like as much. However, parents who give their deceased baby the name they had already chosen are usually glad to have done so and find that naming subsequent children is not the problem they had anticipated. As one mother who had suffered two losses revealed, "After we named both babies, we wondered if there would be a name left we liked. But as soon as we named the next baby, who lived, we loved that name, too."

The issue becomes more complicated if religious tradition and family expectations maintain that children should be named for a beloved relative, living or dead. Couples may feel they are not providing the proper honor in bestowing the name on a child who has already died or has no hope of living. Lisa, whose Jewish tradition of naming babies after a deceased relative meant a great deal to her, explained her thoughts when she knew her baby would live only a few hours:

> We had picked out names after our grandparents. When we knew she was not expected to live, I didn't want to use the names. We started thinking that she should be named after both of us, her parents, because she was such a part of us. That's not the Jewish tradition, but it was important to us. So we gave her two names, each one starting with our own first initials.

If you had decided not to name your child and now have regrets, it is a decision you can change. One couple who had ended a pregnancy for chromosomal problems was so distressed by the event that they chose not to name their baby. Their hospital chaplain saw the couple several months later at the medical center's yearly memorial service and found their attitude had changed. "During the service, the father read a poem and dedicated it to his son, whom he named at the end of the reading," said the chaplain. "It was very powerful."

Burying or Cremating Your Baby

If a loss occurs late in the pregnancy, parents must make arrangements for the baby. If they do not indicate a specific choice, hospitals may automatically provide cremation, sometimes with the option of a funeral service in the hospital chapel. Other hospitals arrange burial through the city or county in a common grave, or potter's field, but parents are usually not notified of the exact date or site of the burial and cannot attend the interment or visit the plot later.

Increasingly, hospitals are requiring parents to make all the arrangements themselves for babies over twenty weeks' gestation. Private burial or cremation is then necessary and can be handled through a funeral home. This can be costly, so it is best to contact the hospital social worker or chaplain, or the head of your own congregation, for help in making arrangements through a sympathetic funeral director who might reduce his fee. If a private funeral home is too expensive, contact one of the religious burial societies mentioned under individual religions later in this chapter.

If you are still in the process of making these decisions, there are many issues to consider. You need to ask yourself if you will be able to visit a distant cemetery, or if having the baby cremated and the ashes scattered close to home would be more suitable. Perhaps you live in a new town where you feel you have no roots, leading you to choose cremation, which allows you the flexibility of arranging a service at a later date or in another community. It's difficult, but important, to consider what is right for you in your moment of sorrow and what will be the best choice for you in the future.

If you are considering cremation, it is important for you to know what the ashes will look like. Instead of the fine gray powder, like fireplace ash, that most people expect, there are little slivers of bone, some of it charred, mixed with the powder. With a baby the amount of ash is quite small, and when you transfer it to the ground, it poofs in the air. Disposal of ashes is not governed by most states, so the burial or scattering of ashes can be done almost anywhere that is meaningful to you. You may also want to purchase a small, polished wooden or metal box that can be engraved with the baby's name and birth date, or a little porcelain jar rather than the large brass urn funeral directors market for ashes.

Should you choose to bury your child, you will need to decide where the baby will be buried and what kind of service would be appropriate. Some couples prefer holding a service for immediate family and friends in their house of worship followed by a simple burial or committal ritual at the grave site. If you wish to hold your child before the burial, it is important to know that the baby will no longer be warm, which many parents do not expect and find upsetting. Caskets for babies are very small and are usually made from a white polyurethane material, giving them a potentially offensive likeness to a soda cooler. Specially designed "burial cradles" are available from organizations listed in Appendix B.

You may find it comforting to pick out a little outfit for the baby to wear or to select objects to be placed in the casket by you or by the funeral director. Making these small but important arrangements may provide you with a needed connection to your baby. "I dressed her in an outfit with little ruffled socks and put in a couple of toys and a blanket," remembered Irene about the day before her stillborn daughter's burial. "It was hard purchasing them, but it meant something to my husband and me to have those things with her."

Funeral director Ronald Troyer suggests that bereaved parents plan a meal or other informal gathering following any burial or cremation, to give family and friends the chance to share in the open recognition of the couple's grief. He feels that giving the parents the opportunity to bond with their family and friends "can assist in reducing the conspiracy of silence parents often feel at future family and social gatherings."

When Ritual Is Denied

If you feel you need a traditional ritual, it is upsetting to have a member of the clergy try to dissuade you. When the clergy are not well trained in pregnancy loss or newborn death, or when they are overwhelmed by their own feelings of sorrow and helplessness, they tend to lead bereaved parents away from rituals. They may discourage you from using ritual as a means of expressing your grief and suggest that you get on with your life by planning another pregnancy. Although this advice comes from good intentions, it is misguided.

Members of the clergy may also deny grieving parents rites because of theological constraints or confusion over the appropriateness of employing certain standard rituals for the death of a baby. Catholic priests and Protestant ministers may refuse to baptize a stillborn baby, since baptism is a sacrament reserved for the living. The Jewish tradition of sitting shiva, in which mourners receive visitors at home for seven days, is not encouraged. Jewish parents may be dissuaded from having a funeral for a baby who did not live the requisite thirty-day period beyond birth established by Jewish law, although burial is required.

Adelle asked to see a rabbi after her premature daughter died shortly after delivery at twenty-one weeks. She wasn't sure what she wanted to do or what was even proper, but Adelle knew she didn't want her baby simply disposed of by the hospital without some religious ritual:

> I wanted to know if there was any special prayer we could say. The rabbi said
> there wasn't any. He also tried to talk us out of a funeral, saying it wasn't nec-
> essary and would be too expensive. I got the feeling he says this to all women,
> but he didn't realize how much I had committed to the pregnancy and what I
> had been through.

Laurel found that the absence of religious ritual for her premature
baby made it more difficult for other people, especially those in her
congregation, to cope with her loss. Even though she eventually convinced her rabbi that she needed to have a funeral, the ceremony
included only the immediate family:

> If we had been allowed to have a ritual recognized by the whole community, it
> would have given others a way to acknowledge our grief. Since we couldn't sit
> shiva, there was no way for people to share our grief, so they said nothing,
> which was worse.
>
> My pain and attachment to this baby would have been validated if there
> had been a prescribed way for people to respond to us. Without rituals, I felt
> embarrassed and ashamed, as if I had done something wrong because my
> baby had died.

If you doubt that religious rituals are meaningful, their value
becomes clear in their absence. Omission of rituals can be an attempt
to erase the painful reality of your loss. With time, you may realize these
efforts were futile, and you might even feel negligent toward your child
for not having provided a service. If this happened to you, you can still
name your baby or hold a memorial service at a later date to help bring
expression to your grief.

THEOLOGY AND RITUAL

As you search for meaningful rituals, you may question certain dogmas
and traditions. You may need help in understanding some of the theological limitations of particular rituals and how they can be adapted to
suit your need for solace. As one mother said after being refused rituals
she wanted:

> I eventually had to accept that my clergyman's interpretation of what was
> acceptable was just that—an interpretation. His view. I had to do what was
> right for me, what gave me comfort.

Jewish Traditions

Customs vary depending on whether the congregation is Orthodox,
Conservative or Reform. According to Orthodox Jewish tradition, if a
loss occurs within forty days of conception, the pregnancy is considered

"watery tissue" and no burial is warranted. After forty days, it is customary to bury any products of conception that resemble human form, but usually without a formal funeral service. Well-established Orthodox traditions surrounding death and burial are observed only if a baby has lived thirty days or more.

The Conservative rabbinic leadership adopted new recommendations regarding rituals and newborn death in 1992. Any child born alive, no matter what the gestational age, can be recognized with a traditional burial service and full mourning rituals for parents and siblings, including sitting shiva—observing seven days of mourning in the home—and saying the Kaddish, a prayer recited by families in mourning. However, the Conservative Jewish leadership does not recommend these rituals for stillborn babies.

Some scholars have interpreted the traditional avoidance of ritual as a kindness to bereaved parents, who would have spent their entire lives mourning one loss or another during most of history, when infant mortality and pregnancy loss were rampant. But this explanation is of little comfort to modern parents, who may feel the need to mark their losses with a ritual. Ancient Talmudic references do exist to support the observance of mourning rites for stillbirth. Sensitive rabbis may draw from these traditions to help congregants say good-bye to an infant with meaningful rituals, such as a funeral service or saying the Kaddish.

If you prefer to have a burial without making the arrangements yourself, you may contact a Jewish burial society, or Chevra Kadisha, in your community, which will handle all aspects of the funeral and burial in a Jewish cemetery. Cremation is not allowed.

If the baby is a boy and you wish to have a circumcision, it is acceptable to have a posthumous ritual bris. But this practice can be uncomfortable for some parents. After Mark's premature son died, his rabbi recommended circumcision. "I couldn't do it," Mark confessed. "I was bothered by the rabbi's suggestion. I thought God would accept the baby the way he was."

In Orthodox and Conservative Judaism, autopsy is prohibited unless the knowledge gained would directly save the life of another child or a member of the baby's immediate family. It cannot be employed for general scientific inquiry.

The use of traditional rites and the acceptance of new rituals vary among Orthodox, Conservative and Reform synagogues. Parents may find that the degree to which they feel their needs are met depends on the experience and sensitivity of each individual rabbi.

Jewish naming issues. Most Jewish families choose to name a child who dies late in the pregnancy or shortly after birth. If there is a burial, the name is recited at the cemetery and a gravestone is inscribed with the baby's name and the family name. This step helps create the recognition grieving parents might need, because people tend to realize the extent of the family's loss when they see a traditional engraved headstone.

Some families bestow the name they had originally chosen for their child, but an ancient tradition in the Jewish code of law has made it customary to name a deceased infant based on a variant of the Hebrew words for "mercy" or "comfort." This custom implies that God will have mercy on the child and that the parents should be comforted in knowing and loving their child, however briefly. Rachamim is the masculine form of the name meaning "mercy," and Ruchama is the feminine form. Nechama is the feminine form of "the comforting one," which for boys becomes Nachum or Menachem .

Jewish babies are usually given both a secular name and a Hebrew name at birth. The secular name is often derived from the first initial of a deceased family member's secular or Hebrew name. When a baby dies, parents may prefer to choose a name beginning with the same initial, but not use the name they had originally selected.

Islamic Traditions

Muslims believe that the greatest burden a mother can bear is the death of her child. Families should therefore be counseled and comforted following any form of pregnancy loss. According to Islamic tradition, a child lost during pregnancy or before puberty belongs to God and is guaranteed entry into paradise. A baby entering paradise is a credit to its parents and will ensure them of a place in the hereafter, although bereaved mothers and fathers are still expected to lead good lives and keep their faith.

Islamic belief maintains that the soul is breathed into a baby 120 days after conception. Losses before this period do not require a service, but the baby may be buried if the parents wish to have this comfort. A stillborn baby or a baby lost shortly after birth may receive the traditional preparation and burial. The baby should be washed and shrouded in a single white sheet, a ritual that is usually performed in the funeral home, but can also occur in the hospital, the family's home or the mosque. It is customary for families, especially both parents, to participate in this rite. The baby may be buried with the traditional funeral prayer recited at the ceremony. Burial should occur within twenty-four hours of death, but concessions can be made depending on the individual circumstances.

The parents should be at the burial, offering supplications to God. The tradition of not allowing women at the funeral and graveside ceremony is considered a cultural limitation, not a religious one. There is a current movement to reexamine the relationship between men and women in light of the teachings of the Prophet Mohammed, who considered the two genders to be equal, like the two halves of a whole. Many imams and practicing Muslims regard Islam as a religion of common sense, so they believe it is reasonable and proper for a mother to be present for the burial of her baby.

Cremation is not allowed, and autopsy is permitted only in certain instances. Islamic religious leaders believe that faithful Muslims can maintain a sensible and compassionate view toward life when dealing with modern technology. Prenatal testing is therefore sanctioned, and ending a pregnancy is possible, especially if a baby is diagnosed with an impairment which is incompatible with life. It is also permissible if the mother's life is at risk.

Islam acknowledges that people grieve at different rates and intensities, so there is no prescribed mourning period; however, a traditional forty-day bereavement period is often observed. The family's role is vital in comforting and supporting the bereaved during this time. For further guidance, it is best to speak with an imam who is on the hospital chaplaincy staff, or contact your local Islamic Center.

Islamic naming issues. Naming is considered a rite for the living, a way of honoring the character of the baby so that the child will live up to its name. There are no special names for miscarried or stillborn babies because they are not considered born into this world, but babies who live even a few seconds should be named. Babies may be given names chosen to honor family members, living or deceased, or may be given other traditional Islamic names. According to custom, the mother always has the first choice of naming a newborn because she already knows the baby's nature after carrying her child for nine months.

Catholic Traditions

One of the dichotomies devout Catholics face is that although their faith regards human life as beginning at conception, few rituals and blessings are traditionally employed for most forms of pregnancy loss. Part of the problem lies in the issue of baptism, the sacrament of being welcomed into the faith and community of the Church, which is reserved only for the living.

The Church has no other rituals for babies that carry the weight of blessing and honor inherent in baptism. Parents often request baptism because it is so basic to being Christian and to being welcomed into the fellowship of the Church. Many members of the Catholic clergy recognize this problem and offer what they call "conditional baptism," in which the rite is celebrated on the chance that some flicker of life exists that is not discernible to the hospital staff. If the baby is born in an emergency situation, anyone may baptize the infant—the parents, an ambulance driver, or a nurse—including non-Catholics. This can be done by pouring ordinary water on the baby's forehead and pronouncing the baby's name followed by the words "I baptize you in the name of the Father and of the Son and of the Holy Spirit. Amen."

Theologians have recently returned to a newly clarified and amplified older theory. If the parents have faith and would have wanted the baby to be baptized, then the baby was automatically baptized before its death in what is termed a "baptism of desire." Some Catholic clergy have created new liturgies rather than applying the sacrament of baptism when it is not considered appropriate. See Appendix B on sample religious rituals for a version of these blessings.

If a baptism wasn't performed, sensitive priests and chaplains realize that parents still need something tangible, such as a baptismal certificate, to take home with them and treasure as a keepsake. Some offer a "certificate of life," which can be used for any birth or loss. The small scroll has spaces for the baby's and parents' names and the baby's birth date, along with the inscription "Your child entered eternal life."

The concept of limbo, traditionally a place of neither punishment nor heaven for innocent unbaptized souls, arose to help account for deceased babies in the universe of God. But limbo is not an official dogma of the Catholic Church and is no longer recognized.

A funeral Mass or a memorial service offered in your baby's name may be of great comfort, although it is not required. A funeral and burial can be observed as long as there is something to inter, even if the baby has not been baptized. Some Catholic churches hold yearly services to commemorate babies lost to miscarriages, ectopic pregnancies and other forms of loss that might not have warranted a funeral or other more formal mourning ritual. Your local diocese or archdiocese will have information about where such services are held. Appendix B will provide you with ceremonies, and Appendix D with additional resources.

You can have your baby buried in a Catholic cemetery, and your parish priest may encourage you to do so. If you do not wish to purchase a stone or to attend a service, you can choose to have the burial handled by the St. Vincent de Paul Society, which buries the baby in a common grave without the family present. Cremation, once frowned upon, is gaining in acceptance. Wakes are not considered necessary for babies, but if parents wish to hold a wake, they may. Some clerics, especially those who serve in hospitals, are willing to be creative in developing meaningful liturgy and rituals following pregnancy loss.

Catholic naming issues. Catholic parents usually give their children two names, one of which honors a particular saint. If the couple doesn't wish to give their baby the name they had originally chosen, priests and nuns may encourage them to honor the baby with the name of a member of the Holy Family. "Our babies' plot has many Marys and Josephs buried there," admitted one Catholic hospital chaplain.

Couples who wish to honor their baby boy by naming him after his father might consider switching the first and middle names so they can still use the father's name with a subsequent son. Some Hispanic parents give the name Angel to a baby who died during gestation or shortly after birth, which represents a compensation for the difficulties the child has been through and the comfort of knowing that their baby is with God.

Protestant Traditions

Cremation, burial, memorial services and honoring the baby in a Sunday morning pastoral prayer are some of the many rituals that are used to express the loss of a baby in the Protestant faith. Clergy and congregants alike are encouraged to develop new and personal liturgy to suit the needs and desires of the bereaved.

Although Protestants have fewer dogmas to confront than Catholics, the issue of baptism is the same: It is a sacrament for the living and generally is not used for a miscarriage or stillbirth. Your denomination's interpretation of baptism may vary, so you should discuss your wishes openly with your minister.

Protestant naming issues. There are no restrictions on the naming of babies lost during gestation or shortly after birth. Protestant couples who planned to name a firstborn son after the baby's father might consider reversing the father's first and middle names, either for the baby they lost or for a subsequent son.

Mixed Religions

If you and your partner do not share the same religion, suffering a pregnancy loss can pose special problems. You may have had to deal with religious differences for your wedding, but it was an event you had the time and inclination to plan. In the crisis following a pregnancy loss, neither of you may know how to approach two distinct members of the clergy. You may also worry how they will respond to your need for a ritual that acknowledges both religions.

Some couples of mixed faiths have discovered that they are caught in a judgmental bind. When Jesse, who is Jewish, and his Protestant wife, Irene, had a stillborn daughter, they knew they wanted to bury their baby with suitable rituals. But they also realized that Jewish tradition would not allow a family of mixed religions to be buried together in a Jewish cemetery. Fortunately, Jesse and Irene found a sympathetic rabbi who guided them without judging their mixed marriage. He helped them locate a cemetery that accepted all faiths, and he created a simple graveside service for their baby girl that included readings from Psalms and Proverbs that were comforting to both Christians and Jews. Irene in particular was grateful for his compassion:

> He wasn't casting guilt on either one of us or on Jesse's family for letting him marry outside his faith. He reminded us that our love for each other would help us through this. He talked about the grandparents and their grief. He was sensitive toward everyone's feelings.

If you prefer to contact two clerics of different faiths to help you bless your baby, do so. Hospital chaplain Catherine Garlid recalled a Jewish mother who went into labor knowing her baby would not live long. She called a rabbi and her husband called a priest, both of whom agreed to be present in the delivery room. When the baby was born, he was blessed by the rabbi and baptized by the priest, a remarkable gesture that Reverend Garlid remembers clearly:

> It was a wonderful experience for the couple and the two members of the clergy who participated. The baby lived only a few hours, but the feeling between the priest and the rabbi was amazing. The collegial opportunity to minister together in an interfaith context was something they both still talk about many years later as being one of the most powerful experiences in their ministry and rabbinate.

If you wish to acknowledge each of your religions in commemorating your baby, by all means reach out to members of the clergy you know or whom the hospital may recommend or have on staff. Explain the unity of love you and your partner have for your child, and your desire to have the baby's presence in your lives acknowledged and blessed in each of your faiths.

THE NEED FOR SPECIAL RITUALS

If you have decided that traditional rituals are not a suitable way to commemorate your loss, you may still feel the need to have some observance that is personal and meaningful. You may find solace in honoring your child's birth date or due date, perhaps by reading aloud a letter or poem you have written to your baby, as well as setting aside time just to recall the brief moments you shared, even if they existed only during your pregnancy.

Planting a tree or perennial flower in honor of your baby may provide the sense of ritual and symbolism you need. A member of the clergy could participate, and this could be another opportunity to read prayers, a poem, or a letter you have written to your baby. You might want to honor your baby by committing yourself to a meaningful volunteer project or by making a charitable donation in the baby's name. Some hospitals have plaques they will inscribe with your infant's name if you choose to make a contribution. You may want to mark the anniversary of your baby's death and birth by visiting the plaque.

The personal ritual you create might change over time once your loss is more integrated into your life. After Wendy buried two newborn babies, she placed flowers on their graves every week. Later she began to feel she had gotten past the need to make the weekly trip to the cemetery, but she still wanted to commemorate her children in a tangible way, to show that they were with her in spirit. So each Monday she has fresh flowers delivered to her office. "I think of the flowers as a gift from my children," she says warmly. "It helps me to look at my flowers every day and for people at work to see them, too. It's as if my children are still spreading joy." See Appendix B, on rituals, for additional suggestions.

Rituals for Early Losses

> All but one of my losses were so early we didn't even consider rituals. But we regret not doing something more. We didn't put the emotional energy into grieving that we should have.
>
> —Vera

If you suffered an early loss and feel the need for a ritual, do not hesitate to speak to the hospital chaplain or the spiritual leader of your congregation. Because you will have little more than blood or "fetal tissue," services such as funerals and burials are often discouraged by the clergy as being too expensive and unwarranted, but this does not mean your loss should go unacknowledged or your baby unblessed. Some parents choose to bury the products of their conception with a simple ceremony in a place of special meaning, such as their backyard or a garden, with family or friends and a member of the clergy present.

Ellen had experienced several first-trimester miscarriages and only gradually realized her need for ritual was growing with each loss. By the time she suffered her fifth miscarriage, she felt compelled to acknowledge her sorrow in some religious way. As she sat bleeding and cramping in a hospital emergency room, Ellen was startled when a patient representative came up to her and asked if she could bring her anything:

> It just sort of popped out of me, without much forethought, that I wanted to speak with a chaplain, who arrived a few minutes later. He was a kind, soft-spoken Episcopal priest who asked what he could do for me. I told him I wanted a prayer for the baby who had died inside of me. He stood quietly by my chair and said a gentle, simple prayer that acknowledged my love for my baby, no matter how small it was. Few religious services in my life have touched me more deeply.

If you feel the need to commemorate your early loss, please read the prayers, poems and rituals—including naming ceremonies—in Appendix B, and contact a member of the clergy if you wish to express your grief in a more formal way.

Rituals for Ending an Impaired Pregnancy

Few situations present a more searing theological problem than ending a pregnancy. As entire populations struggle with this issue, people from all walks of life, including lawmakers and doctors, as well as members of the clergy, are drawn into the conflict. But as long as prenatal testing exists and the dilemma is borne privately in the hearts of bereaved parents, religious leaders must accept that mothers and fathers who are ending their pregnancies need and deserve the comfort of their faith.

This does not pose a problem for liberal Protestant or Jewish denominations, but the Catholic Church, Orthodox Judaism, Islam and fundamentalist Christian sects are generally opposed to most forms of abortion. However, people of these faiths are still entitled to spiritual help and rituals to assuage their grief when they decide to end their pregnancies. "So many people feel guilty about the decision, they don't feel they deserve to be sad," explains Catherine Garlid, a Protestant hospital chaplain. "But that can really complicate the grieving process. It is just as crucial that these parents get help and comfort, too."

You have experienced a real and painful loss rendered more agonizing by the issue of choice. You need to mourn, and if this includes seeking out the comfort of your religion, you should be able to find solace within your faith. You should be allowed to bury or cremate your baby and to have a memorial service, funeral or anything else you need to acknowledge your sorrow.

Even the more conservative lines are softening somewhat on this issue. One Orthodox rabbi explained that although his denomination rejects the idea of ending a pregnancy, in "no way is a fetus to be rejected or despised." He insists that burial of an Orthodox baby under these circumstances is still possible and that no sanctions are implemented against the parents for making the choice to end their pregnancy.

Devout Catholics and fundamentalist Christians may have the most difficulty, since any termination is forbidden by their religion. Many of them simply forgo prenatal testing as a result. However, certain routine prenatal examinations can indicate defects that are incompatible with life. If these parents wish to end a pregnancy, they should be encouraged to seek out private counseling with a compassionate priest or minister.

A nationwide Catholic ministry called Project Rachel offers postabortion support services and counseling for parents who wish to be reconciled with their religion after ending a pregnancy. Information on Project Rachel is provided in Appendix D, and a ritual for ending a pregnancy is included in Appendix B. Also read Chapter 8, "Prenatal Diagnosis and the Burden of Choice."

If you cannot find a helpful member of the clergy who understands your need for religious acknowledgment of your loss, ask a hospital social worker for guidance. She should be able to put you in touch with an understanding clergyperson, perhaps one of the hospital chaplains.

YOUR RETURN TO FAITH

Even if you have become a lapsed practitioner of your religion, you may turn to old beliefs for comfort in the desolation of losing your baby. Your experience may deepen your faith and commitment to God. For some parents, the joy of a subsequent baby gives them a renewed trust in their religion. For others, the loss itself becomes the key to a restoration of faith.

Wendy struggled with her faith when she lost two newborn babies. With the first loss, she was overwhelmed by guilt that she had done something wrong, and she blamed God for punishing her. After her second loss her attitude shifted, and she began to believe that she could try to learn something from her sorrow instead:

> Little by little I am returning to my faith. I want to have faith in something. I want to believe in something again. This has really shattered my life. I can't believe this is the only life my children have had. I want to believe my children are in a better place.

Even with a renewal of faith, religious doubts can continue to plague you. But doubts can strengthen faith, just as questions advance learning. You may find the experience of grappling with the issues—even if they sometimes remain unresolved—has a positive effect on your life. Ellen recalled talking to a minister in her community when she was a teenager, a conversation that had remained forgotten for years until after she had endured several miscarriages:

> He said the point of religion was not to explain away bad things but to equip us to handle them. So what it came down to for me was not what all my pregnancy losses meant in a religious sense, because ultimately I don't think they happened for any real purpose. There was no Divine Plan, no Ultimate Test.
>
> But what I made of the losses, how they affected my life—that was the real test of my faith. Could I do some good as a result of my sorrow? Would I be able to overcome my bitterness and still love life? That was the challenge—and the final comfort I'll probably spend the rest of my life striving for. God was within me with the babies I lost, but I am the only one who can build into my life a memorial to the children I will never see grow up.

KEY POINTS TO HELP YOU FIND SOLACE IN YOUR RELIGION

The loss of your baby can make you doubt your belief in an orderly universe overseen by a loving, compassionate God. Sensitive members of the clergy may have guided you and helped you grieve, but if others failed to offer you the comfort of rituals, you may have felt disappointed.

There are many ways to seek solace from your religion. Here are some suggestions to help you find comfort within your faith:

- If you turn to a member of the clergy who does not offer what you need, consider looking further. There are compassionate clerics and funeral directors who can guide you toward the rituals and comforts for which you yearn. Consider contacting a social worker or chaplain at the hospital where your loss occurred.
- If you would like a prayer offered on your behalf, consider asking a member of the clergy to do so as part of a regular religious service or during her private devotions.
- Consider naming your child to give the baby an identity, so you can refer to your infant with the specific warmth and affection parents reserve for their children.
- If you decide to bury your child, contemplate buying a little outfit for him to wear or toys to be placed in the casket.
- If the mother cannot attend the funeral or burial service for medical reasons, try to postpone it until she is able to attend. If this is impossible, schedule a memorial service after she has recuperated, or tape the burial for her. Be sure she has someone to stay with her during the ceremony if she cannot attend.
- Consider composing poems or prayers to your baby that can be read aloud at a funeral or memorial service. You may want to plant a tree or a perennial flower in honor of your baby that you can watch grow over the years, or make a charitable donation to honor your baby's memory.
- If you received thoughtless care from a member of the clergy, think about writing to explain what would have helped you. Try also to remember what a kindness it is to write a note of thanks when you have received sensitive care.
- Catholics who wish to be reconciled with their religion after ending a pregnancy can contact Project Rachel, listed in Appendix D.
- Endeavor to accept that bad things sometimes happen for no reason at all and that the only meaning you can give your loss is how you integrate it into your life.

11

The Response of Your Family and Friends

During the days following your loss, compassionate friends and relatives may have comforted you, listening to your story and letting you cry. But even those who love you may not understand the depth of your grief or the length of time it might take you to feel better. Pregnancy loss remains a taboo subject in our society, so even the most caring relatives and friends may not know how to help you cope with your sorrow—while you feel equally ill-equipped to guide them.

In the coming days and weeks, you and your partner must justify your absence from work and inform family and friends whom you do not see regularly that you lost the baby. Explaining your loss to this wider social circle can leave you feeling more drained and angry than understood, especially if people's responses seem clumsy or unkind.

This chapter can help you secure the comfort you need from others and enable you to deal with your disappointment when you do not get the support you deserve. You might want to encourage family and friends to read this section of the book, especially if they would like to help you through this difficult time but aren't sure of the best approach.

TELLING PEOPLE ABOUT YOUR LOSS

Breaking the news of your pregnancy loss to others can be a heartbreaking task. Your own immediate reactions of shock and dismay may turn to a sense of embarrassment and failure as you are forced to tell your story over and over again.

Informing Close Family and Friends

Although it is important to reach out to loved ones, your sad news can feel like an intrusion on their lives. If your family recently enjoyed a happy occasion, such as a wedding, you may feel your loss casts a shroud of gloom over their high spirits. On the other hand, if they have experienced recent sorrows, you may feel you are augmenting their sadness. "I don't like calling people with bad news," said Leah as she remembered the first few weeks following the death of her newborn baby, "so I waited for them to call me."

Once you feel ready to talk about your loss, you need willing listeners who can make you feel loved and valued. Your own parents may be the first people you call, but their ability to respond helpfully can depend on your relationship with them.

Jody phoned her mother immediately after she had suffered her second miscarriage:

> She cried as soon as I told her. If I needed her to go anywhere or do anything, she was there for me. She didn't reflect everything back on herself. She just listened to me and dealt with my emotions. My feelings were her concern.

Your parents may be able to put you first and show their understanding by keeping you company or, if you would like, by putting away baby things or taking care of your other children. But pregnancy loss is a misfortune for grandparents as well. They may be preoccupied by their own sorrow or worried about the bereaved mother's physical health. As a result, they may give unwanted advice instead of expressing pure love and concern.

One woman remembered how different her parents' remarks had been when she told them about her fourth miscarriage and D&C:

> My mother openly asked me why I kept going through pregnancies and miscarriages, and she urged me to stop doing this to my body. But my father just told me how much he loved me and that he would support me no matter what I decided to do. Of the two, my father was far more comforting.

For a more detailed discussion of the impact pregnancy loss has on grandparents, please read Chapter 13, "For Bereaved Grandparents."

Close friends pose particular problems. Some may not realize how upset you are and either avoid the subject of the loss or utter thoughtless remarks, a topic that is discussed later in this chapter. Others may truly help, offering to bring over a meal or make necessary phone calls. Sometimes even simple expressions of genuine sympathy can be meaningful. "When I told one of my best friends about my miscarriage," recalled Ellen, "her eyes immediately filled with tears. She didn't say much, but she conveyed her own sorrow, which meant so much to me."

Telling Your Wider Social Circle

Once you have told your immediate family members and friends about your loss, you face informing colleagues and other acquaintances. But their reactions can make you believe they need comforting more than you do. Each person you tell may want to talk about the loss at length, compelling you to repeat your story when you already feel overburdened.

You should feel free to ask close friends and family to call other people, so you will not be overwhelmed by this unhappy task. You can also look for a more protected way to tell others about your loss. Several organizations listed in Appendix D carry cards especially designed for this situation. In gentle, appealing phrases the cards express the parents' sorrow and suggest how the recipient can offer support. They also include a place to record the baby's name, birth date and weight. One bereaved mother sent a card issued by Perinatal Loss that read:

> Acknowledgment of our child's short life may be upsetting to you. You may think the less said the better. Until now we did not know how important it would be for us to tell you of our little baby, even though our baby died. You can help us through this difficult time by letting us talk about our sorrow when we feel the need, allowing us to cry when we want and not pretending that everything is okay ... when it's not. It will take time, but with your support we will make it.

Jesse, whose baby daughter was stillborn, was most comfortable writing personal notes to people outside his immediate friends and family:

> I picked a card with a stark photograph of a bleak landscape, an overcast day with a lone tree clinging to the side of a mountain. I wrote a note explaining what had happened, and I heard back from people, which was wonderful. Most of them wrote me, which was easier than handling all those phone calls.

Comments from well-meaning people who knew about your pregnancy but not your loss can be especially difficult. Try to keep in mind that these people are only showing interest and support by asking about your pregnancy. They do not intend to hurt you with their questions, as painful or awkward as they may be. You cannot avoid embarrassing them a little by telling the truth, but you can ease the situation by making your response simple and brief. Planning what to say beforehand can help you find comfortable phrases that discourage unwanted questions.

Two months after she lost her full-term son to congenital abnormalities, Leah ran into a woman she knew slightly who commented on the fact that she was no longer pregnant and asked if she had a boy or a girl. Leah had thought carefully about how she would handle this predicament:

> I tried to use the gentlest language possible in these situations, not mentioning death or the baby's abnormalities. I just said, "I had a son, but he didn't make it." She got the message that I didn't want to say any more than that.

Telling acquaintances about your loss may be harder than telling family and friends. The people you and your partner feel closest to are probably more comfortable seeing you cry and sharing their own grief. You might feel awkward breaking down in front of people you don't know well, or annoyed by having to comfort them when they become upset about your news. Amelia found herself in this situation when she attended a performance of a theater subscription following the death of her first premature baby. She dreaded facing the couple who had sat next to her and her husband for the series:

> They weren't close friends, but they were aware of our baby's illness and I knew they would ask about her. I knew I was going to have to tell them, but it seemed so unfair to say "She died" right before the lights went out and the curtain went up. What would they be able to say to us at intermission? I couldn't avoid making them uncomfortable no matter how or when I chose to tell them.

Opening with a phrase such as "I know this will come as a shock" or "I have sad news to tell you" gives people a little time to prepare themselves for their own reactions. It is inevitable that they will still feel uncomfortable or upset, but try not to take on the burden of their feelings in addition to your own.

Mothers can find it especially helpful to alert colleagues before returning to work full time, perhaps telephoning and asking a supervisor to inform the rest of the office. Molly, who worked in a large advertising agency, was relieved to discover that her boss had sent out a letter to all of their clients after her baby was stillborn. "I actually appreciated it very much," she recalled. "Not only was I spared having to tell the news myself, I got so many letters of condolence in return. People really poured their hearts out to me in those letters."

Arranging lunch with coworkers before returning to work full time can also make your transitions easier. It gives your colleagues the chance to ask the usual questions and enables you to answer without having to turn immediately back to your desk and work responsibilities.

Even if you and your partner take these precautions, be prepared for some slip-ups. If this happens, try to explain your story in terms that are easy for you to handle. This will keep you from having an overly emotional response at an awkward time.

Leah had alerted most of her colleagues about her newborn son's death, but word had not spread throughout her company by the time she returned to work:

> When one of the managers in another department saw me, she exclaimed, "Oh, you're back so soon! How's everything going? What did you have?" I pulled her into an empty office and told her in scientific terms what had hap-

pened. If I had told her more of the emotional elements, I would have broken down, and I didn't want to.

If you are a single woman, you may have additional concerns about announcing your loss to this wider social circle, even if you had planned your pregnancy. The awkward silence of colleagues and supervisors can make you feel an unspoken disapproval of your pregnancy instead of sympathy for your loss. If you need additional sources of comfort, a psychotherapist or pregnancy loss support group should be able to provide you with the nonjudgmental consolation you deserve. Please see Appendix D for a list of resources available to you.

Special Issues

If your baby suffered from birth defects, you probably want to avoid insensitive remarks or prying questions from friends and family, as well as colleagues and acquaintances. You may find it helpful to decide how much you want to reveal to each person on an individual basis.

Adam, whose baby had a fatal congenital disorder and lived only a few hours after birth, felt this approach eased the strain of each encounter:

> We didn't know how necessary it was to tell all the details about the loss to people, especially to those who didn't know us well, but you do need to express the truth at times. We decided differently with each person we told.

If your loss involved ending your pregnancy, you may be exposed to unintentionally hurtful remarks. Paula had leaked so much amniotic fluid during her fifth month that her doctors urged her to abandon the pregnancy by inducing labor. She was upset when she returned to work to find people saying how sorry they were that she had to have a "therapeutic abortion" rather than expressing their sadness over her loss. "After that," admitted Paula, "I just told people I leaked fluid and lost the baby, without even mentioning inducement."

Think about the explanations you want to give each person individually. Try to convey what the loss meant to you so that others may respond compassionately.

FINDING THE SUPPORT YOU NEED

> *You can't expect people who have not gone through a pregnancy loss to understand what it is all about.*
>
> —Eric

Shortly after your loss, you may begin to feel bereft of solace from friends, family and the entire community. Standard religious customs and ceremonies are often not available to parents following pregnancy loss and newborn death, a topic that is explored more fully in Chapter 10, "Finding Solace in Your Religion." You may find this lack of societal comfort upsetting, as if the world had forgotten how to reach out to you in your grief, making your loss a truly silent sorrow.

If friends and family seem unsure of what to say or do, it is probably because they have not experienced a similar tragedy. People seem to have lost a common thread of custom, as well as a willingness to share misfortunes with each other. The fact that pregnancy loss can be a taboo subject is also partly to blame. Even family members who suffered a loss may have kept it secret until you told them about yours.

The Reverend Dr. Vienna Cobb Anderson, an Episcopal priest who served an urban congregation in Washington, D.C., remembers from her own childhood in the southern United States how important social customs surrounding death used to be. The clothing people wore, the sprig of flowers or the purple wreath on the door enabled everyone in the community "to know that a family was in need and required special attention and care. People knew about the death and cooked meals, or called and just came by."

In ministering to her own parishioners, Dr. Anderson has seen how we've lost that important sense of community around death, especially that of an unborn or newborn child. By relying on the telephone to spread the news, Dr. Anderson believes, people end up feeling even more removed from the event:

> So often I hear members of my congregation say they didn't bother to visit people in mourning because they would probably cry and upset everybody, without realizing that this is exactly what should happen, that people are more upset if they *don't* see their friends and relatives crying with them.
>
> Most of us feel we have to keep life nice. We are afraid of pain and vulnerability and the tenuousness of life. And nothing seems to leave us feeling more vulnerable or tenuous than the death of an innocent baby.

When people overcome these obstacles and reach out to you, it can be especially meaningful. Even if your friends and family have never shared a similar sorrow, they can help you by offering to put away baby items or calling a store to cancel a layette order. One grieving mother remembered a friend who brought a meal for her and her husband while she was recuperating from an early miscarriage:

> We weren't up to going out yet and we hated the idea of cooking for ourselves, so it was a wonderful gesture. She even stayed to clean up afterward in the kitchen. She could never know exactly how I felt, because she had never suffered a miscarriage, but what she did was so loving and thoughtful.

Handling Thoughtless Remarks

You may feel exhausted and frustrated by the effort to reach out to people after your pregnancy loss, especially when you are still immersed in your own grief. Unfortunately, family or friends you may have counted on to comfort you may disappoint you deeply.

Family members and close friends usually want to be helpful, but they may sometimes blurt out preposterous statements instead. However well-meaning, comments such as "It happened for the best" or "You can always have another baby" do not acknowledge your loss.

People often overlook the simplest statement when trying to say something comforting. Even conveying the thought "I don't know what to say" acknowledges your sorrow and the inadequacy of any words.

When Eve returned to work after an early miscarriage and a colleague said to her, "I'm so sorry, I know how much you wanted that baby," it brought tears to her eyes. "But that was okay," Eve recalled. "The important thing was that she recognized my sense of loss. I was very touched by her sympathy."

Ellen was less fortunate when she called her brother following an early loss in a pregnancy that would have been due at Christmas:

> He said that was a terrible time to have a baby anyway because kids who have birthdays near Christmas always get cheated on presents. I know he was trying to make me feel better, but I just wanted to scream at him that I would have welcomed a baby at any time of the year.

Loved ones may also fail to respect the choices you make about honoring your baby with a name or a religious ritual. Adelle's brother was in close touch with her following each of her two losses, but when he discovered that she had named her second child, he objected. "I thought you would have learned after the first one and not bothered to name the second one," he told his sister. "I did learn," Adelle replied. "I learned you need to name your children."

Chance encounters with people you care about can be awkward, especially if they occur in a public place. Annette and her husband ran into close friends on the street shortly after her early miscarriage. Their friends knew about the loss, but this was the first time they had met face-to-face. "The woman said to me, 'I heard what happened to you,'" recalled Annette. "Then she visibly shuddered and said, 'Yuck!' The four of us were frozen there, not able to say anything."

Tactless comments from people you do not know well can be infuriating—so much so, that you might say the first thing that comes to mind. Ellen attended a company picnic where she encountered the wife of one of her husband's employees:

I barely knew this woman, but she came up to me and said, "I just heard about your most recent miscarriage. My God, what are you going to do, adopt?" "That's none of your business!" I snapped at her as I went back to spooning potato salad onto my plate.

Some grieving parents are caught completely off guard by calls from vendors selling baby products. Diaper service companies, baby photographers and magazine salespeople can descend on unsuspecting parents after a loss, assuming that all went well with the pregnancy. Molly was upset by solicitations she received after her baby was stillborn, but found a way to cope with the onslaught:

When one salesman opened the conversation with "How's your new baby?" I simply said, "My baby is dead." I felt it was okay to shock them a little, and I didn't feel guilty about directing my anger toward them, since I didn't care about these people. I actually appreciated the opportunity to try to educate them about pregnancy loss, explaining that everything doesn't always go perfectly.

Your friends and family may err by assuming you don't want to talk about the loss because it will be too painful for you, so they avoid mentioning it. In fact, this lack of response can be especially difficult to handle.

Molly found it hard to bear when people avoided her out of embarrassment or said nothing about her loss when they did eventually encounter her:

Some friends are no longer friends because they thought we didn't want to talk about our baby. The pain we felt when people ignored our loss was terrible. For us, it was another way of ignoring our son, whose existence we desperately needed to acknowledge.

Try not to be overly concerned if you have occasional angry outbursts when people ignore your loss or say the wrong thing. In a relationship you care about, you can always call the person later to explain your response. True friends can usually absorb both your anger and their own embarrassment.

A few weeks after her friend had said "Yuck" to her, Annette spoke with the same woman by phone and explained why she had become speechless after their encounter. "She apologized for having been so tactless and really showed much more sympathy this time," Annette recalled. "After that conversation, a lot of my anger toward her dissipated."

You may derive a sense of accomplishment by being frank with people whose responses are inconsiderate. Thoughtless comments or silences present an opportunity to educate others about pregnancy loss and how it should be handled in our society. "I felt so passionately about telling people how important it was to make a connection to us in our grief," said one mother, "it became almost a crusade for me. I became one of the 'militant bereaved.'"

Coping with Social Pressures

After the initial shock of your loss, you must face many awkward or stressful social situations. If friends or family had given you a baby shower, you may be wondering what to do with the gifts. It is important to keep in mind that this was still your pregnancy and your baby. Try to find the approach that makes you feel most comfortable and that honors your memories of the baby as well as your future plans for a family.

Leah was in her twenties and her first pregnancy had progressed normally, so she welcomed baby showers from friends and coworkers. She was about halfway through her thank-you cards when her son was born, only to die four hours later:

> It was difficult to continue with the remainder of the thank-you notes, but I wrote people that I hoped my next baby would enjoy the gift, or explained that I was keeping the present because I was not going to give up on having children. I didn't want to return any of the gifts because I knew I would have a baby by some means. What would my friends have done with the returned gifts, anyway? It may have been more painful for them to get them back, too.

If your baby was born gravely ill, you may have been subjected to a different set of disconcerting responses from others. The conventional congratulations surrounding a normal birth may have seemed empty and insincere.

Amelia was saddened by the flower arrangement friends sent when her first baby, a daughter who eventually died, was born three months prematurely. "It was a traditional bouquet, with a vase in the shape of a pink baby shoe, that I associated with feeling happy and congratulatory," she explained. "A critically ill baby is not a joyous event."

If your infant was very ill at birth, you may have wondered if sending out birth announcements was appropriate. Many parents have found that a simple handwritten note on a plain piece of stationery is more in keeping with their mood and the actual news about their baby. You may have been equally uncertain how to respond to gifts you received, especially items of clothing meant for an older, healthy baby.

One option is simply not to respond to the gifts. Once the baby has died, most people would not expect a response, and if they don't understand, let it be their problem, not yours. As one bereaved mother who did not send thank-you notes decided, "It was a time when I had to give myself some kind of a break. I needed to forgive myself for changing the rules of etiquette."

When family and friends do come through with thoughtful gifts for gravely ill newborns, your gratitude may extend beyond your baby's death. Amelia appreciated a little brass picture frame she received from a friend who had suffered her own losses:

> We put a photo of Olivia in there immediately, while she was still in the hospital. It touched us, because it was a gift that acknowledged our first baby and the important person she was to us. That little framed picture became even more meaningful after Olivia died.

You may find that family and friends who talked about the loss early on become less willing to listen as time passes. It may be difficult for you to bring up the subject weeks or months after the loss. One mother who suffered several first-trimester miscarriages remarked that after her first loss people sent flowers and little notes of condolence. But her second and third losses were greeted by silence. "It was as if they didn't know what to do with me if I was going to keep losing babies and demanding their sympathy," she recalled.

You may also begin to perceive that some people don't want to be near you, as if pregnancy loss were communicable or unlucky. This "jinx mentality" may seem especially strong if you live in a community where large families are the norm. After her second miscarriage, Iris went to a community center she frequented in her town. "I felt I started losing friends there because pregnant women didn't want to bother with me," she admitted. "I was the failure, the one who couldn't have a second child. I seemed to frighten them."

You probably feel unprepared to grapple with these distressing encounters. Silence drops over your conversations, while embarrassment replaces the kind words you need. One father found that he had to keep reminding himself that people just didn't know what to say. "I wonder if my response toward a friend's pregnancy loss would be comforting without having experienced a loss myself," he confessed. Try not to take hurtful remarks personally, but it is understandable if someone's thoughtless comments make you angry.

You will probably need to let friends and loved ones know that you miss your baby and want to talk about her sometimes. Talking about your baby is part of grieving, and silence or isolation can fuel depression. If those close to you don't offer you solace, be sure to get other help, from a psychotherapist or a pregnancy loss support group. Appendix D can help you locate a pregnancy loss support group near you.

Being with Pregnant Women and Little Children

Right after your loss, you may be able to sequester yourself from the outside world, staying home as much as you need. Eventually you must venture out again, first on short errands, and ultimately back to work or your regular routine, bringing you in touch with people who are pregnant or who have small children.

Casually visiting the children of friends and family who helped you during your ordeal may be more bearable than encountering the children of strangers. However, even these informal get-togethers can be distressing.

Shortly after one of her early losses, Vera and her husband were scheduled to visit close friends who had a newborn baby. They had planned to go out with their friends and the baby, but cold weather prompted the new parents to insist they all stay home. Vera suddenly felt trapped in their apartment:

> If we had been outside, there would have been distractions all around us, but we had to sit there and look directly at the baby the whole time. And all they talked about was the baby. I was on the verge of tears the entire time we were there.

One way to avert this kind of situation is to let friends with babies know in advance that you will get together only if they hire a baby-sitter and go out with you, away from the confines of their home. You may choose not to get together at all for a while, until you are feeling better. You probably wish your friends and family would come up with these solutions by themselves, but as Vera admitted, "Their own happiness interferes with their ability to be sensitive to someone who is unhappy."

The pressure to attend joyful events involving the children of loved ones, such as birthday parties, christenings and brisses, can be especially difficult after your loss. In addition to grappling with feelings of anger, resentment and jealousy, you may fear bringing a shadow of gloom to the celebration. One mother, who debated attending her nephew's christening shortly after her miscarriage, lamented, "I hated the thought of being the sad person at a happy event."

It is important to do what feels manageable and to respect your grief. If you think an event will be too upsetting for you, excuse yourself. Usually a reminder of your circumstances will help the hosts understand your decision. You might say something like, "I appreciate the invitation, but I'm still feeling sad about my loss and I'm not up to a party." If you are uncomfortable explaining this, ask a close friend or relative to express your regrets.

Once you open up about your feelings, people's compassion may surprise you. Annette recalled feeling pressured by her sister-in-law to attend her niece's first birthday party, which occurred shortly after Annette's early miscarriage:

> We didn't go, and I even refused to look at the pictures of the party when we visited my sister-in-law a couple of weeks later. She was not offended at all and really seemed to understand my feelings, for which I was truly grateful.

An invitation to a celebration can be paralyzing after a loss: You want to share the joy, but your distress makes this feel impossible. Make a decision that is respectful of your grief. One woman who had just suffered a midterm loss agonized over an invitation to her cousin's upcoming wedding. When she couldn't decide what to do, she discussed it in the pregnancy loss support group she was attending:

> The people in my group said I had permission not to attend, or that if I went, I could leave anytime I couldn't handle the pressure. Just knowing I could leave actually enabled me to stay through the entire wedding, even the reception.

Sometimes the only way to take care of yourself is to avoid celebrations that include babies or small children, at least for a while. It may be too upsetting to socialize when you feel envious of someone you care for, and angry because they have what you don't. It is exhausting to be friendly and polite when you are hurting in the face of their joy.

It is especially hard to cope when pregnancies occur within your immediate family. Wendy's newborn daughter died while her sister was still in the early stages of her own pregnancy. Wendy found it very difficult to face her sister's advancing pregnancy while grieving her own loss. "I hated my sister for having what I didn't have," conceded Wendy, "and then I hated myself for hating her."

You may feel guilty that your loss has altered your loved ones' perceptions of pregnancy. Wendy felt her baby's fatal congenital defect affected her sister's experience of her own pregnancy:

> My sister was suddenly aware of everything that could go wrong. I felt that I had taken away her innocence and joy about pregnancy. And I felt responsible for making her feel guilty about having something I so desperately wanted. It was hard for me on many levels.

The intensity of your anger, guilt and jealousy can be so extreme you may worry that you will never recover some of your close relationships. Bereaved parents sometimes do lose friendships following a loss, or become temporarily estranged from even close family members. Amelia was afraid she would become "this bitter, hardened woman" because her feelings of resentment toward friends and relatives with children were so strong. "I thought my jealousy of others would seal me off from people for the rest of my life," she said. "I did feel better eventually, but I also formed new friendships with other couples we met who had similar losses."

Time does help, especially if you give your anger and jealousy outlets that allow you to talk about these natural responses to losing a pregnancy. Gulfs can be breached, wounds can be healed and a new appreciation for friends and family can emerge.

KEY POINTS TO HELP YOU WITH FAMILY AND FRIENDS

You and your partner may have found a comforting seclusion in your home immediately after your loss, but eventually you have to face the outside world. Once you start informing colleagues and acquaintances about your loss, you may have to grapple with well-intentioned but hurtful remarks. Friends and family with children may expect you to attend events that involve their youngsters, as if nothing had happened to you.

Here are some suggestions for talking with others about your loss:

- Let others know that you need help. Friends and family usually respond well to a specific request when they otherwise wouldn't know what to do or say.
- Respect your need to talk and be heard, and choose good listeners who care about you. It is vital that you reach out to others during this sad time.
- Plan how you will phrase the news of your loss to colleagues and acquaintances, in a simple, brief manner. Respect your need to decline discussing details you don't want to share.
- Allow your feelings of upset to surface if someone makes an insensitive remark. If you feel like it, take the opportunity to educate others about pregnancy loss, telling them how they could respond more helpfully.
- Consider telling those close to you who are pregnant or who have small children that it will be difficult for you to socialize with them for a while. If you feel you can't attend celebrations because you are too emotionally raw, send your regrets. Relatives and friends who care for you will probably understand.

The Five Worst Comments You Might Hear

"It happened for the best." No matter what caused your loss, it is unlikely you believe it happened for the best. This statement negates your loss and sorrow.

What you can say in response: "I know you mean to be comforting, but I don't think bad things happen to people for the best."

"Don't worry, you can have another baby." You need to mourn the baby you lost. Children are not replaceable.

What you can say in response: "I'm very sad about losing this baby, who meant so much to me.

"You didn't really know the baby, so it's not like losing a child who has lived with you a while." Although there is a distinction between these two losses, this is not a comforting comment. You have lost the dream of

having that particular child. Although your loss may be *different* from losing an older child, it should never be deemed unworthy of grief.

What you can say in response: "I'm sad *because* I will never know this baby."

"I know exactly how you feel." Unless the friend or relative has been through a similar loss, this phrase may ring false and make you angry. You probably wished they had asked you how you felt instead.

What you can say in response: "It's hard to know how this feels unless you've been through it yourself."

"What are you going to do now?" You may be too stunned by your loss to make plans about your future family. This question is an invasion of your privacy unless you volunteered to talk about it.

What you can say in response: "I really don't feel like discussing that right now. I'd rather talk about the baby I just lost."

Having people say nothing at all hurts deeply because it negates your loss and the impact it has on your lives. On the other hand, simply saying "I don't know what to say" is honest and acknowledges the dimensions of your sorrow.

What you can say in response: "I realize you don't know what to say about my pregnancy loss, but I don't mind talking about it, and it helps me to remember my baby."

The Five Best Comments You Might Hear

"I'm so sorry. I know how much you wanted to have that baby." This statement acknowledges your sorrow and gives you permission to grieve.

"It's okay to cry." This response validates your feelings and your need to express them without embarrassment or guilt.

"Would you like to talk about it?" The friend or relative who responds with this sensitive question offers the best support possible—a willing ear, a comforting shoulder and a healthy respect for your needs.

"Is there anything I can do for you?" Family and friends may offer consolation through practical help. This allows you to say what you need, whether a home-cooked meal, help with difficult phone calls or assistance dismantling the baby's room.

"May I call you back in a few days to see how you are doing?" After a while you may find that others no longer want to talk about your loss. Family and friends who assure you that they will continue to listen and comfort you in the months to come are truly loved ones.

12

Helping Your Children at Home

Our four-year-old came into my bedroom after the stillbirth. I was lying in bed, depressed. "Mommy," she asked, "do you want me to stay with you?" I told her I would like that very much. "Okay," she said, "but you have to do something." She told me to lie on my side in an S position and crawled into the space by my tummy.

—Christine

After your pregnancy loss, your children at home need to know what has happened, even though it is hard to take care of yourself, let alone break the news to them. By talking with your children in a way that is sensitive to their feelings and their ages, you can help the entire family accept the loss and begin to heal.

Children may feel angry and cheated after a pregnancy loss because their expected sibling will not be coming home. They can also feel guilty for having had mixed emotions about the baby their parents are so sad about losing. Often they are confused and alarmed when their daily routines disappear in the wake of a family crisis.

You may be tempted to hide your emotions from your children, but this will only confuse them, as they will sense your feelings. Weeping in private or with your partner may feel more natural, but it is all right for your children to see you cry sometimes. When you are tearful, you may want to explain that you are sad about the baby but otherwise are fine and that your sadness will get better.

Sharing your feelings about the baby can help your children open up and can reassure them that you accept their emotions, even anger or jealousy. If you avoid the subject, your youngsters may misinterpret your distress and assume *they* have done something to upset you.

Children may react to a loss through behavior changes more than through tears or words. A toilet-trained preschooler may start wetting

159

the bed, or an older child's school performance might decline. Children sometimes have nightmares or become withdrawn and depressed, experiencing your sadness as "proof" that they are not good enough or important enough to prevent your grief. On the other hand, young children in particular may become hyperactive, or may giggle when family members talk or cry about the baby. Silly behavior can be disconcerting if you do not realize these are uncontrollable outbursts of anxiety, not expressions of happiness.

Children have their own ways to express sadness. Youngsters may be playful and involved in their usual activities much of the time, expressing anger, anxiety or sorrow only occasionally. This is not because they are unfeeling, but because they may play and be sad at the same time. They might also recover more quickly or simply need a break from feeling sad. As long as their unexpressed emotions are not being held in or masked, your children's return to their usual mood and activities is fine.

Sometimes children feel guilty for playing or enjoying an activity while the rest of the family is grieving. You can reassure them that you accept and understand their behavior by saying, "It's okay to feel sad and still play," or, with a hug and a smile, "I'm glad you had a nice time at your friend's house."

HOW TO TALK WITH YOUR CHILD

Your child's reactions to your pregnancy were probably laced with both love and resentment. If the pregnancy was showing, your young child may have alternated between angrily pummeling or affectionately rubbing your growing tummy. Her anger about the potential rival for Mommy and Daddy's love can make your child fear that her negative thoughts really caused the loss. Your child may have been so excited— or indignant—about the expected birth that breaking the news can be especially difficult. One woman's three-year-old had been very absorbed in her pregnancy, which ended in a stillbirth. "My first thought when I learned the baby had died," she recalled, "was, 'Whatever will I tell my son?'"

It is best to tell your child about the loss as soon as possible and reassure her that Mommy is fine, though sad. If the mother was hospitalized, explain that she will be home soon. Share information about the cause of your loss in simple, direct terms, since a young child's imagination can make her far more anxious than the facts will. You may want to say something like "The baby's lungs were not working right" or "The baby's body did not grow properly from the very beginning, so he died."

Florence explained how her husband broke the news of their baby's stillbirth to their three children, ages four, seven and eight:

He told the children the baby had died, that the cord had wrapped around
her neck and she couldn't breathe. He told them I was fine. He kept it truthful
but simple.

Let your youngster's questions guide you as to how much detail to
give. If your child listens to your explanation and asks nothing more,
you have probably said as much as she can absorb for the time being.
An older child may ask for more concrete information, such as when
the problem occurred or why the doctor couldn't save the baby. Be
frank with your answers: "We think the cord wrapped around the baby's
neck a week before she was born, when I noticed she had stopped mov-
ing," or "When the baby was born she was no longer alive. There was
nothing the doctor could do." If the cause is unknown, be honest about
this as well, explaining that sometimes even doctors don't know why
babies die.

Since a child of any age may blame herself for the loss, reassure her
that nothing anybody thought or did caused the loss. You might say,
"Most kids feel both happy *and* jealous when a new baby is coming.
Then if the baby dies, they can worry that their jealous thoughts hurt
the baby. But *nobody's* thoughts or wishes can hurt a baby. The baby
died because his body didn't work properly."

You may find that reading children's books on loss and grief with
your youngster gives the child words and permission for her feelings
and helps you understand your child's experience as well. *Thumpy's
Story,* by Nancy C. Dodge, is a book geared for preschool and grade-
school children. It tells about the death of a newborn in a rabbit family
and depicts with sensitivity the emotions of a sibling. The story also
portrays the healing process that gradually takes place as the family
grieves, yet still remembers the baby. Teenagers may appreciate reading Mark Scrivani's *When Death Walks In,* a book that describes the difficult feelings of grief and how loss can also bring growth.

You may be better able to reach out to your child, and help with her
feelings and fears, if you understand the special concerns youngsters
have at different ages.

Toddlers and Preschoolers

Your very young child may have some awareness of both your pregnancy and your loss but will not understand the permanence of death.
You can help by explaining the loss in terms your child can grasp and
by responding patiently to his repeated questions. One mother
explained her miscarriage to her preschooler by reminding him of
seeds he had planted for a nature project; some germinated, but several did not. The mother told him her miscarriage was like one of the
seeds that had not sprouted, an explanation he was able to accept. You

can use other examples from your child's experience, such as the death of a family pet or a baby bird that has fallen out of its nest, to help explain the finality of a pregnancy loss.

Rabbi Earl Grollman, an expert in family bereavement, suggests explaining to the child that "dead" means that the body doesn't work anymore, that the baby cannot move, cry, see, eat or feel anything, including heat, cold or pain. Even in the face of these explanations, your young child may continue to ask if the baby will be coming home. Be patient and consistent with your answers, and as the child absorbs your explanations and matures, he will come to understand the permanence of the loss.

Six months after having a stillborn baby, one father found his two-year-old son looking through drawers in the "baby's room" for the baby:

> We talked to him and told him the baby would not be coming. When he turned three he started to understand. Every year we light a candle in church, or do something special to commemorate the baby. So now he knows.

Since your young child will take explanations literally, it is important to avoid euphemisms such as "We lost the baby," "The baby went away," "Being dead is like being asleep," or "God took him for an angel." To your preschooler, something that is lost can be found and someone who goes away can come back. If told that being dead is like being asleep, your youngster may become fearful of going to bed, and if God took the baby for an angel, your child may be scared that God will take him next.

Your young child can fear for his own safety following a pregnancy loss. His sense of security depends on the well-being of you and your partner, since you provide his physical and emotional care. When Mommy and Daddy are upset, the child's world is threatened. He will probably react strongly to being away from either of you, so try to keep separations to a minimum.

Your preschooler can also be anxious after a pregnancy loss because children make connections between events that are completely unrelated. A young child may fear that since your baby died, someone else in the family will die soon, too, a thought that can make him especially worried about the safety of a hospitalized mother. Whether or not your child verbalizes these fears, reassure him that the problem the baby died from was different from sicknesses other family members can get and that the rest of the family is going to be fine.

Don't be too concerned if your young child becomes short-tempered and prone to sudden impassioned outbursts after your loss. One four-year-old boy had a friend over a few weeks after his baby brother was stillborn. One minute he was playing and seemed to be fine; then suddenly he threw himself on the ground and shouted, "I want my baby!" While outbursts like this can be upsetting for you, your child is letting you know he feels distressed and needs comforting. With time, these emotional displays should become less frequent and then stop.

Your youngster may also surprise you by expressing love and concern for you with spontaneous, poignant gestures. Karen became depressed after a miscarriage and was touched when her two-and-a-half-year-old daughter responded to her mood. "I was lying down, and she came over to me and said, 'Mommy, are you having a hard day?'" Karen recalled, "and then she put her security blanket on me to comfort me."

You can help your preschool child adjust to a pregnancy loss by giving him lots of attention and care. Tell your child that you love him and that you are going to be fine. With your help, he can feel reassured that while the expected baby has died, the sadness at home will get better, and he is safe, valued and loved.

Children Age Six to Eleven

> Our seven-year-old thought she had caused the stillbirth. Before the delivery, she had a dream that the baby had died. One day she got very upset and finally asked us, "Do you hate me because I made the baby die?" We explained to her that nothing she dreamed or thought about could cause a death.
>
> —Florence

Between the ages of about six and nine, a child begins to understand the finality of death, a concept that can be abruptly brought home after a pregnancy loss. As Dan Schaefer and Christine Lyons point out in their book *How Do We Tell The Children?*, grade-school youngsters "often look on death as a *taker*, something violent that comes and gets you, like a burglar or a ghost."

Florence noticed that her eight-year-old daughter seemed to understand the loss better than her younger siblings:

> Rosemary knows something that dies will never come back. She had a pet gerbil she was very attached to and it died. We got her another one, but it wasn't the same thing. Her younger sister thinks, "If Mom gets another baby, things will be fine." Rosemary knows another baby won't replace our baby who died.

Allowing your child to express a full range of emotions can help her overcome anxieties. Ellen was shocked when she told her six-year-old son she had suffered a miscarriage, and he blurted out, "I didn't want a baby anyway!" He complained that he dreaded visits from a neighbor's baby, who ruined his drawings and Lego creations. Ellen assured him she understood his feelings but reminded him that when his little sister had been that age, they used to put his creations out of her reach. "I do remember that!" he said. This discussion allowed her son's mixed feelings to surface, instead of only negative ones that could have left him guilty and afraid of his anger.

Grade-school children may show anger or anxiety by picking fights with siblings and schoolmates or by challenging their parents' and teachers' authority. It's a good idea to let your child's teacher know about your loss and keep in close contact with her, to make sure your child's behavior has not changed at school even if it seems fine at home.

Your grade-school child might become protective of you after your loss. Florence recalled how her eight-year-old sprang to her defense for months when anyone mentioned their stillborn baby:

> My daughter got upset with people who talked about the loss because she thought it would upset me. If someone mentioned the baby and my eyes got teary, she would say, "That was really smart. Now look what you've done!"

You will probably feel grateful for your child's obvious love and concern when she attempts to keep you from feeling sad. At the same time, you may want to remind her that crying sometimes about the baby is still okay.

Because your school-age child is learning so much about her world, she may be interested in the biological details of what happened, such as what part of the baby's body stopped working and why. If you know the medical causes for your loss, share them with your child, using her questions as a guide for how much detail to give.

Like other children her age, your child is also in the process of developing a sense of right and wrong, morality and fairness. The death of an infant can greatly upset the child's emerging sense of justice and order in the world, and you may find yourself struggling to explain the loss.

Florence had no ready reply to her daughter's pointed questions about her stillborn sister: "The baby was so young, Ma, she never hurt anybody. Why did she have to die?" Florence could only answer truthfully, "I don't know why. There isn't a reason for everything. We all have trouble understanding why it happened."

There may be no simple answers you can give a youngster who is struggling with the notion of fairness and the realization that death is an inevitable—and irreversible—part of life. You can foster trust by honestly sharing your own emotional struggles and by letting her see how much family relationships can mean at a time of loss.

Preteens and Teenagers

Your adolescent child will not need help understanding what death means—he knows it is inescapable and irrevocable. But a pregnancy loss can be very painful to your teenager, who is already struggling with the mood swings and feelings of vulnerability that go hand in hand with adolescence.

Since many families who have teenagers when a pregnancy loss occurs are remarried families, your adolescent may already have experienced complicated feelings about the pregnancy. He may have felt jealous or torn by conflicting loyalties, or might have hoped the baby would firmly unite the tentative bonds within your newly blended family.

Confronted with a pregnancy loss, your teenager may feel his world has been turned upside down. Angry, guilty and helpless, maybe even embarrassed by having to acknowledge his parents' sexuality, an adolescent may be overwhelmed by the loss and by his own emotional tumult. He may also believe the loss is a punishment for his ambivalent feelings about the baby.

Your teenager may have a hard time accepting his anger and sorrow over your pregnancy loss. Since it is natural for teens to be concerned with their image, your adolescent may hate to cry and might consequently develop physical symptoms instead, such as headaches, stomach pains, or sleeping too little or too much.

Talk with your teenager honestly about your sadness and anger over the loss, and don't be afraid to show feelings or tears. Whether your adolescent had expressed excitement or ambivalence about the pregnancy, talk over the hopes or anxieties he shared with you and how the loss has changed your plans. You might recall with your teenager, "We talked together for so many months about having a new baby, and you worked so hard with Dad getting the room ready. It's hard to believe after all those hopes that the baby died," or "I know it was difficult for you to get used to the idea that a new baby was going to come into our family. But I can see how upset you are that the baby died." Recalling the pregnancy and the shock of the loss can open up discussions and help your adolescent accept his ambivalence and grief.

Be on guard if your adolescent seems unable to talk about his upset and instead seeks relief through the use of alcohol or drugs or through sexual activity. These behaviors can be perilous and can block the grieving process. If you are concerned that your teenager is using these risky outlets to relieve stress, seek professional advice.

SPECIAL ISSUES FOR YOU TO CONSIDER

Children face special emotional challenges after your pregnancy loss. If you suffered a midterm or late loss, your children may wish to see their baby brother or sister and say good-bye. You may question if they should participate in religious rituals or wonder how to help them tell their friends about their sibling.

Saying Good-bye to a Baby Sibling

You may be uncertain at what age it is beneficial, rather than frightening, for your child to see and say good-bye to a dying or deceased baby sibling. This decision is highly individual and depends on the needs and maturity of your child. Families with children as young as four have found that their youngsters expressed a strong wish to see a dying or deceased infant sibling. If your child wants to see the baby and you think she can handle it, it is important to explain the death and describe the baby's appearance before gently giving your child the choice.

Oliver remembered when his five-year-old, Margo, insisted on seeing her brother who had died one hour after his premature delivery:

> After the baby died I went to Margo's day care and brought her to the hospital. My wife was holding the baby. Margo looked at him, touched him, held him, got to know him in a way. She cried. Over the next six months she would break out crying occasionally; otherwise she was fine. I feel it really helped her to say good-bye to the baby.

If your child did not see her baby sibling, you can still help her to accept and mourn the loss. If you saw the baby, you can describe what he looked like; otherwise you might show her the baby's footprints or a photograph of the baby. Your young child may want to draw pictures or make clay models of a baby, whether or not she saw the infant. By showing interest in your child's creations and letting her talk about them, you convey acceptance of her feelings. Your child's expression of emotions through art, talking and play are all healthy efforts to accept the reality of a confusing and upsetting loss.

Mementos can help a child born after the pregnancy loss understand who her baby sibling was. One mother explained how she envisioned telling her infant son about his older sister, who died shortly after birth two years before he was born. "My husband and I have already discussed it and agreed that we will tell our son about his sister," she revealed. "Someday I'd like to show him his sister's photo album filled with pictures from her brief life."

Your Child and Religious Rituals

The aftermath of a pregnancy loss can be a time for sharing your religious beliefs with your child. It does not help to mouth doctrines you do not believe, as children of any age will sense this. However, by expressing true religious convictions, you can share with your child the comfort these beliefs give you.

It is important to acknowledge the finality of physical death even if you want to convey your belief in the afterlife of the baby's spirit. Otherwise a young child might think the baby is physically alive somewhere and able to return.

You may feel unsure if it will be helpful or upsetting for siblings to attend a religious ritual for your baby. In his book *Talking About Death: A Dialogue Between Parent and Child,* Rabbi Earl Grollman suggests that children of four or five and older be given the choice to attend a funeral, memorial service or burial for the baby, because "[t]he funeral is a rite of separation . . . the bad dream is real. . . . It is an opportunity to say good-bye." Children of grade-school age and older are likely to be concerned about having proper ceremonies for the baby and may insist upon attending.

If your child wishes to attend and you feel comfortable about having him there, explain to your child what to expect during the service and how long it will be. Describe the appearance of the room, who will be there and the likelihood that some people will cry. Consider arranging for your child to sit with someone he knows well so they can leave early if the child wants to. You can ask your child if he would like to give a gift to be placed in the casket, such as a flower, drawing or toy of his choice.

It is important for your child to be allowed to change his mind about attending a funeral service, even at the last minute. Have a close friend or relative available that day, just in case your child suddenly decides to stay home.

An adolescent will probably benefit from attending a religious ritual. By including your teenager, you convey that sadness is acceptable and that a funeral, amid the comforting presence of family and friends, is a time to grieve and say good-bye.

Your Child's Peers

Your child's friends may not know how to respond to your pregnancy loss. With your guidance and encouragement, and with the help of social customs, young friends can learn to express sympathy for your bereaved child.

One sensitive third-grade teacher suggested that each classmate write a note of condolence to Luke, whose baby brother had died after an emergency delivery. Months after the loss, Luke still talked about those notes, especially one of his favorites, a heartfelt but humorous limerick written by a classmate:

> Once Luke's mother gave birth to a brother.
> It didn't come out so she gave a shout,
> But maybe she'll have another.
> Your pal, Brian

Christine, whose baby was stillborn, found the religious rituals her family observed provided young friends with an opportunity to demonstrate sympathy for her four surviving children:

> We had a burial, coffin, grave. We had an obituary, and a special Mass was offered. It was wonderful for the children. Their friends came and they all cried together. They felt the peer support keenly.

Once you have helped establish communication between your child and her friends about your loss, you may also notice that the youngster has an increased empathy for the grief of others. One little boy, whose premature baby brother had died, invited over a friend who had recently lost his father. The little host's mother was amazed and touched by the boys' conversation:

> They sat together, talking at dinner like little adults. The friend talked about his deceased father. My son said, "I know what it's like. My brother died."

AFTER THE CRISIS

Children of any age derive a sense of security from their routines. A pregnancy loss, with separation from one or both parents, visits from family and friends and everybody's emotional upset, throws a family's—and a child's—schedule into upheaval.

While your child may continue to have questions or worries about your pregnancy loss for weeks or months afterward, you can help her regain a sense of security by restoring her routine as soon as possible. Perhaps you can pack your child's lunch or help with homework, if this is what she is used to. Keeping to the same bedtime rituals, such as reading a story and having the regular lights-out time, also helps.

You may find that caring for your surviving child helps you as much as it helps her, that the child's love and need for you reaffirm your role as a parent. When you feel ready, you may even want to plan some special activities with your child that can help both of you heal emotionally.

Ellen had her fourth miscarriage only three days before her son started kindergarten. After the loss, she volunteered to do an art project with his class that was so successful she continued the activity through the school term. "My son loved having me in his classroom," Ellen remembered, "and I enjoyed getting to know his teacher and classmates. It was such a positive channel for me after the loss, and it helped him, too."

Make sure you have adequate support for yourself so you can help your surviving child. For mothers especially, it is difficult to deal with a child's anxiety or anger when you are upset and physically depleted.

Accept any extra available help—from your partner, relatives or familiar sitters—to ease the stresses during the early weeks after your loss. "You have to take care of yourself," one bereaved mother expressed. "Otherwise I believe it will backfire later."

A youngster needs time to understand what a pregnancy loss means and to absorb her own feelings about it. You can help by keeping the lines of communication open. A young child in particular will often ask the same questions over and over, or as time passes will come up with new questions. This process, which can go on for months, reflects the child's efforts to assimilate your family's loss.

Just as your youngster may need to repeat a question, you may also want to reopen a discussion about what happened, or about your child's feelings and worries. Choose a relaxed time other than bedtime. For instance, while out driving together, you can recall aloud, "Remember how we used to talk about the baby when we were driving places, thinking what it would be like to have him along? I still think about him at times like this. Do you sometimes think about him, too?" Sharing your feelings about the baby can help your child open up as well, allowing you to convey acceptance of her emotions, whatever they may be.

If You and Your Family Need Extra Help

Your child's reactions will depend on his age and personality, on the circumstances of the loss, and on your own grief responses. It is common for a child to experience both physical symptoms and behavior changes after a pregnancy loss in the family.

In most cases, a child's symptoms will diminish and behavior changes will disappear over a few weeks or months. But sometimes behavior changes, either at home or at school, continue without showing signs of improvement. This can happen for many different reasons, and when it does occur, it is wise to seek professional help.

You may be consumed by your own grief after a pregnancy loss, making it especially difficult to respond to your child's demands. For some parents this difficulty persists, and the child begins to react to the changes in routine and to the parents' lack of involvement with him.

Lonnie and her husband had a healthy, five-year-old son, Warren, followed by two early losses and a stillbirth. After the third loss, her husband would not talk about his grief and withdrew emotionally for several months. Lonnie became seriously depressed. Sometimes she resented Warren for surviving when the other babies didn't. Her relationship with her son suffered. "I was ignoring Warren," she recalled. "I wasn't taking him to the park or anything. I stayed in bed all day, so he just had to watch TV."

Understandably, with his mother depressed and his father unavailable, Warren's behavior changed, and in ways Lonnie found hard to take. "He cried with no explanation and wouldn't say what was wrong," Lonnie explained. "He made a fuss about everything, like taking a bath or going to bed."

After these difficulties went on for several months, Lonnie finally went to her priest for help, which was a turning point for both her and Warren:

> My priest helped me to realize that I was paying more time and attention to the babies who died than to the child I had. This helped me start to accept the losses more. I started to feel so grateful for my son.
>
> Afterward I noticed a change in Warren. He got better after I changed toward him.

A pregnancy loss can be traumatic for a child if he witnessed emergency medical procedures or if his mother's life was endangered. Eight-year-old Luke saw his mother go into full-term labor late at night. Five minutes later, she went into shock and collapsed due to separation of the placenta from the uterine wall. While the ambulance rushed his mother and father to the hospital, Luke followed in a police car, sirens blaring.

After the emergency delivery, Luke overheard doctors saying his mother had a fifty-fifty chance of survival and that the baby's chances were even less. His mother recovered, but the baby died.

Not surprisingly, Luke's mother noticed behavior changes that lingered long after these frightening events:

> A few months after the loss, Luke was still eruptive. He had a short fuse and got frustrated more easily than before. If his drawing wasn't going well, he threw down his pen. He was more aggressive than we had ever seen him.

Six months after the loss Luke's parents consulted a family therapist on how they could help their son with his distress. The professional encouraged them to talk openly with Luke about the loss and his mother's medical crisis, so he could share his own feelings and fears. Luke's behavior gradually improved.

If your loss involved a medical emergency, you can help your child by talking about what happened, by giving realistic assurances that the danger has passed and by giving the child opportunities to express what these events were like for him. Children are emotionally resilient, and with your help, and professional support if needed, your youngster should gradually come to terms with your pregnancy loss and return to his usual behaviors and activities.

KEY POINTS TO HELP YOUR CHILDREN AFTER A LOSS

Dealing with your child's response to your pregnancy loss is emotionally taxing. Children of all ages might experience mood and behavior changes after a loss. You can help your child by explaining the baby's death in simple, frank terms and by being truthful about your own sorrow. Children need opportunities to express their anger and anxieties as they gradually come to terms with the loss.

Here are some suggestions that can help your child after a pregnancy loss:

- Tell your child about the loss as soon as possible, simply and directly. Try to avoid euphemisms such as "The baby is sleeping" or "We lost the baby," as a young child in particular may take these statements literally and may fear going to sleep or expect the baby to be found.
- Your youngster might feel sad and vulnerable after your loss and need lots of love and attention. Parents, other relatives, close friends and familiar sitters can all help.
- Assure your child that nothing she or anyone else thought about, said or did caused the pregnancy loss. Explain that the rest of the family is healthy and that the problem the baby died from is different from other sicknesses.
- If you hold a funeral service or other ritual for the baby, and your child wishes to attend, you may want to give her that option. Children four and older are more likely to show an interest in these rituals, but again, this is very individual.
- Try to get your child's routine back to normal as soon as possible. Planning special time or activities together, when you feel ready, can help both of you during this difficult period.
- Be prepared for your child to ask the same questions over and over, or for different questions to arise as she grows and matures. Try to respond to your child's concerns so she feels free to talk about this significant event in her life.
- If your child has symptoms or behavior changes that continue for many weeks after a loss, she may need additional help. Be sure you have adequate support for yourself, and consult a qualified psychotherapist if your child's difficulties continue. See Appendix D for help in locating a psychotherapist.

13

For Bereaved Grandparents

*The initial shock was to know there was no grandchild. We had looked for-
ward to another grandchild so much; they are so rewarding. We felt terrible.*

—Sid

*The hardest thing about going through a loss with your children is the grief
you feel for them, because you can't do anything. I am conditioned as a
mother to fix things, make things better, and I couldn't.*

—Maureen

Grandchildren bring a treasured feeling of family continuity and a
unique gratification to you, their grandparent. They often create a
new and cherished bond between you and your adult children as well,
so when an unborn or newborn baby dies, you grieve doubly, for yourself and for your children. It is especially difficult for you to feel so
helpless and sad when you see your grown children suffer.

When a pregnancy loss occurs, you may initially feel shock and disbelief that an expected family joy has turned into a sorrow. Sid was upset
when his adult daughter and son each had a baby die near term:

The pregnancies had really traumatic endings. It was a terrible shock; there
was no way of being prepared. Then my wife and I realized this had really happened, that there was no way to go back and make it different. We had to
concentrate on how we would get through it.

As a grandparent, you may not know how to respond. You may have
been raised with the attitude that one doesn't talk about a pregnancy
loss, that one puts the loss in the past and gets on with life. If your children are openly upset, this can leave you worried and confused. You
may be tempted to help by urging the young couple to have another

baby or, if they are already parents, by encouraging them to be grateful for the children they have. While well-intentioned, such comments are likely to be hurtful rather than comforting. The more you are able to accept that mourning is a painful but useful means of healing a loss, the more helpful you can be.

Your reaction will be individual and will depend on the relationship you already had with your adult children before the loss occurred. You may feel the loss deeply but wonder if sharing your grief will only further burden your bereaved children. As one grandmother expressed:

> I could cry for them, but should I, so they know how bad I feel? Or should I try to keep cool so they don't feel they've utterly disappointed me by not giving me grandchildren?

Your children will probably appreciate knowing you also feel the loss, as long as you do not expect them to be your primary source of support.

As a grandparent, you can help your bereaved children more than anyone else, a help that may permanently deepen family ties. If you have survived a pregnancy loss yourself, you may be able to reach out and sustain your children in especially meaningful ways.

Lenore had experienced a miscarriage and a stillbirth as a young woman. She found that memories of her own losses resurfaced when her daughter, who suffered from infertility, became pregnant and then miscarried. Lenore's ability to listen created a closeness that helped both mother and daughter cope with their grief:

> I told my daughter about my own losses. I wanted to prepare her so she would know it's a hard time emotionally. I do tell her I am sad about her baby, and for her. I talk to her at least once a week. If she's feeling low, she'll say so. I can tell if she's been crying.

Your children may ask you to dismantle the baby's room and store the baby supplies before the sad homecoming from the hospital. One grandmother had the unhappy task of going to her daughter and daughter-in-law, in turn, after each lost a newborn. When both mothers asked her to put away their baby things, the grieving grandmother recalled, "The afternoon I packed up the second set of baby items, I thought that no grandmother should have to do this twice."

You might want to talk over your feelings about the pregnancy loss with your spouse, relatives or friends. If you are religious, you may wish to speak with a member of the clergy or friends from your congregation. It is especially important for you to be sustained in your grief so you can be strong enough to help your children.

GRANDPARENTS' GUILT

Like many bereaved grandparents, you may suffer from feelings of guilt when your unborn or newborn grandchild dies. Sometimes this takes the form of "survivor guilt," in which you feel the order of your life has been profoundly upset, that it is somehow "wrong" for you to be alive when a new life in the family has ended.

Painful though it may be to let your spouse or children know you feel this way, the honest sharing of feelings with your loved ones is best. Otherwise, guilt or resentment can create barriers in your family relationships when you need each other the most.

Pregnancy loss can be especially difficult if a genetic cause is identified and you wonder if you passed along the "bad" gene. You may feel particularly guilty if you are a grandmother who took DES, a medication that was prescribed to pregnant women from the 1940s through the 1970s in the belief that it could prevent miscarriages. Unfortunately, DES did nothing to forestall miscarriages and has now been implicated in pregnancy losses and infant deaths in the daughters of women who took it.

If a genetic or DES-related problem contributed to a loss, don't blame yourself, as you had no control over the problem or were following your doctor's advice in an effort to protect your own pregnancy. In either case, it is important for your children to have the facts of your medical history, as advances in the early diagnosis and treatment of some genetic and DES-related disorders have enhanced the chances of a successful pregnancy. As one DES daughter expressed:

> My only anger was that my mother did not at first acknowledge that she had taken DES because she felt so guilty. All I wanted was medical information, so my doctor could help me. I wasn't judging or blaming her; she had only tried to hold on to me and do what her doctor told her to.

Rather than dwell on self-blame, acknowledge the problem, but then focus on ways you can help the couple during their bereavement or a subsequent pregnancy.

Grandmothers who had problem-free pregnancies may have a different fear, that their children will resent them for having had babies so easily. One grandmother of eight grown children wanted to be comforting to her daughter, who had miscarried three times, but questioned whether her vastly different experience would get in the way. "Sometimes I wonder if she could be angry with me for 'popping off babies' so easily," she explained. "I can't say 'I know exactly how you feel,' because I don't."

However different your experiences with pregnancy may have been, your genuine sympathy for your children's plight will probably be much appreciated. Sometimes simply saying "Do you feel like talking?" or "Is there anything I can do?" will allow your children to open up about their loss so that you can begin to understand their worries and frustrations.

Even if you have a close relationship with the bereaved couple, they may be reluctant to talk with you about their pregnancy loss because they want to spare you their grief. One grandmother said:

> I was concerned because when my daughter had her miscarriage she didn't tell me right away. She tried to spare me. I found out from my son, who told me she had not called me right away because she had wanted me to get through the weekend undisturbed.

If you think your bereaved children are trying to protect you, let them know that you are available to talk with them, and while you are sad, you are more concerned about them than about your own grief.

HELPING YOUR ADULT CHILDREN

If you visited your children during or shortly after their pregnancy loss, your simple presence probably meant a great deal to them. Perhaps you helped with household tasks such as shopping and cooking, or you accompanied the grieving parents to the funeral home, phoned relatives or cared for other children. This assistance may have seemed insignificant to you, but it is meaningful to bereaved parents, who are physically and emotionally drained.

If your children suffered a stillbirth or newborn death, you may have seen and held the baby with them. Your contact with the infant may have intensified your feelings of loss but might also have given you a treasured moment with your children and grandchild. Maureen spoke of how seeing her tiny granddaughter affected her grieving daughter-in-law, Tina, and herself:

> I felt such grief for this baby. I saw her; she lived for four days. I told Tina how badly I felt, for her and for us.
>
> I could tell Tina cared I was there. It meant so much to me to know I could give help and she could accept it.

If you were unable to visit your children after their loss because of geographical distance or other constraints, it is still possible to show you care. You can acknowledge their loss by sending a card or flowers, or by making a donation to a charity in memory of the baby. If there is a funeral, you may want to help with expenses if you are financially able to do so.

You can also make a point of keeping in touch through letters or telephone calls. If your children named their baby, they will appreciate your referring to your grandchild by name. Let your children know you are willing to talk about the baby when they want to. You may want to mark the dates of the birth or loss on your calendar, so that you can acknowledge these anniversaries in the future.

Differences in opinion between you and your bereaved children can easily arise around practical decisions, such as putting away baby things, making funeral arrangements and planning for another pregnancy. While it is natural for you to have your own views, the bereaved couple must live with their decisions and need to make these choices themselves.

Both parents and grandparents, for example, can have strong feelings about how to handle a nursery when a baby dies. When Amelia and Charles found out that their first baby, a premature daughter, would probably be coming home soon, they quickly prepared a room for her. When their baby died unexpectedly, they chose not to dismantle her room right away. To the young couple, putting away the baby things meant giving up hope of ever having a child, but as Amelia recalled, her parents disagreed:

> They implied that our daughter's room should be changed into something else, like a den or guest room, and that we were weird or unhealthy to keep it a baby's room. We resented their opinion and their feeling entitled to ask us about it. It was an invasion of our privacy. The next time my parents came to visit, I remember locking the door to the baby's room for the first time.

In contrast, Leah turned to her mother immediately after her newborn son's death and asked her to help store gifts from several baby showers that filled the baby's room:

> My mother cleaned out the baby's room and put everything in her attic. When I came home from the hospital it was just an empty room with pastel curtains. I assured her I would be a parent one way or the other and that I wanted her to keep the things. She kept everything until our next son was born. I was really grateful.

FAMILY CELEBRATIONS AND HOLIDAYS

You will probably be part of family and holiday gatherings where the presence of babies is obviously painful for your bereaved children. As one grandmother, Maureen, recalled:

> My daughter Janice and her husband came here for Christmas a few months after the death of their newborn son. Two sisters-in-law had babies the same year. It was very hard for Janice to watch these mothers with their little children.

Family events such as baby showers, christenings or brisses heighten the sense that a baby who should have been there is missing. Quietly let the bereaved couple know that you, too, miss their baby and that you will understand if they wish to be excused from any of the festivities. If the couple wishes, you can offer to talk to the party's hosts to explain their reason for not coming, making it clear that you respect their decision.

PREGNANCY AFTER A LOSS

You might have strong feelings, either positive or negative, about a future pregnancy. One grandmother confessed she hoped her son and daughter-in-law would keep trying to have children in spite of miscarriages and infertility problems. A grandfather expressed the opposite concern after both his son and daughter had losses followed by one successful birth each. "They have good marriages and we don't want them to rock the boat," he admitted. "When we hear they are planning to have more children, we worry. What if something happens again?"

When another pregnancy does follow a loss, you may experience anxiety while feeling there is little you can do to help. Maureen and her husband felt apprehensive throughout the high-risk but successful subsequent pregnancies of both their daughter and daughter-in-law. "I think they were the longest months of our lives," Maureen admitted. "But the end results were wonderful!"

Your anxiety over the possibility of another loss can make you wary of becoming emotionally involved with the pregnancy until the baby arrives safely. Nevertheless, you can help your children by maintaining a positive but realistic attitude about the pregnancy and by encouraging the couple with cards, letters and telephone calls. It is all right to acknowledge your own anxiety and admit that this difficult pregnancy is tough for you, too.

STRENGTHENING FAMILY TIES

Pregnancy loss is an event that changes a family permanently; however, if you and your adult children are able to share your grief, you may find that your relationship deepens. As one grandfather explained, "We all joined forces; we were all in it together. This is what helped me and the others the most." As you share your sorrow and rally to help one another, you may also develop richer ties and a strong mutual appreciation.

Lenore, a mother of several grown children, was geographically distant from her two daughters who had experienced miscarriages and infertility problems. But she kept in close contact and let them know of her love and concern for them. As a result, she noticed a change in her relationship to each of them:

> I feel I have more closeness with these two daughters, even though both live out-of-state. But somehow or other we are the really close ones, maybe for having shared all their troubles and losses.

Maureen described a positive change in her relationship to her daughter-in-law, Tina, after the death of an infant granddaughter:

> I suppose in a way I feel closer to Tina. I always felt close to her. I felt so blessed to have her for a daughter-in-law. There is even a greater bond there now, since we shared the loss.

KEY POINTS FOR BEREAVED GRANDPARENTS

Since your children's pregnancy loss, you may have been grieving doubly, for their pain and for the loss of your grandchild. You might feel guilty and helpless, as you are unable to protect the grieving couple from their distress.

Your love, concern and shared sorrow, however, can bring comfort to your children as they slowly put their lives back together after their loss. Here are some suggestions for getting the support you need while helping your grieving children:

- Allow yourself to talk about your feelings with your spouse, family or friends, or within your religious community. A pregnancy loss in your family may be deeply upsetting to you, as you lost a grandchild and are suffering for your own children as well.
- Be honest with your bereaved children about your sorrow, but because of their own distress, do not expect them to be a primary source of comfort to you.
- Offer to help your bereaved children, if you can. You might suggest that you telephone other relatives, prepare meals, care for their other children or help financially.
- Let the bereaved couple know you are thinking about them and their baby, even if you live far away and cannot visit. Telephone them, send a card or make a charitable donation. If the baby was given a name, mention it when talking or writing about your grandchild.
- Respect the couple's decisions about putting away baby things, making funeral arrangements and planning a subsequent pregnancy. You may have strong opinions about these matters, but the bereaved parents need to make these decisions themselves, and live with them.
- If a subsequent pregnancy follows the loss, tell the expectant parents that you are thinking about them. Be encouraging but realistic. It is all right to admit that this is an anxious pregnancy for you as well.
- You can strengthen family ties and deepen your appreciation for your loved ones by living through your children's pregnancy loss and sharing their grief.

Section IV

Special Circumstances

As you recover from your pregnancy loss and make plans to return to work, or begin to consider having another baby, you and your partner may feel renewed hope for the future. This initial sense of recovery can leave you unprepared for the impact your loss might have on other aspects of your life. Women can find themselves unable to concentrate at work, and both partners may discover they are unexpectedly fearful of conceiving another child. Should additional reproductive problems arise, both of you may be devastated just when you thought you could begin to enjoy life again.

The following chapters will help prepare you for these issues before they arise so you can deal with them effectively, even as you struggle with the far-reaching consequences of your loss.

14

The Impact of Pregnancy Loss on Your Career

L ike many bereaved mothers, your pregnancy loss affected you both personally and professionally. You may have postponed pregnancy until you were older and well established in your career, adding the pressure of time constraints to your hopes for a family. Your entire perspective on the importance of work in your life may shift as you endure the setbacks and uncertainties imposed by your loss. If future pregnancies will be high-risk, you face the major challenge of maintaining your career while putting work on hold, perhaps for a long time.

The contrast between your professional success and the out-of-control experience of pregnancy loss can be especially frustrating. As psychiatrist Elisabeth Herz has noted, career women who lose a pregnancy are "conditioned to set a goal, work hard toward it, and succeed." Being faced with an ambition that may be beyond your immediate reach creates feelings of confusion and helplessness that do not fit your self-image. You may experience the normal crying spells and decreased level of work performance during bereavement as a total loss of control over your life.

Your partner may also react to this change in your self-image. Accustomed to seeing you as independent and accomplished, he may resent your temporary helplessness and vulnerability after your loss. One woman who stopped working for several months during a difficult pregnancy that ended in a loss said, "My husband felt that a lid had been put on my development and career. He saw another loss, my loss of self-esteem, and it troubled him greatly."

MAKING CAREER DECISIONS
The leave you take from work after your loss can depend on whether you had an early miscarriage or a later loss. If you were well into the

pregnancy and had already arranged a maternity leave, returning to work means an abrupt change in these plans, a shift that can be a painful reminder of your childlessness. As one mother lamented:

> I didn't know what to do about anything, my work, my leave. Should I find a new job or go back to the old one? I loved my work, but when I was pregnant with our daughter I set my mind to being at home and leaving work for a while. Then suddenly I had to go back to not being a mom and think about work again. That was hard for me.

Your return to work after a pregnancy loss can be an emotional step, but it may help focus your thoughts and energies and bring you some relief from mourning. Marianne, who had three pregnancy losses, found this to be the case. "It was very hard coming back to work, especially the second time," she recalled. "But going back to work was best and helped me cope with the losses."

If you had to put your career on hold because of your pregnancy loss, you may reach a point when you decide that having a baby will have to wait so that your career can come first for a while. You might look forward to having an arena in your life where your self-esteem can blossom free from the stress of childbearing problems. "After my third miscarriage I went back to school for my M.B.A.," explained one woman. "I had wanted to do this for a long time, and I really needed to do something for myself."

But this tactic can backfire. Completion of graduate school or a career training program can feel like the seal on your failure to have a baby, as if your career were a substitute for becoming a mother. Natalie enrolled in nursing school after two miscarriages and had a third loss before her graduation. "I thought nursing school would at least give me professional gratification, but the graduation brought home the loss," she revealed. "I shouldn't have graduated in May. I should have had my baby in March."

It can be tempting to immerse yourself in work to elude your grief, a tactic that may postpone but cannot prevent the mourning process. "I used my work as an escape," admitted Vera, who had suffered several first-trimester losses. "I buried myself in work and repressed all my emotions, but it was unhealthy to do that."

If you use work as an escape, you will probably discover, as Vera did, that you still need to set aside time to grieve—with your spouse, in a support group, or with a psychotherapist—before you begin to feel better. Then work can become a true source of gratification rather than an evasion of grief.

A lack of interest in work is common during the mourning period, when depression and discouragement can dominate your mood. Even a career that you once found prestigious and exciting can suddenly feel like just a job. A persistent longing for a child can add to your sense that work is less important than it seemed before. "I can't shake the feeling that I should be home with a baby now and that I don't really want to be at work," confessed Cecelia. "My job is rewarding, but I want to be doing it in conjunction with the other piece of my life—the baby I want. So I'm mad. I'm angry about work."

Some mothers find sadness and longing for a child recede only with the birth or adoption of another baby, or through the acceptance of a child-free lifestyle. Once your desire for a baby has been resolved one way or the other, your career can again feel stimulating and important.

Making decisions about your career in light of a pregnancy loss may compel you to think carefully about what is most important to you. You might discover, in the process, that your priorities have changed. You may clarify and pursue career goals that you had put on hold, or choose to cut down on professional commitments to give more time to family and friends. "Clearly my child and family were the most important things to me," explained Naomi, a high-powered professional who had cut back to part-time work after three miscarriages and the birth of a healthy baby. "I might not have felt this if I hadn't had the losses." Balancing your career and plans for a family after a loss is a vitally important process.

MEN AND THEIR CAREERS

Men usually find the importance of their careers remains unchanged or increases after a loss. They most often return to work after no leave, or a very brief one. Work can give men a welcome refuge from grief and allow them to feel helpful and productive by providing financial security for their families.

Sometimes, however, a pregnancy loss has a direct impact on a man's career. He may experience extra work pressure after a loss because of additional financial burdens due to medical expenses or the temporary loss of his partner's income. If he had a career change in the offing, he may feel he has to postpone or abandon his plans because of the uncertainties at home.

Jeff, a clinic physician whose wife had suffered three miscarriages, had been planning to start a private practice, but became concerned about the timing of this career move:

> Starting my own practice has been a goal of mine for some time. Now I have a lot of anxiety and find it scary to contemplate. My difficulty with this decision is related to the losses, in the sense that I wish our plans to have a family were secure so I could start my new practice with other aspects of my life under control.

Occasionally pregnancy loss can be the impetus for a man to make a positive career change. The couple's shared grief can alter the father's priorities so that new career decisions become possible.

Eric discovered inner resources after he and his wife, Annette, lived through infertility problems followed by a pregnancy loss. When Annette then became pregnant with twins, Eric felt capable of making a significant career change to put his family on a sounder financial footing:

> I went from being a freelance writer to a computer programmer. I was a champion of Annette when she went through the infertility treatments and then the miscarriage. She was a champion for me when I went through this radical career switch. We gave each other strength because, having lived through the losses, we had learned how to do it.

YOUR CAREER CHOICES AND HIGH-RISK PREGNANCY

> *I am in a never-never land now. One part of me needs a job that is challenging and absorbing so I don't feel sad all the time because I don't have a child. My whole life is set up now for having a child, and I don't have one. We are saving money for my being pregnant again and being out of work and on bed rest. I have been putting my life on hold for two-and-a-half years.*
>
> —Peggy

When you face a future high-risk pregnancy that may include months of bed rest, you are compelled to alter your career plans with no guarantee of motherhood. Your employment may not accommodate a leave for bed rest, or you may find it difficult to arrange coverage for your work responsibilities during your absence. Even if you are able to find and train someone to fill your job, you will probably find little appreciation from your colleagues for the complexity of the task.

Peggy spent a great deal of time planning her leave, since she knew she would be coming back to her job and wanted it to be well organized when she returned. "Making all these arrangements was like having an extra job," she remembered, "but I felt it was my responsibility, and my colleagues expected it, too."

You may face painful dilemmas about career opportunities that are incompatible with the care you need while pregnant. It can feel unfair to have to decide whether to make a good career move that could imperil a future pregnancy or whether to forgo career satisfaction while your reproductive future remains uncertain. Natalie was well established in a highly stressful profession when she suffered her losses, which forced her to consider the effect a future high-risk pregnancy would have on her career:

I now have to decide whether to stay in bed for the next pregnancy; this is having a major impact on my career. I was just offered an excellent job, which I turned down because I thought it would be too stressful. I am so afraid that stress on the job is going to make me miscarry.

If you must take a pregnancy leave, check with your employer to find out which benefits might cover your absence. You may be entitled to certain disability payments or be able to return to the same position and salary after your leave. The social worker at the hospital where you plan to deliver can assist you if your employer is not helpful. If you are self-employed, your situation may be more difficult. Try to be realistic with clients and colleagues about when you can get back to your previous schedule and workload.

Even if leave for bed rest is not required, a high-risk pregnancy can still have a major impact on your work. While previously accustomed to keeping your personal life separate from work, you must inform your employer and colleagues of your pregnancy earlier than you might like. This invasion of your privacy is unfortunately necessary to ensure coverage of your work responsibilities should you suddenly have to take a leave.

It is also stressful when care for your pregnancy takes precedence over your work routine, as you take time off for medical exams, sonograms and other tests. "It was awful to have to choose between my pregnancy and my work," recalled a financial consultant who had two previous miscarriages. "Sometimes I would have to decide whether to get up in the middle of a client meeting to keep a doctor's appointment." You may find that these obligatory shifts at work have a negative effect on your status, productivity and professional self-image.

If your career is in a male-dominated field, you can feel especially torn when a high-risk pregnancy obliges you to put the care of your unborn baby first. You probably entered your field knowing you would be under pressure to demonstrate your equal ability and productivity to your male colleagues. When your job performance is affected by a high-risk pregnancy, you can feel that you are confirming the bias that men are more reliable than women in these positions, an attitude you had hoped to combat.

Tina, a research psychologist, lost a full-term pregnancy due to undiagnosed diabetes. During her next pregnancy, she was maintained on a strict regimen to stabilize her blood sugar. This required pricking her finger for a blood sugar test at regular intervals, eating meals and snacks on a frequent and precise schedule and giving herself insulin shots at specific times throughout the day, all of which affected her career:

I wasn't producing the way I had been; I knew it, and my boss knew it. That felt stressful, and stress makes diabetes worse. My lower productivity affected my job status, too. I was given the worst office, in an out-of-the-way location. I couldn't participate in the Friday social hour because I had to get home to eat an early dinner instead. Those social contacts provided important work contacts as well, and I really felt the impact of missing them.

If you continue to work while maintaining a high-risk pregnancy, it is essential for you to receive encouragement. You need to hear from colleagues and supervisors that they believe in your skills, understand your temporarily lowered productivity and know you will produce well again after the baby is born. But this kind of emotional backing is rare. Instead of getting credit for managing your work obligations and high-risk pregnancy admirably, your colleagues may insinuate that your work is simply not up to par.

Your boss's attitude in helping you adapt your work to a high-risk pregnancy can make a crucial difference. If your supervisor values your work and wants you to continue in your position after the baby's birth, you can work together to find an acceptable solution.

Ruth, who had previously lost a pregnancy in midterm, had a cervical cerclage and was on partial bed rest at home for much of the pregnancy that eventually produced her healthy daughter. As a vice president of her company, and with her boss's backing, Ruth discovered ways to manage working at home:

My boss was very understanding and he didn't want to lose me, so he had a computer set up at home next to my bed. Most of my customers, whom I dealt with by phone, didn't know I had ever been out of the office. I felt I was still part of something and I kept busy, which helped me keep a positive attitude about my pregnancy.

If you are working during a high-risk pregnancy and do not have your boss's support, try to find at least one colleague you trust whom you can talk to about daily stresses. If this is impossible, try to reduce emotional stress by talking with a friend or relative or through the help of a pregnancy loss support group or sessions with a psychotherapist. If you are bedridden and live in a major metropolitan area, find out if there is a support network such as SIDELINES that offers phone contact and counseling to pregnant women on bed rest.

In spite of the impact pregnancy loss has on your career, you may discover that practical aspects of your struggle give you confidence to cope with your future. As one woman remarked, "I think coping with my losses and managing difficult pregnancies have improved my ability to handle almost anything."

KEY POINTS WHEN PREGNANCY LOSS AFFECTS YOUR CAREER

As a mother, you may find that your work is affected by your pregnancy loss. Although working may provide solace after your loss, you might also discover that your career has temporarily lost meaning and has become an upsetting reminder of your absent baby.

If you face a future high-risk pregnancy, you must deal with putting your career second or placing it completely on hold as you accommodate medical appointments or bed rest. Making career decisions after a pregnancy loss, or in view of a future high-risk pregnancy, requires good support from family, friends, bosses and colleagues.

Here are some additional suggestions:

- Consider taking some of your planned maternity leave as a personal leave following your loss.
- If you are working during a high-risk pregnancy, talk to your boss about your special circumstances and the adjustments you will need to make in your work routine.
- Contact SIDELINES, a national support network for women enduring high-risk pregnancies, listed in Appendix D.
- Seek out at least one understanding person at work whom you can talk to. If this isn't possible, look for emotional support outside of work, with your family, friends, a pregnancy loss support group or a psychotherapist.
- As grief lessens, your career can again provide a sense of purpose, a means of self-expression and a source of self-esteem.

15

Pregnancy Loss and Infertility: A Twofold Sorrow

When you experience infertility—difficulty in conceiving and sustaining a pregnancy—and pregnancy loss, you endure a double blow. Both may deny you the number of biological children you want. They can turn the years in which you and your partner plan to have children and raise a family into an epoch of heartache and frustration. This double loss probably affects every aspect of your life, sometimes for years, as you withstand medical interventions and efforts to conceive, followed by hope and perhaps disappointment again.

One in six couples in the United States is affected by some form of infertility, and the number is rising. Although infertility is usually defined as an inability to conceive after one year of unprotected sexual intercourse, other distinctions are made when it occurs in combination with pregnancy loss. Primary infertility, in which the woman has never conceived, can be followed by pregnancies that end in loss. Secondary infertility occurs when an inability to conceive follows a conception, whether the pregnancy ended in a loss or a healthy birth. Women who repeatedly lose pregnancies, usually within the first trimester, are considered to be infertile, since they are unable to carry a pregnancy to term. Couples who choose to undergo pregnancy reduction when infertility treatments result in multiple gestations face a particularly difficult form of loss.

If your pregnancy loss was followed by an inability to conceive or carry a pregnancy, you may experience a profound sense of frustration and disbelief. After all, you were pregnant before; why not again? If you chose to end a pregnancy for any reason, disbelief can be compounded by immense guilt and the feeling that your infertility is retribution.

In the case of a newborn death followed by infertility, where you had a chance to parent your infant, however briefly, not having your own baby becomes a loss you can almost taste and feel. "I think parental instincts are aroused when you hear your baby cry, see your baby, touch your baby," explained one woman. "For me, that brief experience of mothering has made my infertility more poignant, has given an edge to my frustration."

If a couple does not have a subsequent successful pregnancy, they may be grateful for having had the experience of carrying a baby, even for a short time. A woman's sense of herself and her femininity may seem more complete than if she had never been pregnant at all. Bess experienced three early losses before she was diagnosed as having premature ovarian failure:

> I am very sentimental about my pregnancies. I felt sick and horrible, but blooming with fruit. I'm so glad I experienced what it is like to be pregnant. I would have been very sorry to have missed it.

The experience of pregnancy loss is intensified if it comes after years of infertility. You may have felt you had conceived a "miracle baby," that your patience and persistence had finally been rewarded. To lose a baby after such major investments in time and effort can feel unspeakably unfair. You may also find you are already emotionally depleted from your infertility problems as you struggle to cope with the tragic outcome of your long-awaited pregnancy. "We had spent six years of our lives in a futile quest that continued to bring us ever greater agony," remarked one man whose wife finally conceived and carried a pregnancy to term, only to have their newborn infant die. "We felt very betrayed by fate, as if we were under a cloud of doom."

If you have a child and then experience a loss, a pregnancy reduction or secondary infertility, you face additional problems. You may feel cut off from understanding people and informal networks, which can be a lifeline for many infertile couples. Infertile couples without children have no sympathy for you, and parents who have the size family they want may tell you to be satisfied with the number of children you already have.

But losses related to secondary infertility and pregnancy reduction are very real. If you wanted more children, you must live with the disappointment that your family feels incomplete. You may have definite opinions about *not* wanting to raise a small family or an only child and may worry that you have cheated your offspring doubly, first by being emotionally unavailable during your efforts to conceive, and then by not providing a sibling.

COPING WITH A PREGNANCY REDUCTION

Certain infertility treatments and drugs greatly increase the likelihood of high multiples in a single pregnancy. This can present infertile couples with a particularly heartbreaking form of loss called pregnancy reduction. By eliminating the fetuses that have implanted in the least favorable spots within the uterus, pregnancy reduction gives the remaining babies a better chance of survival and optimal health.

Although some parents who have given birth to a large number of babies from the same pregnancy have been treated like heroes in our society, many people, including infertile couples, medical ethicists and fertility specialists, have a different perspective. Allowing too many embryos to develop can retard the growth of each baby and lead to premature birth, which in turn can cause severe complications, even death. Mothers who carry multiples are also at greater risk for developing serious medical problems, such as high blood pressure and diabetes. Babies born of large multiple births will never receive an adequate amount of their mother's breast milk, crucial in helping premature infants thrive. Nor can such babies survive at home without the aid of many additional grown-ups, either paid staff or volunteers, options not available to all families.

Some specialists refuse to allow couples who are unwilling to undergo pregnancy reduction to participate in fertility treatments that will increase the likelihood of multiple conceptions. This poses a conflict, since most infertile couples who conceive multiples are already discouraged by their ongoing struggles and may not wish to consider such an option. One mother who had ended a genetically impaired pregnancy and then experienced infertility expressed her predicament:

> One of the major reasons that I am reluctant to undergo a course of Pergonal, as my doctor recommends, is that even though I remain pro-choice, I cannot bear the idea—much less the reality—of choosing selective reduction.

Pregnancy reduction presents already disheartened parents with a terrible predicament: Sacrifice some babies to save others. Since pregnancy reduction itself involves potential dangers, such as infection and premature labor, couples who use the procedure to give some of their babies the best chance of survival still risk losing the entire pregnancy.

If a couple decides in favor of pregnancy reduction, medical staff, as well as family and friends, may overlook their accompanying grief. One mother who chose to reduce her pregnancy from four fetuses to two said:

> I felt like the mother in Sophie's Choice, saying good-bye to some babies to give the others a better chance. But when I told one friend about the reduction, she judged me and said, "How could you do that?" So I didn't tell anyone else. Everyone thought I was only having twins and I never got sympathy for the other babies.

If you and your partner choose a pregnancy reduction, try to concentrate on the positive elements of your decision while still expressing your sadness over losing some of your babies. Consider finding a peer support group or psychotherapist trained in these special bereavement issues. If these alternatives are not available, ask your doctor to put you in touch with other couples who have made this choice. Contact with others in similar circumstances will help you feel less isolated by your particular sorrow.

Appendix A includes additional information that will help you understand pregnancy reduction. Once you have decided to reduce your pregnancy, consider reading about rituals in Appendix B or following the suggestions in Chapter 8, "Prenatal Diagnosis and the Burden of Choice" and in Chapter 1, "When an Unborn or Newborn Baby Dies," under the section entitled "Grieving Loss in a Multiple Pregnancy." Mourning and saying good-bye to the babies you lost will enable you to consecrate and eventually celebrate the life you granted your remaining children.

WHEN TO STOP TRYING TO CONCEIVE

> *People have different thresholds for the sadness of pregnancy loss and the rigors of fertility treatments. For some couples, it is very important not to give up. Others are ready sooner.*
> —Robin Fleischner, adoption attorney

When prolonged efforts to conceive and maintain a pregnancy fail, your cumulative disappointment can be overwhelming. In addition to losing one or more pregnancies, you are deprived of your hoped-for future children, who may never be born. Phyllis Lowinger, a social worker with the New York City chapter of RESOLVE, a nationwide self-help network for infertile couples, forcefully captures what these losses mean to would-be parents. "A couple must actually mourn their pregnancy losses and infertility, grieving and 'burying' their unborn, wished-for children," she insists. "Only then can they be ready for other life-affirming possibilities, such as adoption or child-free living."

It is important to decide at what point to stop trying for a biological child and take stock of your alternatives instead. This stopping point can be elusive, because continuing medical advances hold out new treatment possibilities and hope. Infertility specialists often feel their mission is to help you become pregnant, and rarely help you recognize when to stop trying. Even if you do stop, you may be haunted by the possibility that your next attempt might have succeeded.

Iris had a healthy son followed by three miscarriages before she was diagnosed as having an antibody abnormality that resulted in her body's rejection of her pregnancies. The efficacy of treatment was uncertain, but she was determined to try:

> If I give up and never have a second child, then I'll have a feeling of failure forever. I hope I will have the good grace to know when I should stop, but at this point I need to keep trying.

Family and friends who fail to respect your personal timetable and decision may urge you to abandon your hopes for a biological child or push you to keep trying when you're ready to stop. Rebecca, the mother of two adopted children, resented hearing others' opinions on the choices she and her husband faced:

> During the time we were so disappointed about not getting pregnant, friends and family would say, "Why don't you look into adoption?" or "Why don't you at least get on the adoption lists while you keep trying to have a baby?" But I was so hurt that they had given up on us when I wasn't ready to give up.

Discontinuing efforts to conceive when you deeply desire a child can leave you sad and defeated, especially after suffering a pregnancy loss as well. "I feel unfinished," admitted the mother of one healthy child who had endured a late pregnancy loss and infertility treatments. "My reproductive years have been long, and I've been through a lot. But I want to feel the completion of our efforts, and I don't."

You may find that continuing protracted and expensive attempts to conceive and hold on to a pregnancy exact a heavy toll, controlling all aspects of your life, from your sexual relationship to your personal finances. "I am constantly thinking, 'What are my ovaries doing? What are the sperm doing?'" one woman recalled. "It makes it hard to enjoy anything."

At some point the treatments and relentless preoccupation with trying to conceive and maintain a pregnancy become worse than the problem, and the cost, both emotionally and financially, becomes too high to bear. Insurance may not cover infertility expenses, and a couple can risk economic ruin in their pursuit of a biological child. Financial realities can force a decision and another grief reaction.

A woman may be ready to stop treatment before her partner, partly because it often involves a regular invasion of her body and usually demands more of her time than his. Doctor appointments might be taking precedence over all other commitments, including her career. A woman may simply reach her limit and decide to stop treatment for her own well-being, even if her partner would like to keep trying. "I couldn't bear it anymore," one woman confessed. "Mentally, I could not go on. I had to think of myself—to *save* myself, really."

Partners sometimes reach the stopping point together, particularly if a medical risk arises. Jody, who had suffered repeated early miscarriages, almost didn't come out of anesthesia after her last D&C. The couple agreed that one more attempt would be their limit. As her husband said, "I don't feel I have the right to risk her life with more pregnancies and would rather adopt instead."

Sometimes a man is ready to consider alternatives to pregnancy first. He may feel powerless over his partner's physical and emotional ordeal as he witnesses the monthly cycle of hope and anxiety.

Philip and his wife developed infertility problems after a complicated delivery and newborn death. He found his willingness to consider alternatives to pregnancy grew with their repeated, failed efforts to conceive:

> I would like to have a child, but I do not want to have a child at all costs. It is hard to lie in bed and hear my wife crying because her period came. Sometimes I think it would be better to adopt.

A couple may find it easier to come to a joint decision about when to stop trying if they go together to as many medical appointments as possible. The man's sympathetic presence can help the woman endure the demands placed on her and may enable him to empathize with her eventual decision.

You may decide to stop trying as you see prime years passing you by, realizing that you have given up other interests or that you no longer enjoy yourself, each other or your other children. For Jody, the cumulative sacrifices she and her husband endured brought about a major transition:

> Infertility and losses had been running my life. Getting pregnant was a problem. Holding on to the pregnancy was a problem. I want to have fun with my husband again. I want to talk about other things besides infertility tests and sonograms. We share so many other interests that we haven't enjoyed lately. I don't want this issue of having a baby to run our lives. My marriage is more important than just having a biological baby.

Having been pregnant before, you may find it difficult to stop efforts to conceive, especially when medical advances can entice you to keep trying. When you do stop trying, you may feel as if you are quitting or failing.

New York City psychologist and infertility expert Dr. Joann Galst helps couples with this impasse by suggesting that a decision to stop does not make them "quitters" or "failures," but instead is a constructive choice when the toll outweighs the likely benefits. The questions she has her clients ask themselves may help you to clarify your own readiness to make this choice:

- Do I know the likelihood of success? How can I find this out?
- What am I currently sacrificing to pursue this goal? How much am I willing to sacrifice?
- Are previously unacceptable options becoming more acceptable, such as adoption or child-free living?
- Would I feel a sense of relief if I skipped my next appointment with the infertility specialist or threw out the basal thermometer and sperm collection jar?
- Have I just had enough? If it isn't time to stop, for me or for us, when will it be?

It takes a tremendous psychological leap to give up the dream of having a biological child. When you make this shift and are truly ready to stop trying, infertility and pregnancy losses will no longer define your existence. You might set new career goals, arrange special activities with an only child, take on a hobby, make exotic travel plans or take steps to adopt a child. You may also experience renewed pleasure in your sexual relationship once you are released from the burden of sex on a timetable and obsessions about conceiving. A woman may feel particular relief once she is freed from the tyranny of the infertility and pregnancy loss cycle. She can take pleasure in her body, exercising or losing weight for her own sake instead of preparing to carry a baby.

Once you have made your decision, you may also rediscover a refreshing capacity to empathize with other people who have different troubles. "When you are going through infertility and losses, you feel the worst off in the world," explained Edna. "When it's more resolved, you can again be sensitive to problems others may be having."

ENDURING UNCERTAINTY

You may need to develop a number of coping strategies to help you endure the stress and uncertainties of both pregnancy loss and infertility. If you try to understand each other's depth of feeling, as well as your individual motivations to conceive, you can help each other and respect your mutual differences. "I am willing to trust my wife's instincts about how important having a biological child is to her," one husband explained. "If she said three months are enough trying, I would trust that she knows what she needs to do."

Men are often more optimistic about conceiving, while women frequently remain worried, making the kind of help each needs from the other very different. A woman usually wants her partner to listen to her worries, sympathize with her and hug her. If he offers reassurances that ring false, or advice about what might solve the problem, he may genuinely mean well, but he runs the risk of leaving his partner even angrier and more depressed than before.

Russell felt that undergoing a loss and infertility treatments had taught him a great deal about himself and the support his wife needed:

> I came with the attitude that this was a problem we could fix. I gradually realized I was incapable of fixing it, that if it could be fixed, the doctors would do it. I needed to play a different role than fix-it man. I had to be supportive in a different way, to listen. And my wife learned to tell me what helped her.

Although it is important for a couple to communicate, it may also be essential, at times, to limit discussions about infertility and losses. Psychotherapist Merle Bombardieri proposes "the twenty-minute rule" for couples who have trouble matching one partner's longing to talk with the other's willingness to listen. Under the twenty-minute rule, the couple sets a timer every day so that each partner can take a turn venting current preoccupations for ten minutes. After the timer goes off the second time, no further discussion is allowed for that day. This rule encourages the couple to become aware of each other's concerns, while protecting each partner from being overburdened by the other's turmoil.

Both you and your partner may find outside help essential as you grieve your losses and weather the uncertainties of infertility. Help may come from others with similar problems, which can give you a sense of community in your struggles. "When I talk to my friends who are also trying to become pregnant," said one woman, "I feel this incredible rush of relief."

Once you begin to put your troubles in perspective, you may feel more stable and reassured. Instead of dwelling on your disappointment, you can eventually realize that you and your partner will have a good future together even if unexpected problems arise. You may realize that although your difficulties in having a family are serious, they are among the many challenges couples encounter in life. Other families might not have this particular problem, but they still have their share of misfortunes.

You may find the heartache of not having a biological child is transformed over time with your capacity to grow and adapt to a difficult reality. You can emerge with a sense of inner strength, with humility, wisdom and a sense of humanity that are expressed in your dedication to make the most of the gifts life has given you. As Jessica expressed:

> What I have been through is a blessing in a very peculiar way. I always had felt I would never be up to a major tragedy. I felt I would dissolve, shatter, not be capable of surviving a terrible loss. I find I am made out of concrete. I have been changed. This has given me a good sense of myself.

Philip's view of becoming a parent, of his personal needs and goals, changed in significant ways after suffering a late pregnancy loss followed by infertility:

> Part of having a child is a selfish feeling, wanting to have a child for *me*, to make me feel good. Before we got pregnant, our thoughts were more to have a child for us. Now we tend to think more of having a child to give to, to teach and to raise to be a good human being.

KEY POINTS TO HELP YOU COPE WITH PREGNANCY LOSS AND INFERTILITY

The cumulative impact of pregnancy loss and infertility is immense. You have endured heartache, frustration and anxiety-ridden pregnancies, sometimes over a period of years. In addition, your career and finances may have revolved around infertility treatments or attempts to maintain precarious pregnancies.

You are likely paying a high price in time and emotions as efforts to conceive take over your life, leaving little energy for your relationship or other interests. This combination of problems is particularly heartbreaking as you struggle to make the best decision about treatments and when to stop trying to conceive, either accepting the number of children you have or considering alternatives to pregnancy.

Here are some suggestions to help you endure the combined stresses of pregnancy loss and infertility:

- Find a specialist by contacting the American Society for Reproductive Medicine, listed in Appendix D.
- Suggest that your partner go to doctor appointments with you to increase mutual understanding of the strain involved.
- Try following "the twenty-minute rule," in which each of you takes ten minutes daily to unburden feelings about your losses or treatment.
- Seek outside support. No one experiencing both pregnancy loss and infertility should have to go through this ordeal alone. Consider seeing a psychotherapist and contacting your local chapter of RESOLVE by checking with the national office listed in Appendix D.
- Read material to stay current on diagnostic and treatment options, as well as books on alternatives to pregnancy, such as adoption or child-free living. See Appendix D for suggestions.
- Stay involved with outside interests, which can be a welcome distraction and can help you discover new creative outlets.
- Know that it takes courage to continue trying to conceive, but that it also takes courage and wisdom to know when to stop

16

Becoming Pregnant Again

The biggest negative impact of my losses has been that each subse-
quent pregnancy is a fearful time instead of a happy one. I wish I could
have that innocent feeling, that I could fly through pregnancy not realiz-
ing the risks. I am envious of women in that position. They are having
such an easy, joyous time!

—Jody

A pregnancy that follows a loss can be fraught with anxiety instead of being the carefree, joyous experience you may have had with an earlier pregnancy. While you would love to feel elated, you are simply too apprehensive.

Enduring a loss may affect your decision to conceive again, your perception of carrying the new baby and your experience of giving birth. It can have an impact on your relationship to your partner and on the way you raise your children. Understanding and accepting how your life has been altered can help you make decisions about future pregnancies and child rearing that are right for you.

MAKING THE DECISION

Researchers have discovered that if parents conceive too soon after a loss, they may be unable to express their grief, thus delaying and complicating their emotional recovery. Women in particular fare better emotionally if they wait at least six months before conceiving again. Grieving your baby is an absorbing process that may interfere with your ability to bond with your new child. If you fail to mourn before having another child, you can fall into the trap of hoping to replace the baby who died. You may also become unduly fearful during the next pregnancy.

Michael and Judi Forman have written about the importance of their own mourning period after the death of their newborn son:

Before we could open ourselves up to the possibility of having another child, we needed to reach some understanding of why Robin died, what his death meant to us in terms ranging from the most concrete to the most spiritual. Without that awareness it is unlikely that we could have become loving or effective parents to another baby.

The Right Timing

A couple's readiness to conceive again depends on the kind of loss they suffered, the mother's age, and each parent's emotional progress. Doctors generally recommend that a couple wait two or three full menstrual cycles before trying to conceive again following any loss. This passage of time permits the uterus to return to its normal size, the lining to grow back and the cervix to close, all of which can improve the chances of success in a subsequent pregnancy.

But a doctor's clear-cut medical permission to try again does not take into account all the issues a bereaved couple must weigh. Lisa had lost a newborn daughter and felt nervous about conceiving again. Even after the requisite three-month period had passed, she fretted over being physically and emotionally ready:

> When my husband and I started discussing getting pregnant again, I was very hesitant about sex or even trying to conceive at first. On one hand I said, "Yes, I want another baby," and on the other I said, "No, I'm too nervous, scared and confused."

Some parents are afraid that if they conceive again quickly, they will be too vulnerable if they suffer a subsequent loss. Others feel surprisingly relaxed about trying to conceive again. One mother had been panicky about conceiving her first pregnancy, which ended with the death of her newborn baby. Keeping track of temperature charts and fertile periods had taken its toll before that first conception, so when she and her husband agreed to become pregnant after their loss, the pressure was off:

> At least I knew that I had been pregnant before, so I was much more relaxed. The fact that I wasn't quite ready also made me a lot less anxious about conceiving. If it happened, it happened. If it didn't happen right away, that was okay, too.

Older mothers may feel pressure to conceive quickly after a loss because they realize their childbearing years are nearing an end. They run the risk of neglecting their emotional recovery and physical readiness if they become pregnant right away. "Waiting was the hardest," one thirty-six-year-old woman recalled. "I wanted to fast-forward my life so I could just start trying to get pregnant again."

Young women may find they are not immune to feeling similar pressures, even if they have many childbearing years ahead of them. Karen had experienced several first-trimester losses while in her twenties and found that with each disappointment, the urgency to conceive again increased. "I feel I've got to make up for all the losses and the lost time," she admitted. "It's an indescribably urgent feeling."

If a conflict arises between you and your partner about when to conceive again, try to discuss this openly and make a decision both of you can live with. You will need each other's emotional support during your next pregnancy, especially if it will be high-risk, so it is important to wait until both of you are truly ready.

Once you have agreed to conceive again, you may find that every aspect of your life is refracted through the prism of planning a subsequent pregnancy. "My husband and I had to plot out his business trips to coincide with my fertile periods," remarked one woman, "and then we had to make sure he was around during the critical first trimester, when I usually miscarried. It placed a tremendous strain on both of us."

It is difficult to anticipate all the issues and to predict the best time to conceive, but being honest with yourself, your partner and your doctor about your feelings can help you arrive at an acceptable decision.

Finding Out You Are Pregnant Again

Once you have decided to conceive again, you await the arrival of each menstrual period with mixed emotions, cautiously hopeful and yet fearing another loss. Confirmation of a new pregnancy brings hope for a happy outcome, but it also can begin months of anxiety as you wait for the birth of your new child. This pregnancy may remind you of your loss more than you had anticipated, especially when you reach the point at which you lost the previous baby.

Some parents are reluctant to believe in the pregnancy or its outcome, refusing even to fantasize about the baby. Natalie, who suffered several first-trimester miscarriages, felt that by not allowing herself to commit her hopes to each pregnancy, she might be more prepared to handle a possible loss. "Because of the miscarriages," she confessed, "I was not entirely invested in each of the subsequent pregnancies."

Additional stresses can be placed on a marriage once the new pregnancy is confirmed. Doctors may advise a limit on sexual relations during a subsequent high-risk pregnancy for several reasons. Uterine contractions associated with female orgasms and certain components in semen, such as prostaglandins, have been implicated in the onset of preterm labor. Since semen occasionally carries infections that may harm a precarious pregnancy, physicians may recommend the use of condoms, further reducing a couple's spontaneity and pleasure. The slight possibility that sex could harm the pregnancy can make one or both partners reluctant to have sexual relations.

Other stresses can emerge because the woman may be feeling vulnerable in her newly pregnant state and may make more demands on her partner's time and attention than usual. Even if she had been an independent, confident woman before her loss, she can feel insecure and defenseless during a subsequent pregnancy.

Neil, whose wife had lost three pregnancies in the first trimester, at first welcomed the time-consuming nature of his career once their new pregnancy was confirmed. He was grateful for the haven from anxieties his work provided, but his wife felt he wasn't spending enough time with her or giving her the support she needed. When she called Neil at his office one day, he suddenly realized why he needed to change his attitude:

> I said I was busy and couldn't talk to her. I didn't even take the time to find out what was bothering her. It turned out she was staining and was frightened. Whenever she called me after that incident, I always asked if it was important. If she said yes, I just dropped whatever I was doing and talked to her.

Once you have adjusted to the new pregnancy and the anxiety it provokes, you may be able to achieve a certain closeness to your partner by sharing your concerns for each other and the pregnancy. Neil eventually found a new role for himself that felt comfortable and important:

> Once I accepted that Jody required extra help during this pregnancy, I found I had a tolerance for her needs and anxieties that wasn't there before. It was good knowing I was needed and that we could be there for each other.

The decisions and stresses you face begin to multiply as the pregnancy advances. You wonder when to tell other people about the pregnancy, and you question whether you are receiving the right medical care. Perhaps most difficult, you begin the long weeks of anxiety, hoping against hope, but never quite believing that all will go well.

Telling Others

The joy you felt with your first pregnancy may have grown as you shared your good news with family and friends. In a pregnancy following a loss, this eagerness is often stifled by a sense of caution and privacy. "We held off telling even immediate family until the beginning of the third month," explained Neil. "I couldn't go screaming to the world about how happy I was with the pregnancy, or enjoy it with other friends and family the way I would have liked to."

Keeping the pregnancy a secret becomes a way of trying to contain the tension and fear that you might lose this baby, too. You may also wish to spare loved ones who will worry about you and your new pregnancy.

But this caution can backfire because it deprives you of a support network of family and friends during this anxious time—and in the event of another loss. Ellen and her husband had agreed to wait to announce their subsequent pregnancy until after the results of the amniocentesis were in, well into the fifth month of pregnancy. But by the time she had reached twelve weeks, Ellen had changed her mind. "I felt I needed more support from everyone around me by then," she recalled, "so my husband and I talked it over again and we agreed to start telling at least close friends and family that week."

Not everyone you tell about the new pregnancy will necessarily be happy. They may be so personally concerned or professionally dubious that they cannot be encouraging. Gayle and her husband experienced two full-term losses of babies with rare congenital anomalies and had to change doctors to find one who would support their efforts to try again.

The few people who knew Gayle and her husband were trying to conceive again thought they were being irresponsible, including her parents. "But it was impossible to get mad at my parents," she conceded, "because they basically were just so worried and anxious about me and my husband. My father couldn't even talk about the new pregnancy, not even after our healthy son was born."

A different problem can occur when relatives and friends who were understanding at first lose patience with your continuing anxiety once the pregnancy is progressing nicely. They do not realize how much is riding on the pregnancy or how fearful you are about the outcome. Annette, who had suffered infertility problems and a miscarriage, felt criticized by friends for her ongoing worry:

> All the anxieties overrode the joy, and I started to berate myself for that. But I feel I was wrong to berate myself. It is natural to feel anxious after a loss, and I should have been kinder to myself.

Some people may even tell the pregnant mother that worrying during a subsequent pregnancy could cause another loss or produce a high-strung baby. As one woman said:

> These remarks were not only cruel but also unfounded. After two miscarriages, all I could do was worry during my next pregnancy. But from the day we brought our healthy son home from the hospital, he slept through the night. He was a relaxed, happy baby in spite of all my anxieties while pregnant.

If a Loss Occurs Again

> *After the second loss, I fell apart. I had no self-esteem. I kept thinking, "Everyone can do this and I can't. This is going to keep happening." I didn't know if I could keep trying and having more losses.*
>
> —Amy

With a subsequent conception, most couples face the same 31 percent chance of losing a baby as the rest of the population; however, if they suffer more than one pregnancy loss, they may begin to feel like a statistical oddity. "It was as if lightning had indeed struck twice," lamented one mother. "We felt we had been singled out in some awful way."

The most important step you can take at this point is to seek thorough and thoughtful medical care to optimize your chances for a healthy future pregnancy. Exploring the physical causes and treatments for your loss can help your frame of mind as well, enabling you to take meaningful action when your life feels out of control. "The more we learned and the more we understood," recalled Neil, "the easier it became for us to cope with our situation."

When you and your partner schedule a consultation with your doctor, plan for the meeting by discussing and writing down your questions beforehand. If you still feel your questions are not being answered, consider changing doctors or at least obtaining a second opinion from a medical specialist.

If a subsequent pregnancy ends in another loss, you and your partner may need time to reestablish your lives and priorities. Two losses are traumatic, and psychotherapy or a pregnancy loss support group may be helpful. A support group in particular can console you and enable you to reach out to others when you thought you had nothing left to give.

After her third miscarriage, Neil's wife became a lay counselor for couples who had suffered pregnancy losses. "I think she basically transformed her sorrow into something positive," recognized Neil, "by trying to do something meaningful for others."

RECONSIDERING YOUR MEDICAL CARE

A pregnancy loss may force you to reevaluate your choice of doctors and the management of your medical care during your next pregnancy. In some instances, the loss itself may have created high-risk complications that require specialized care for any subsequent pregnancy. If you stay with the same physician, you may need careful monitoring or medical interventions. Another option is to change doctors so that you are under the care of a specialist.

You may be so upset by your loss that you and your partner feel compelled to switch physicians, even if you thought your original doctor was medically competent. You may be dissatisfied with the lack of comfort your doctor provided, or may feel that returning to the same doctor could stir up painful memories. Seeking the care of a new, well-qualified physician can bring a feeling of fresh hope for your next pregnancy.

Changing Doctors

If you decide to change doctors for a subsequent pregnancy, there are several issues to bear in mind. Try to get solid recommendations from other patients and physicians for a board-certified specialist. Schedule a consultation with the prospective doctor, and be sure to bring your medical records with you. Ask pertinent questions that will reveal the physician's attitude about pregnancy loss and your particular case. Also find out how the physician stays up-to-date with the latest clinical practices and research. You may want to write down your questions and notes on your medical history before the appointment, so that you and your doctor can refer to this information. Even though you are sitting in his office and paying for his time, you are the one who is considering hiring him as part of your medical team to help you have a baby. If he rushes you through your questions and dismisses your concerns, he is probably not the right physician for you.

"I refused to go to one specialist who told me in the consultation not to worry, that I would have a baby," said one woman who had experienced several miscarriages. "I knew enough to realize that wasn't necessarily true and thought that his attitude would be all wrong for me."

Keep in mind that highly skilled doctors do not necessarily have the best bedside manner. Both your doctor's competence and your feeling of being in a partnership with him are vital. During your consultation, ask the doctor if you may call for reassurances or come into the office without an appointment so the nurse can let you hear the baby's heartbeat. If the answer is no and you live in a large enough city to find another doctor, consider doing so.

When Molly changed doctors after her baby son was stillborn, she knew she would be extremely anxious throughout her next pregnancy and questioned her new physician about his availability. "He made it clear that if I needed to, I could go to his office anytime I wanted," she recalled. "He told me if I needed to see that the baby was alive on a particular day, to just come on in."

Discussing all options and making the patient a part of the decision-making process can also help dispel a feeling of helplessness. Jody had several first-trimester miscarriages before she switched to a high-risk-pregnancy obstetrician. He supported her quest for information and worked closely with her throughout her subsequent pregnancy, which resulted in the birth of a healthy daughter. "We discussed everything," she recalled, "from how much Clomid I should take to what dosage of progesterone I should have. I felt this doctor was partners with me."

Use of Technology

You may want your doctor to examine you more frequently and make greater use of available technology in a subsequent pregnancy. Many parents find the knowledge technology provides to be encouraging following a loss. "I didn't have testing in my first pregnancy because I was so young," explained Lisa, who was nervous after her full-term baby died from a congenital disorder, "but I had three ultrasounds in my next pregnancy. It was a relief to know that the new baby was developing properly."

You may want to be under the care of a doctor who has testing and monitoring available but who discusses your individual situation with you, so that you can decide together which procedures are necessary. You may agonize over the risks and benefits of tests in a subsequent pregnancy if your loss may have been triggered by a medical procedure. It is essential to know that you and your doctor are partners in these hard decisions. If you have concerns about specific tests, be prepared to take the initiative in bringing them up with your physician.

Paula and her doctor suspected that she lost her second pregnancy in midterm because her uterus did not tolerate an amniocentesis due to DES exposure. Even though she had since slipped into a higher-risk age group, she was reluctant to have the procedure in her next pregnancy. When her doctor assumed Paula would opt for amniocentesis because of her age, she confronted him:

> I forced the issue and said to him, "I can't sleep at night thinking about having an amniocentesis. Let's just sit down and go through the pregnancy I lost and see if this could have been caused by the amniocentesis." We went over everything and he finally said, "You're right. I've been nervous about it, too." I felt it was important to talk about not just the probabilities in amniocentesis, but about my particular case.

Even if your next baby is at risk for genetic or chromosomal abnormalities, you may decide against having a procedure because it presumes a willingness to end an impaired pregnancy. "It seemed inconceivable to have an abortion at twenty weeks if the amniocentesis revealed a problem," recalled Lidia, who had suffered two losses and was thirty-six at the time of her subsequent pregnancy. She also recognized that the likelihood of genetic problems occurring was slightly less than the chance of losing the baby from the procedure itself. After talking it over with her husband and her doctor, Lidia decided against having amniocentesis.

These decisions can shift, however, in subsequent pregnancies. When Lidia found herself pregnant again at age forty, she recognized that both her chances of conceiving an impaired baby and her inability to cope with a handicapped child had increased significantly. "We were still reluctant to use amniocentesis because it is done so late in the pregnancy," she concluded, "so we opted for chorionic villus sampling, which is performed much earlier."

If you decide to have prenatal tests that reveal the baby's sex, consider having your doctor give you the information in a sealed envelope so you may carefully weigh the impact this news might have on you.

Some parents believe that knowing the gender will enable them to bond with their new baby and think about their expected child as an individual. Others feel that knowing the sex of the new baby would make them sad, as they would compare this pregnancy to the one they lost. Try to do what feels best, and realize that your decision about having this information may change with later pregnancies.

Your involvement in medical care as a couple can also change following a loss. You and your partner may want to attend prenatal visits together, to support each other during these stressful months. "Going to doctor appointments together during the next pregnancy helped us enormously after the stillbirth," one woman said. "It enabled us to keep communication open about sexual relations and what tests to have, really all the issues that affected us as a couple."

Whatever your decisions may be—to stay with your current doctor or to choose a new medical practitioner, to use more technology or less—you may still change your mind during the pregnancy. Open communication with your partner and your doctor will help you and your baby receive the best possible care.

SURVIVING THE NEW PREGNANCY

> I felt I was walking on eggs and just kept hoping this time it would be okay.
>
> —Kimberly

When you conceive after one or more losses, the new pregnancy can create hopes, anxieties and unexpected conflicts. You may be unable to concentrate at work or to enjoy leisure activities. If you have other children, they may provide welcome comfort and distractions, but you might sometimes resent their intrusions when you are focusing on the new pregnancy. If your children are old enough to know about your loss and the new pregnancy, they may increase your anxiety by asking in all innocence, "Will this baby die, too?"

Continuous worry may keep you from bonding readily to the expected baby for fear of suffering another loss. On the other hand, a mother in particular may become devoted both quickly and intensely, believing that if the pregnancy fails, she will have experienced her unborn baby as much as possible. "I want to bond immediately with this baby, because if it doesn't work out, I want to enjoy it as much as I can," one woman explained. "I like to think this baby senses that commitment, too, and wants to stay with me."

This special subsequent pregnancy can become a dominant concern in the expectant mother's life. Some women practically memorize pregnancy books, carefully following every suggestion, or curtail activities even beyond what their doctors recommend. Others debate whether to stop work or forgo regular exercise routines, and let their partners, relatives or friends take over meal preparation and housework.

A woman may even keep herself housebound because she feels this protects the pregnancy. Jody had experienced three miscarriages, and when she became pregnant again she simply stayed home. "I felt very fragile," she admitted. "I feared going out of the house to the point where I was almost phobic."

During a subsequent pregnancy, you and your partner may become overly cautious about making plans for the new baby. The layette you eagerly set up during the previous pregnancy may stay hidden away until the baby is safely born. You may refuse baby showers, put away gifts unopened, and not discuss names for the new infant until your baby arrives. If avoiding preparations for the baby helps you get through the new pregnancy, respect your feelings. You can ask a friend or relative to shop right after the baby is born or set up the crib in time for your homecoming.

Some expectant mothers and fathers find their approaches to coping with a subsequent pregnancy are at odds. Neil attempted to find strength within himself during their most recent pregnancy. "I didn't have much difficulty with the lack of assurances during this last pregnancy," he declared after his wife safely carried to term following several miscarriages. "I prayed that the pregnancy would work out, and had faith that if it didn't, I would be able to deal with it."

But this feeling of strength was in stark contrast to his wife's experience, as she envisioned a variety of ways a loss could happen again. "As a result," Neil confessed, "my wife felt more prepared for problems than I did, but she also lived in constant fear that something could go wrong."

If you suffered an early loss, your new pregnancy may be fraught with both dread and optimism as each day passes without a problem. These mixed emotions intensify as the point of your previous loss arrives and then passes. As the baby continues to grow and you receive good prenatal test results, you may feel increasingly hopeful and confident that the pregnancy is advancing properly and that your baby will be fine.

Eric felt that his concern disappeared rapidly once he heard the heartbeat and saw the baby on the sonogram screen. "I felt the pregnancy was on its way, that it was really going to happen," he admitted. Other parents find their sense of security peaks around the seventh month, when the baby has a good chance of surviving outside the womb.

If you endured a late loss, no time in the pregnancy may ever seem safe, and your anxiety can increase as the due date approaches. Adam, who lost a full-term baby shortly after birth, remembered how anxious his wife became in her subsequent pregnancy. "She waited and waited until the baby was big enough to feel his kicks," he recalled. "But then if the baby didn't kick for half a day, she would go crazy."

Until particular medical or psychological hurdles have been passed, bereaved parents often try to assuage their anxiety by doing anything in their power to give their subsequent pregnancy its best chance. Some expectant parents pray daily or bargain with God, pledging, "If you give me this baby, I'll do anything you want!" One mother used meditation tapes to help her go to sleep every night for three months until she got beyond her critical first trimester. Other women learn breathing and relaxation exercises to do several times a day, or whenever their anxiety starts to rise.

Otherwise rational and scientifically minded people have been known to seek out faith healers or mystics and to wear charms that are supposed to help maintain a pregnancy. Old wives' tales are revived and ancient customs dusted off in an attempt to defy the fates—or at least lessen anxiety—during the months of waiting and worrying.

Parents may freely admit that submitting to such talismans is like believing in magic, but they adhere to the customs steadfastly. Karen felt that visiting a religious faith healer was only part of the total process of trying to secure her subsequent pregnancy. "I felt we were seeing all these doctors and using medical interventions," she said, "and this didn't seem all that different to me." When the healer suggested she wear a magnet around her neck throughout the pregnancy, citing ancient biblical references to lodestones, Karen eagerly complied. "I've been wearing one around my neck under my shirt since I found out I was pregnant," she conceded. "I worry about someone noticing it and having to explain it, but I wear it all the time."

Endurance may come from unexpected sources. Keeping a diary can be a wonderful outlet for your worries during a stressful subsequent pregnancy. Even a sense of humor can be key to helping you cope. "What is life without being able to laugh at it?" one woman asserted. "I try to suppress my very satirical side most of the time, but I let it out when I'm pregnant. It really helps me deal with the stress."

As you approach the new baby's due date, you may wish to take a childbirth course but find the thought of being in a room full of expectant couples unnerving. Consider arranging private lessons for yourself and your partner through the International Childbirth Education Association, listed in Appendix D. You may also want to ask your doctor if you may have a specially trained labor assistant, called a doula, or some other helpful professional with you at the birth, in addition to your partner.

No matter what kind of loss you suffered, you will probably need to hear the cry of your healthy newborn, and see for yourself that she is strong and well, before you begin to relax and enjoy your baby and parenthood.

For Mothers Who Must Manage a Subsequent High-Risk Pregnancy

If you are a mother who has experienced a medical crisis in a previous pregnancy, such as preterm labor or high blood pressure, your subsequent conceptions may require additional interventions and vigilance. The increased doctor visits and monitoring for a high-risk pregnancy may elevate your anxieties, affecting your relationships at home, your productivity at work or both. The overpowering impact this can have on your work life is discussed in Chapter 14, "The Impact of Pregnancy Loss on Your Career."

Bed rest is the most trying intervention required by some high-risk pregnancies. Women who must stay on complete bed rest may resent the dependency this entails, whether at home or in the hospital. Nicole, an active and self-reliant woman, was in need of constant care during her pregnancies because of recurrent preterm labor. She couldn't afford professional home care, but having her mother-in-law come to help was not a problem-free solution, either:

> Having someone help who has always seen you as independent is embarrassing. It's hard to keep bothering a family member to get you lunch or something to drink. As willing as my mother-in-law was, I felt uncomfortable constantly asking her for things.

Although you are physically dependent, you can still find ways to exert some control. If you are at home with a relative or under hospital care, make an effort to assert your needs. One hospitalized woman felt guilty about asking for nursing help in getting her dirty dishes cleared away. Yet the atmosphere in her room was important for her morale, so she overcame her reluctance to ask. You, too, will probably feel better if you act on the choices you do have.

After one midterm loss and a miscarriage, Peggy was put on home bed rest for her next pregnancy. The complicated, long-range planning her situation demanded actually helped Peggy feel she was exercising some control. She matched people who were willing to help with the tasks that needed to be done:

> My sister and friends who enjoy cooking just loved creating meals for me and putting calories on someone else. Figuring out what needed to be done and who could do it best was a benefit to the people who wanted to help as well as to me.

If you have a young child, managing bed rest at home becomes even more of a challenge. It is frustrating to have your child want to play with you or get into things she shouldn't when you aren't supposed to leave your bed. Make an effort to arrange adequate child care so you don't have to choose between caring for your youngster or your unborn baby.

The loneliness and isolation of bed rest, especially in a hospital, can be immense. You may find that bringing attractive framed prints, throw pillows and pillowcases from home lifts your spirits during the weeks or months of your hospitalized pregnancy. "Wearing my own brightly colored T-shirts helped me feel better about myself," one woman asserted. "So did putting on earrings and a little makeup each morning."

It may be especially helpful to give some structure to your day by waking up and bathing by a certain hour, as well as scheduling time for projects. Make appointments with friends and family who want to see you, so you avoid having too many visitors at once or none at all when you want the company. Planning visits also prevents someone from walking in when you are having a sponge bath.

See if you can think of innovative ways to keep occupied. Needlepoint, knitting or other crafts can keep your hands and mind engaged. You might arrange for tutoring on a topic that is enjoyable and interesting to you. "I had always wanted to brush up on my French," remembered Peggy, "but I never had time. So that was one of the first things I planned when I knew most of my next pregnancy would be spent in the hospital." Try keeping a selection of your favorite music and comedy CDs or videotapes on hand as well.

For women who need to be hospitalized at a medical facility far from their homes, the feeling of seclusion only increases, and the courage and effort needed to cope can become monumental. Marianne suffered from an incompetent cervix and was hospitalized for several months in a medical center about an hour and a half from her home. Her husband endured the commute three times a week and stayed with friends near the hospital on weekends. Friends and coworkers visited her, sent notes and called. "There wasn't a spot on the wall that wasn't covered by cards," she recalled.

If you are bedridden, consider contacting SIDELINES, the national network of lay counselors who can provide emotional support during high-risk pregnancies. Their number is listed in Appendix D.

Extended bed rest decreases strength and muscle tone, which can drastically affect your self-image. "I could barely walk after my son was delivered at thirty weeks," said Amelia, who spent most of the pregnancy in the hospital. "I hadn't gained weight so much, but it was as if my leg muscles had collapsed and slipped down around my ankles. As thrilled as I was about my baby's birth, I felt and looked terrible."

If you are a new mother who has just come off bed rest, try to be patient with yourself, since it will take time for you to get back into shape. For every week in bed you will need about three weeks to regain your former condition. Talk with your doctor, nurse or physical therapist about exercises to do daily that will gradually increase your strength and muscle tone.

PARENTING AFTER YOUR LOSS

Once you and your partner deliver a healthy baby, the vestiges of your loss may continue to color your experiences of parenthood. From the moment of birth through your child's first illness, you may find yourself more anxiety-ridden than other parents. Even red-letter events occurring years later, such as your child's first day of school or first sleepover away from home, can bring back uneasiness related to your pregnancy loss. Understanding the source of your concerns can help you overcome them and allow your living children to emerge from the shadow of your sorrow.

Experiencing the Birth of a Healthy Baby

The delivery of a healthy baby may be highly emotional, as memories of your previous pregnancy crowd your mind. Thoughts of your earlier pregnancy may upset you or may be a bittersweet reminder of the baby you lost.

When Molly gave birth to her daughter, she found she needed to think about her stillborn son, in spite of remarks she felt were intended to deflect her thoughts away from him. "People tried to say uplifting things about the new baby, like 'She's so healthy,' but all I could think was, 'Now I know what we were missing with our son.'"

The birth experience may trigger worries that had been repressed while you coped with the new pregnancy. Because of her past history and loss, Paula had scheduled a cesarean delivery, which proceeded in a very orderly fashion. "But when our son emerged alive and healthy, my whole body suddenly shook with this enormous sigh of relief," she recalled. "I hadn't realized how tense I had been during the entire pregnancy until my son was born and I knew he was fine."

Many parents realize that not all babies cry instantly at birth, but mothers and fathers who have suffered a pregnancy loss may feel panic-stricken when they don't hear their babies holler as soon as they are born. Lisa recalled yelling at the delivery room staff, "Why isn't my baby crying? Do something!" When he finally cried a few moments later, she felt enormous relief.

This disbelief in your baby's safe arrival is not an unusual reaction after a loss. You may need to grieve the baby who died once again as you gradually realize that this new, different baby is going to be strong and well.

Problems with Child Rearing

The effects of your pregnancy loss can persist long after your new baby is safely delivered. Disciplining long-awaited children can be a problem after living with the fear of never becoming a parent. You may find yourself reluctant to reprimand your children properly, even when you know the youngsters need constraints. One mother conceded that her son became hopelessly spoiled because of her fears. "But once I realized that discipline could be an act of love, that I could make my child adapt better to the world around him if he accepted limits," she confessed, "we both did much better."

You may feel protective of your children's health and welfare, running to the pediatrician sooner than parents who haven't had losses. "I still get nervous whenever my son gets sick," acknowledged one mother. "I know I overreact and am a little obsessed."

If vigilant medical care for your baby gives you peace of mind, you are entitled to those precautionary doctor visits. Explain your concerns to your pediatrician and consider arranging telephone consultations to determine when your child needs to be seen. Your feelings of panic when your child gets sick should diminish as he grows.

Pregnancy loss, and the poignant recognition of how fleeting life is, can leave you a positive legacy as a parent as well. "I'm more patient with our son than I think I would have been if we had not lost our daughter the year before," concluded Jesse. "I guess I'm just mindful of his preciousness even when he is driving me nuts."

Responding to Awkward Questions

As your subsequent pregnancy advances and after the new baby is born, you might receive unintentionally provocative comments from well-wishers who ask, "Is this your first baby?" or "How many other children do you have?"

Molly, who suffered a full-term stillbirth, had difficulty responding to these questions after her healthy daughter was born. Sometimes she would just say that her daughter wasn't her first child and leave it at that, without saying anything more unless people asked further questions. Some did. If they persisted, she would say something simple, such as "My son died." For Molly, these answers became another way of establishing her son's existence. "He *was* real," she asserted, "even more so after our daughter was born."

How you decide to handle these questions is very individual. Talk over your feelings with your partner, and try to answer depending on how well you know each person and what feels most comfortable. You may choose to say you had a baby who died, or you may prefer not to tell strangers or acquaintances of your loss. Not mentioning the baby to others does not mean you have forgotten your child.

Your answer may change with time, as your family grows and the loss becomes less painful. You might struggle with feelings of guilt at first, because you are not always publicly acknowledging the baby who died, but eventually you will come to a private peace about your relationship to that child. Lisa had lost a daughter and then had a healthy son, whom she sometimes told people was her first child. She recalled, however, saying to herself, "Lara, we haven't forgotten about you; we still love you."

KEY POINTS TO HELP YOU SURVIVE A SUBSEQUENT PREGNANCY

Pregnancy after a loss is a roller coaster of joy and anxiety. Once you have agreed to try again, you may face worries about new medical treatments and concern that the outcome of any subsequent pregnancy is uncertain.

When you conceive after a loss, you must resolve how and when to tell other people about your pregnancy. Even the experiences of giving birth to a healthy child and taking her home can be colored by your loss.

Here are some suggestions that may help ease the tensions of a subsequent pregnancy:

- Keep in mind that emotional readiness and physical readiness to have sex again are not always in sync, nor do partners always agree on when to become pregnant again. Be frank with each other about your readiness for both.
- Decide how and when you will tell others about a new pregnancy. Try to keep your own comfort uppermost in your mind.
- Work out a plan to have access to your doctor or to change physicians if you feel this will give your subsequent pregnancy the best chance of succeeding.
- Be patient with yourself if you feel anxious at times, even with the best possible medical care and emotional support. Consider using relaxation tapes or exercises to increase your comfort and reduce stress.
- Give yourself time to grieve if your subsequent pregnancy ends in another loss. Consider involvement in activities that will comfort you and honor your baby.
- Respect your need to exert control if you are bedridden during your pregnancy. Create a schedule and make your environment as pleasant as possible. Find projects to keep you busy, and practice asking for what you need.
- Contact SIDELINES, a national support network for women enduring high-risk pregnancies, listed in Appendix D.
- When well-meaning people ask you and your partner how many children you have, find a response that is comfortable for you at the moment, understanding that it may shift with time as you integrate your loss into your life.

Appendix A

Managing Problem Pregnancies

Once a diagnosis of a problem has been made, there are a variety of approaches to treating specific kinds of threatened pregnancy loss and preparing for a subsequent high-risk pregnancy. Some tests and procedures are well-accepted practices that are readily available; others are new and sometimes controversial, and may require treatment in a specialized medical center. This appendix also includes a brief discussion of prenatal diagnostic tests and procedures for ending an impaired pregnancy.

GENETIC AND CHROMOSOMAL PROBLEMS

The accidental rearrangement, realignment or numeric changes in the twenty-three pairs of chromosomes in each cell, such as with Down syndrome, are called chromosomal abnormalities. Genetic anomalies can be traced to one or more of the one hundred thousand genes within the chromosomes that store information about bodily characteristics such as sex or eye color and are responsible for such disorders as Tay-Sachs disease and hemophilia. Both chromosomal and genetic abnormalities can cause defects in a baby and pregnancy loss.

Probable treatment. Chromosomal and genetic defects are not preventable. The adverse effects of certain genetic defects are treatable, but many are not. Once a genetic or chromosomal defect has been determined, the couple may want to consult a genetic specialist about the probability of the same flaw recurring and about tests that can reveal its presence in a subsequent pregnancy.

Some chromosomal irregularities that lead to pregnancy loss can be discovered in the parents' bloodstreams or in fetal tissue. In either case, the chromosomal arrangement within the individual cells is photographed and examined in a procedure called karyotyping, which is expensive and is recommended only in specific cases.

213

Rh-INCOMPATIBILITY DISEASE

Blood types are classified by letters (A, B, AB and O) and by being positive or negative. Rh-incompatibility occurs when an Rh-negative mother, or a mother who has developed Rh-antibodies from a previous pregnancy, becomes pregnant with an Rh-positive baby. If this incompatibility is not recognized and treated, the mother's body mounts a protective immune attack against the baby, which can lead to serious complications. Rh-incompatibility is easily detected during each pregnancy and can be effectively monitored and treated before and after birth.

Probable treatment. Once a mother is identified as Rh-negative, she is inoculated with Rh-immune globulin at about twenty-eight weeks into the pregnancy. Another dose must be given to her upon the baby's delivery or following any type of pregnancy loss.

HORMONAL PROBLEMS

Some hormonal problems that result in pregnancy loss can be determined by a blood test. Endometrial biopsy is the most effective method of determining the presence of the major hormonal imbalance, called luteal phase defect or LPD. If the uterine lining is improperly developed for the day of the cycle on which it was gathered, the assumption is that a luteal phase defect is responsible. A single endometrial biopsy can misrepresent this condition, so two biopsies from two separate cycles are usually compared. A luteal phase defect is accompanied by low progesterone levels and occasionally by elevated levels of prolactin. These hormonal imbalances probably impede implantation of a fertilized egg.

Probable treatment. Some of the drugs used to correct hormonal imbalances are considered controversial, and their use should be evaluated carefully for possible side effects. Clomiphene citrate, marketed under the brand name Clomid, is one of the major fertility drugs used in treating LPD because it increases progesterone levels. Progesterone injections or vaginal suppositories are also used, although the effectiveness of these treatments has not been clinically proven.

The primary treatment for prolactin imbalances is a drug called bromocriptine, which does not cure the causes of elevated prolactin but reduces levels for as long as it is taken, usually up to ovulation or through conception.

UTERINE PROBLEMS

Uterine malformations can interfere with a growing pregnancy in a number of ways, some of which are more readily treatable than others. The major uterine disorders and their treatments are:

Abnormally Shaped Uterus

About one in every seven hundred women has some uterine abnormality that developed before she was born. Instead of the normal, pear-shaped uterus, these women may have a heart-shaped uterus, a uterus divided in half by tissue called a septum, or a T-shaped uterus. Any of these abnormalities might cause miscarriage by preventing the uterus from expanding properly to accommodate the pregnancy.

Probable treatment. Only the uterus divided by a septum can be treated successfully with surgery, although some experimental operations are being developed for other malformations. Many women with a septum can sustain healthy, full-term pregnancies, so doctors usually recommend surgery only after miscarriages attributed to the presence of the septum have occurred.

Tilted Uterus

In most women the uterus usually tips slightly forward, but in over 25 percent of women it tilts backward, toward the spine. Doctors now believe that a tilted uterus is not implicated in miscarriages, since the condition usually corrects itself as the pregnancy progresses. A tilted uterus is probably inherited.

Probable treatment. A tilted uterus is easily assessed during a pelvic examination. Since the condition is harmless, corrective surgery is not recommended.

Fibroids

Between 10 and 20 percent of all women develop benign growths called myomas, or fibroid tumors, in the uterine muscle structure. Elevated hormone levels in a pregnant woman can cause some fibroids to grow excessively, changing the architecture of the uterus and interfering with implantation or growth of the pregnancy.

Probable treatment. Most fibroids are harmless and can be detected during a regular gynecological examination. Fibroids that are causing a problem can be treated by drug therapy or surgery.

Scarring and Adhesions

Excessive scarring and bandlike adhesions, also known as Asherman's syndrome, can build up on the inside surface of the uterus, making it incapable of nourishing an implanted embryo.

Probable treatment. With newly developed microsurgical techniques, removal of the scarring can be effective, allowing the uterus to regenerate its lining. However, pregnancies occurring after this corrective surgery has been performed show an increased incidence of complications, including preterm labor.

IMMUNOLOGICAL PROBLEMS

Three primary forms of immunological disorders occur in pregnant women:

Antiphospholipid Syndrome

This disorder occurs when the mother's immune system turns against its own cells and tissues, including a developing placenta. Antiphospholipid syndrome can also cause blood clots to form within the placenta and may be responsible for as much as 10 percent of recurrent miscarriages. The disease can be diagnosed by a combination of patient history, symptoms and certain blood tests.

Probable treatment. One aspirin a day is the most common drug given, followed by aspirin in combination with prednisone, a steroid, or heparin, a blood thinner.

Lupus

Systemic lupus erythematosus, or SLE, is an autoimmune disorder in which the immune system begins to attack normal parts of the body. The cause is unknown, but SLE affects about one million women in the United States. There are a variety of symptoms, including hair loss, specific rashes, light sensitivity and inflammation, but no single test for this condition is conclusive. Pregnant women with lupus have a higher than average rate of both miscarriages and birth defects and often experience flare-ups during pregnancy or following birth. Lupus can be quite disabling and even life-threatening.

Probable treatment. With neither a cause known nor a cure at hand, lupus is difficult to treat. Some of the symptoms can be controlled by rest, diet and drugs, such as anti-inflammatory agents and steroids, both of which can have serious side effects. Some gynecologists are not familiar with lupus, so a woman who wishes to become pregnant and either knows or suspects she has the disease should consult a high-risk-pregnancy specialist or an obstetrician well versed in maternal-fetal medicine.

Fetal Rejection

Problems can occur when the mother's body attacks the fetus as if it were a foreign object, such as happens with a transplanted heart or kidney. In healthy pregnancies this immunological response is suppressed. However, if signals from the father's genetic material are too similar to the mother's, this suppression may not occur, and the pregnancy is attacked.

Probable treatment. The treatment for fetal rejection is controversial and is doubted by many respected doctors; however, it is being pursued by several hospitals in North America and Europe. For information about hospitals with immunological treatment programs, contact the American Society for Reproductive Medicine, listed in Appendix D.

PRETERM LABOR

Mothers who have experienced a loss from preterm labor will probably be treated with strong medications, called tocolytics, after the twentieth week of a subsequent pregnancy, to curb uterine contractions. Current studies indicate that only the mothers experience the immediate side effects from tocolytics; long-term studies on the babies are also encouraging, especially when compared to the known risks of preterm delivery. The drugs used to help stop preterm labor are administered by one or more methods: orally, by injection into a muscle, by injection under the skin and through an intravenous solution. The success of tocolytic drugs depends greatly on early diag-nosis and treatment of preterm labor. The most commonly used tocolytics include:

Ritodrine. Helps inhibit the contractility of the uterine smooth muscles. It is the only FDA-approved drug currently used to manage preterm labor. It causes an elevated heart rate and other potentially serious side effects that should be monitored closely.

Terbutaline. An asthma medication that is very similar to ritodrine in chemical structure. It, too, increases the heart rate and can lead to bouts of nausea, nervousness and other side effects.

Indomethacin. Primarily used as an anti-inflammatory agent in the treatment of rheumatoid arthritis. Since it also inhibits the hormone prostaglandin, it can slow labor. Use of this drug can cause side effects in the mother's gastrointestinal tract and eyes, as well as serious adverse effects in the fetus, including heart problems and a reduction in amniotic fluid.

Magnesium sulfate. A mineral, similar to the compounds found in Epsom salts, that blocks the effects of calcium in muscles, thus inhibiting uterine contractions. Its primary side effects are muscle weakness and nausea.

Procardia. Initially used to treat certain heart conditions and high blood pressure, procardia may also act to reduce uterine contractions.

CERVICAL INCOMPETENCE

Once a diagnosis of cervical incompetence has been established, the treatment is cervical cerclage. The two most common are the Shirodkar cerclage, in which the vagina is incised and the bladder elevated before a band of material is placed around the cervix, and the McDonald cerclage, in which a drawstring type of suture is pulled through the cervix. Both procedures are accomplished through the vagina, but some techniques, for more serious cases, require an incision in the abdomen. Abdominal cerclages are usually performed between pregnancies and are considered permanent, so cesarean deliveries are necessary for subsequent pregnancies. In certain situations abdominal cerclages are performed after the pregnancy has been confirmed.

MATERNAL ILLNESS AS A FACTOR

Illnesses and medical complications that most women would normally endure without much worry can be sources of extreme danger to a fetus, causing both birth defects and pregnancy loss. No medications for any disease or condition, even over-the-counter remedies, should be taken during pregnancy without consulting a doctor first. The following list is not a complete survey of all conditions and treatments that might be harmful to a pregnancy, but it demonstrates the vigilance pregnant women must maintain.

Diabetes

Diabetes is caused by the body's inability to produce enough insulin, resulting in high blood glucose levels, which in turn can cause a variety of metabolic problems. Diabetes in the mother is a frequent cause of birth defects, as well as excessive growth of the baby while in the womb. Diabetic mothers have a higher risk of preeclampsia, miscarriage, still-birth and premature births. During pregnancy some women develop gestational diabetes, which disappears after delivery.

Treatment. Diabetes during pregnancy involves constant monitoring, usually at a specialized medical center. Treatment of a diabetic pregnancy may involve dietary modification, insulin injections and home monitoring of blood glucose levels. Certain prenatal tests, such as that for alpha-fetoprotein and fetal nonstress tests, can be helpful. As long as diabetics are vigilant both before and throughout pregnancy, the prognosis for delivering a healthy baby is almost as good as for other patients. Paternal diabetes seems to have no bearing on the father's offspring.

Hypertension

Hypertension, or high blood pressure, is one of the leading causes of midterm and late losses. It can also pose a danger to the mother. This illness takes two forms during pregnancy. The first is when the mother had high blood pressure before the pregnancy. This condition can predispose her to the second type of hypertension, preeclampsia. Preeclampsia can develop during the latter half of pregnancy in women who may or may not have had previous hypertension. Symptoms include high blood pressure, protein in the urine and tissue swelling due to fluid retention. In addition to endangering the pregnancy, hypertension can place the mother at risk for potentially fatal convulsions and hemorrhaging.

Treatment. For preexisting hypertension, the mother's need for bed rest and blood pressure medication is closely monitored during her pregnancy. The only treatments for preeclampsia are bed rest, observation and blood pressure medication for preexisting hypertension. If symptoms worsen, the baby must be delivered. The mother is given magnesium sulfate during and after labor to prevent seizures.

Measles, Mumps, Rubella and Chicken Pox

All four childhood viral diseases are generally rare in adults in developed countries because of the high incidence during childhood and vaccination, both of which lead to immunity. Of the four, rubella, also known as German measles, is the most dangerous if contracted by a pregnant woman. It can cause severe birth abnormalities, including mental retardation and deafness, as well as miscarriage and stillbirth. Chicken pox, also called varicella, has been occasionally implicated in preterm labor and birth defects. It can also have the most serious effect on the pregnant woman.

Treatment. A woman who wishes to become pregnant can be given a blood test to screen for these immunities long before conception. If she is not immune, she should be vaccinated months before conceiving. The vaccines, which contain noninfectious live viruses, are generally not administered during pregnancy. A chicken pox vaccine is available, but is not widely used in adults. Women who have not had the disease should avoid exposure during pregnancy.

PKU

Phenylketonuria, or PKU, is a genetic disorder that renders its victims incapable of metabolizing phenylalanine, an amino acid that is present in all protein foods, including meats and some vegetables. If left untreated in pregnant mothers, PKU can cause birth defects and miscarriages. Untreated in newborns, the disorder can cause toxic levels of the amino acid to accumulate in the blood, causing severe mental retardation. This outcome can be prevented with a low-phenylalanine diet, which has enabled many women with the disorder to reach childbearing age and contemplate pregnancy. Ordinarily the low-phenylalanine diet is not necessary for adults afflicted with PKU, but pregnancy is an exception. High phenylalanine levels are passed from mother to baby in amounts the fetus cannot handle effectively, causing birth defects and possibly miscarriages.

Treatment. Women with PKU should resume a low-phenylalanine diet as soon as they begin to contemplate pregnancy and should maintain the diet throughout pregnancy. Aspartame, the low-calorie sweetener known by the brand name NutraSweet, found in many diet foods and drinks, breaks down into phenylalanine once it is ingested, so it should be avoided by all women with PKU. Babies born of non-PKU mothers are routinely tested for this ailment in most hospitals, so effective treatment can begin immediately if necessary.

Toxoplasmosis

Toxoplasmosis, which causes fever and flulike symptoms, is produced by a parasite sometimes found in raw meat or the feces of cats that have ingested infected rodents. Once infected, individuals become immune; however, over 60 percent of childbearing-age women have never contracted the disease. The highest risk from infection is from conception to the twenty-fourth week of pregnancy, when serious problems, including birth defects and some chance of miscarriage, can result. Immunity to toxoplasmosis can be detected by a blood test.

Treatment. Once diagnosed, toxoplasmosis is treatable with antibiotics, some of which are safe to take during pregnancy and may reduce the likelihood that the infection will pass to the baby. Prevention in nonimmune women is difficult but can be helped by not eating undercooked meat and by thorough hand washing, particularly after handling cat litter.

Urinary Tract Infections

Urinary tract infections are common complications during pregnancy. If left untreated, they can cause serious kidney ailments that have been implicated in premature labor, low birth weight and newborn death. Accompanying high fevers might also be dangerous to a pregnancy. Sometimes symptoms, such as pain upon urination, or a need to urinate frequently, do not appear.

Treatment. Doctors should check a pregnant woman's urine for the presence of bacteria. If an infection is present, antibiotic treatment is necessary to prevent the development of more serious kidney complications.

Sexually Transmitted Diseases

Sexually transmitted diseases, or STDs, fall into two basic categories: those that cause pelvic inflammatory disease, or PID, and those that do not.

PID-Related Invaders

The most common and dangerous organisms are gonorrhea and chlamydia, both of which have been implicated in premature rupture of the membranes and late miscarriage. Both diseases can be treated with antibiotics following accurate diagnosis, an often difficult task since infection is frequently symptomless.

Non-PID Invaders

Three of the more common sexually transmitted diseases that do not cause PID are AIDS, syphilis and herpes.

AIDS. Acquired immune deficiency syndrome, or AIDS, is caused by a potentially deadly virus, HIV, that is spread through the exchange of blood or by semen. Women contract HIV by either sharing a syringe or having sex with an infected partner. Before HIV was eliminated from blood supplies, it was also transmitted through transfusions and blood products. Women with the virus can infect their babies during pregnancy or childbirth and through breast milk. A woman who thinks she might have been exposed to the virus should have a blood test to determine if she has HIV antibodies.

Syphilis. Left untreated, syphilis progresses through three phases and ultimately attacks nearly every organ and tissue in the human body. In pregnant women, syphilis has been linked to premature labor, stillbirth, newborn death and birth defects. Proper treatment with penicillin or other antibiotics can cure or stop the advancement of syphilis, and a routine blood test can detect its presence.

Herpes simplex. Herpes is a common viral infection that can be transmitted through sexual contact. The body harbors the virus for an indefinite period, causing recurrent episodes of infection. Babies contract herpes as they pass through an infected birth canal, and a first-time infection in the mother after the twentieth week of pregnancy can lead to miscarriage or preterm labor. Several antiviral drugs are used to treat herpes in adults, as well as in newborns.

AGE AS A FACTOR

The United States Census Bureau reported that in 1996 a total of 33 percent of all American babies delivered were born to mothers over thirty, a marked increase over the 19 percent figure in 1976. The high rate of pregnancy for women in this age group is projected to continue. Women are waiting to start families until their careers are established, but there is an unfortunate consequence: The older the mother, the greater the risk of pregnancy loss from chromosomal problems or other causes.

Because a female is born with all the eggs she will ever release in her lifetime, an older mother is likely to have some eggs that have deteriorated over the years. If these eggs are fertilized, they do not have the internal structure to develop into a healthy fetus and will miscarry. Older mothers may be more prone to pregnancy loss because their hormonal system's ability to function properly might decrease with age. Diabetes and high blood pressure, two factors implicated in pregnancy loss, are also more common in older women.

Less research has been done on the effect of paternal age in pregnancy loss, but there is a correlation for structural defects in babies conceived by older fathers.

EXERCISE AS A FACTOR

For centuries women adhered to the custom of "confinement" during pregnancy, a kind of informal house arrest and enforced lack of physical activity. However, being moderately active during a healthy pregnancy is good for you and your developing baby. Check with your doctor about the exercise level she recommends for you, based on your current health and medical history. If your pregnancy is high-risk, your doctor may recommend limiting your physical activity.

PRENATAL DIAGNOSTIC TESTS

The following tests may be used to diagnose problems in pregnancies:

The Triple Test

The triple test analyzes a maternal blood sample drawn between fifteen and twenty weeks' gestation for three substances found in pregnant women: (1) maternal serum alpha-fetoprotein (MSAFP), a protein (2) human chorionic gonadotropin (HCG), a hormone and (3) Estriol, a form of estrogen. When the test results are examined together and compared to other data, they can indicate the possibility of fetal neural tube defects, such as spina bifida and anencephaly, and chromosomal abnormalities, especially Down syndrome. If a defect is suspected, further testing with an ultrasound exam or amniocentesis is necessary.

Research in the early 1990s established that folic acid, a B vitamin, reduces the risk of neural tube defects in babies, but it must be consumed in the early stages of pregnancy to be effective. The Food and Drug Administration (FDA) requires folic acid fortifications in many food products, such as enriched breads, rice and pasta. More recent studies have indicated that the continued presence of folic acid throughout pregnancy can reduce the risk of premature births and low-birth-weight babies.

Amniocentesis

The most common procedure used for genetic testing is amniocentesis. This is the withdrawal of amniotic fluid, along with fetal cells, to examine the cells' genetic makeup. The procedure is usually done between the sixteenth and twentieth weeks of pregnancy. The doctor visualizes the baby's position by ultrasound, then inserts a needle through the mother's abdomen into the amniotic sac and withdraws some fluid. It is important for the *entire procedure* to be done in conjunction with sonography, as babies can move and change positions quickly. A local anesthetic is sometimes used to numb the site where the needle will be inserted. The sensation felt as the needle enters may be of pressure or of slight pain.

Uterine cramping may occur during amniocentesis. In addition, uterine cramping and spotting often occur for a day or two after the procedure with no long-term effects. Conservative obstetricians recommend that a woman rest as much as possible for a couple of days after having an amniocentesis.

Fetal cells from the fluid must be cultured and examined before results are available, a process that takes between one and three weeks. About 1 percent of the time a culture does not grow and the test must be repeated, creating an additional delay.

There is controversy in the medical field about the chance of amniocentesis causing pregnancy loss. The precise reasons why it may cause losses are not really known. A loss probably occurs in about one in two hundred to one in four hundred procedures as a result of amniocentesis. The risk is likely to be on the lower end of the scale if amniocentesis is done at a medical center that specializes in the procedure or by a physician who performs amniocentesis frequently.

Chorionic Villus Sampling

Chorionic villus sampling, or CVS, is a method of obtaining cells from the developing placenta in the first trimester of pregnancy. Since the placenta is derived from the fertilized ovum, its cells show the genetic makeup of the developing fetus.

There are two kinds of CVS procedures currently being done. In *transcervical* CVS, the pregnant woman has her legs in stirrups and must have a full bladder. The cervix is grasped by an instrument, which may feel mildly uncomfortable. Tissue is obtained by means of a slim, sterile tube, or catheter, inserted through the woman's cervix. Slight suction is applied to the catheter, usually painlessly, to obtain the cells. The entire procedure lasts about ten minutes. In the *transabdominal* CVS procedure, the tissue is obtained by passing a needle through the abdominal wall to obtain the cells.

CVS is not as widely used as amniocentesis because CVS has resulted in a slightly higher rate of miscarriage than amniocentesis, with the degree of risk still under debate. Since most spontaneous losses occur in the first trimester of pregnancy, the true rate of loss for CVS is difficult to establish, but is probably about 1 percent greater than a loss due to amniocentesis. This is considerably lower than the risk couples are generally quoted, often given as a 3 percent to 5 percent chance of miscarriage as a direct result of CVS.

Many prospective parents prefer CVS over amniocentesis, as CVS can be performed early in the pregnancy, with results available within one to two weeks. If the couple is told of a problem, they can end the pregnancy in the first trimester. This is emotionally less traumatic and medically safer than a later procedure.

Amniocentesis is much more widely available than CVS because most obstetricians can perform amniocentesis but not CVS. Rather than refer a woman to a specialist for CVS, many doctors simply recommend and perform amniocentesis.

PROCEDURES FOR ENDING AN IMPAIRED PREGNANCY

You should be aware of the different procedures available to end an impaired pregnancy and discuss the options thoroughly with your doctor. Depending on how far along your pregnancy is, certain methods may be legally restricted in some areas or may pose health risks to the mother. Experts agree that seeing an impaired baby after the procedure, in order to say good-bye and reconfirm your choice, is an important first step toward healthy grieving. Some parents who chose either a D&C or a D&E may later feel that they lost an important opportunity to be with their baby. If you wish to see your baby, only induction of labor provides you with that option. The four basic procedures are:

Dilatation and curettage: In a D&C, the cervix is dilatated and the uterus gently suctioned first to remove most of the pregnancy. Then a long metal instrument with an open spoon-shaped tip is inserted into the uterus, and the sides are gently scraped of placenta or uterine lining. A D&C is usually performed up to twelve weeks of pregnancy and can be done as an outpatient procedure in a clinic or a hospital.

Dilatation and evacuation: A D&E may be done in a hospital or clinic between twelve and twenty weeks' gestation. Laminaria sticks, which dilate the cervix, are inserted into the cervix the night before the procedure. The next day the woman is usually given local anesthesia. A suction pump removes the uterine lining and the pregnancy. The woman can usually go home immediately after the procedure is done and can expect a rapid physical recovery. However, since the baby is usually not delivered intact, it may be difficult to see or hold. Knowing this, many doctors now prefer to avoid this method, so their patients may begin a healthy grieving response by being with their baby.

Induction of labor: Prostaglandin suppositories or injections, with or without laminaria sticks to aid in dilatating the cervix, are the most frequently used methods for inducing labor to end a pregnancy.

When labor is induced, the procedure may take from several hours to a day. As with any labor, it is painful, but medication and an epidural are available to ameliorate the pain. Women who go through this ordeal usually find the presence of their partner or another support person extremely helpful.

Pregnancy reduction: This medical procedure is used in rare instances to induce the demise of some, but not all, of the fetuses in a multiple pregnancy. The technique is employed in two situations: when a fetus in a multiple pregnancy has been diagnosed with a severe impairment, or when a women conceives a large multiple gestation that if brought to term would compromise her health and the well-being of all the babies. Pregnancy reduction is performed only by a highly trained physician in conjunction with sonography, since it involves steps similar to an amniocentesis. The risk of introducing infection or triggering preterm labor is relatively high, so parents must understand that the procedure may jeopardize the entire pregnancy. Pregnancy reduction is usually performed in a doctor's office with topical anesthesia.

Appendix B

Rituals

Planning a good-bye ritual for your baby may be one of the saddest tasks you will ever have to perform. But putting the time and effort into creating a tender, meaningful farewell can give you the chance to release and share your grief. A ritual can help begin the healing process, and continue it with memories you will cherish for a lifetime.

Whether you write your own poems and prayers for your baby, ask a sensitive member of the clergy to create a ritual or use some of the ceremonies suggested here, try to keep several issues in mind. Ask that your baby be mentioned by name. Using the baby's name and referring to the infant as "he" or "she," "our daughter" or "our son," can help you grasp your loss and move through your grief. If your loss was too early to know the baby's gender, try referring to the child as "our infant" or "our baby." Mentioning the baby specifically and personally will also help friends and relatives who attend the service understand the magnitude of your loss.

In deciding what should be said at the service, consider sharing the dreams and hopes you had for your child, since you will not have a lifetime of memories to cherish. Allow time for friends and family to speak or to read poems or selections, which adds to the feeling of community during a service. If your ritual will be held in the hospital, consider inviting members of the medical staff who cared for you or your infant. There could also be time for people to hold hands during the service, or even hug one another. Participants often find the physical expression of emotion during a memorial service both freeing and comforting.

It can be important to acknowledge negative feelings toward God and your faith, as well as the comfort you may feel, during the service. Only by recognizing anger, guilt and frustration can these emotions ever be overcome. Certain passages from Scripture, such as Psalm 51, express the sense that God understands sorrow and anger and accepts our feelings, no matter what they are.

You may want to incorporate symbols and gestures into your service that have particular meaning to you. A symbolic expression Sister Jane Marie Lamb has fostered is the lighting and extinguishing of candles, representing "the fire of life kindled in the womb and the untimely death of the baby." She also has suggestions for the creative and metaphorical use of helium balloons as a symbol of the release of grief and the baby to God; these are outlined in her book *Bittersweet . . . hellogoodbye.*

Whatever form your personal ritual takes, trust your own instincts and judgments. This was your pregnancy and your baby. It should be your good-bye as well.

CHOOSING A PLACE

If your baby is to be cremated or buried, a simple service may be held in the hospital chapel or a funeral home, with another brief prayer and Scripture reading at the grave or the site where the baby's ashes are to be scattered. Parents who are members of a congregation may want to have a more formal service in their regular house of worship; others prefer to gather in an informal setting, such as their own home or backyard, for their baby's service.

If there is no burial, you may still wish to hold a service. If you had the baby cremated and you choose not to scatter the ashes, you may also wish to hold a service. Some parents decide to scatter the ashes at a later time or reserve a portion of the ashes to bury with themselves eventually or to keep with them in case they move from their current home. A ceremony can be combined with a tree-planting in your yard, for which there are specific services in Jane Marie Lamb's *Bittersweet . . . hellogoodbye.* For Jews, making a donation to a synagogue, a charity or the Jewish National Fund, which plants trees in Israel, is a traditional way of honoring the memory of a loved one.

INCLUDING GRANDPARENTS

Including the baby's grandparents during a ritual can be a sensitive way to acknowledge their particular grief, especially if they did not have the opportunity to see their grandchild. You might ask them to read a special prayer, Scripture or poem. Participating can provide grandparents with a powerful expression of their love for your baby, but you should understand if they choose not to do so.

OTHER WAYS TO RITUALIZE YOUR GRIEF

If you wish to acknowledge your baby's importance within a spiritual context but prefer to have the hospital or a religious society handle the burial, you may simply incorporate private prayers in a house of worship during a weekly service or on a special religious holiday. Jews might want to say the Kaddish at any religious service, including Yiskor, the service that especially honors departed loved ones on major holidays such as Yom Kippur. Christians might choose All Saints' Day, an Easter service or a candle-lighting ceremony at Christmas. You could ask a member of the clergy to remember your baby in her own private devotions or during her weekly pastoral prayer to the congregation.

Another way of giving expression to your grief is to create a memory book for your baby. Some of the organizations listed in Appendix D offer books specifically designed for this purpose. A simple baby book or a plain album you could entitle "Baby Memories" would be effective. Some families prefer small, delicate wicker baskets or ornamental boxes that can be filled with baby mementos. Depending on how far advanced your pregnancy was before your loss occurred, you might consider including:

- An early sonogram picture
- A copy of other prenatal test results, such as a photo of the baby's chromosomes from amniocentesis
- Footprints
- A lock of hair
- Naming certificate (certificate of life)
- Birth certificate
- Hospital ID bracelet
- Letters of condolence
- List of baby shower presents
- List of contributions made in honor of the baby
- A dried, pressed flower (this could also be framed) from the funeral
- Photographs of the baby
- A copy of the memorial or funeral service and any poems or prayers that were read to the baby
- Artwork created by family and friends in honor of the baby, such as drawings made by an older sibling or embroidery done by a loving grandmother
- A photograph of the mother while she was pregnant, even if she wasn't yet showing

CREATING A RITUAL

The rituals provided here are meant to be a point of departure for developing a service which is meaningful to you. Most of these prayers, Scripture readings, musical selections and blessings can be adapted to early losses as well as late losses, to Jewish beliefs as well as to Christian or other faiths. If you do not have a member of the clergy present, a relative or friend could take the part of the "leader" or "friend." Even parents who have grown away from their faith, or who are in marriages of mixed religions, may find a ritual comforting, especially if they help design it themselves.

There are books available from some of the resources listed in Appendix D that include more elaborate services and detailed suggestions. The elements of the ritual may be arranged in any order that seems suitable, but here is a suggested format that would last about half an hour:

Musical selection playing as people gather
Prayer by a member of the clergy
Scripture reading by a relative or friend
Song or hymn sung together
Reading of poem by a parent
Reading by a relative or friend
Naming or blessing of the baby by a member of the clergy
Scripture reading by a relative or friend
Prayer by a member of the clergy
            or
Responsive reading led by a member of the clergy
Musical selection for silent prayer
Blessing of the parents by a member of the clergy
Song or hymn sung together
Benediction by a member of the clergy

BIBLE SCRIPTURE

Some parents prefer the older, traditional Bible translations, while others feel more comfortable using inclusive, modern language, even assuming a female aspect to God. Jews may wish to use the *Tanakh,* a modern translation of the Hebrew Bible issued by the Jewish Publication Society; Christians may wish to read from *Today's English Bible,* published by the American Bible Society, or the *New Revised Standard Version* of the Bible, published by the National Council of Churches of Christ. Muslims will find many comforting passages in the Qur'an and interpretations of the Prophet's teachings.

Holy Scripture

(from the shared Jewish and Christian tradition in alphabetical order)

Ecclesiastes 3:1–11; "To everything there is a season ..."
Isaiah 43:1–2; "I have called you by name and you are mine ..."
Jeremiah 1:4–6; God knows babies in the womb and consecrates them
Jeremiah 31:13–17; God will turn mourning into comfort; God hears Rachel weeping for her children
Job 1:21; "Naked I came out of my mother's womb ...The Lord giveth and the Lord taketh away ..."
Job 3:6–16; The nature of stillbirth
Psalm 23; We can be comforted as we walk through the Valley of the Shadow of Death, as God walks with us

Psalm 51:1, 6, 8, 17; God will not despise a broken and contrite heart
Psalm 139:1–17; God knows your feelings and God knows your baby
Psalm 147:3–13; God knows all the stars by name and blesses children in the
  womb
Zechariah 12:10–11; Mourning for a child is overwhelming

Holy Scripture
(from the Christian tradition in order of appearance)

Matthew 5:5; "Blessed are those who mourn, for they shall be comforted"
Mark 10:13–17; "Let the little children come unto me"
John 11:35; "Jesus wept"
I Corinthians 13:4–13; The "love" chapter; "Love endureth all things ... When I
  was child ..."
II Corinthians 1:3–5; God comforts us so we can comfort others; one of the
  secrets to healing is that in helping others you help yourself
Hebrews 5:7–8; Jesus understood tears and learned from his own suffering

—With thanks to Sister Jane Marie Lamb

SCRIPTURES FROM THE QUR'AN

Chapter 2, verse 177; "To be firm and patient in pain or suffering ..."
Chapter 2, verse 286; "On no soul doth Allah place a burden greater than it
  can bear ..."
Chapter 3, verse 17; "For those who show patience ..."

Narrated by Abu Sa'id Al-Khudri and Abu Huraira:

Chapter 1, verse 7–545; "No fatigue, no disease, nor sadness ..."
Chapter 1, verse 7–548; "From whatever direction the wind comes ..."

MUSIC

Musical selections can provide the tender mood you wish to set for your
baby's service. Depending on the setting, there may be a piano or organ
available; if not, an accomplished singer or guitarist can lead the group
in song. Singing together can evoke the sense of community you need.
If you prefer to listen to musical selections, many of the popular songs,
show tunes and classical pieces listed here are readily available on tape.

Classical Selections

Ludwig van Beethoven, "Für Elise"
Leonard Bernstein, *Candide*, Act I, "It Must Be So," in which Candide learns that
  "There is a sweetness in every woe"
Leonard Bernstein, *West Side Story*, Act I, "One Hand, One Heart," in which
  Tony and Maria sing, "Even death won't part us now"
Johannes Brahms, "Cradle Songs," known as "Brahms' Lullaby"

Frédéric Chopin, *Prélude,* Op. 28, No. 7

Gustav Mahler, *Kindertotenlieder* (Songs for Deceased Children), especially No. 4, "Often I think you have only gone out and will return . . ."

Wolfgang Mozart, *Requiem*—especially the "Lacrimosa," "Hostias," "Agnus Dei" and "Lux Aeterna" sections

Henry Purcell, *Dido and Aeneas,* "Dido's Lament," from Act III; Dido asks to be remembered after death

Maurice Ravel, *Pavane* ("On the death of an infant . . .")

Camille Saint-Saëns, *Carnival of the Animals,* especially "The Swan" and "Aquarium"

Robert Schumann, *Scenes from Childhood,* especially "From Foreign Lands and People," "Träumerei (Dreaming)," and "Child Falling Asleep"

Richard Strauss, *Four Last Songs,* especially No. 3

Popular Music

"You'll Never Walk Alone" (from *Carousel*)

"Somewhere Out There" (from *An American Tale*)

"Blessed Are" (by Joan Baez)

"Turn, Turn, Turn" (from Ecclesiastes, adapted by Pete Seeger)

"It's All Right to Cry" (by Carol Hall)

"You Have to Hurt" (by Carly Simon)

"In My Life" (by John Lennon and Paul McCartney)

Christian Hymns and Spirituals

"What a Friend We Have in Jesus"

"Still, Still with Thee"

"Amazing Grace"

"The Day Thou Gavest, Lord, Is Ending"

"Blest Be the Tie That Binds"

"Jesus Loves Me"

"Nearer, My God, to Thee"

"Be Thou My Vision"

"Abide with Me"

"O God, Our Help in Ages Past"

"Now the Day Is Over"

BAPTISMS, BLESSINGS AND NAMING RITUALS

Baptism is a rite of passage for the living, a sacrament of repentance and discipleship. Most members of the clergy therefore feel it should not be applied to early losses or stillbirths. However, a blessing for a deceased baby can be worded so that the profound imagery of water inherent in baptism is maintained without the actual sacrament being given. This blessing can be combined with a naming ceremony.

The person officiating can describe the significance of water in this manner while blessing the baby:

Water, one of the most important elements of creation, is essential for human life in countless ways. In our grief it becomes the symbol of God's cleansing and forgiveness, the power of spiritual renewal and the flow of life throughout the ages. With water we now bless this child:

O God of creation,
Your spirit moved over the waters of the universe
To create life in its first struggling forms.
You led your people through the waters of the seas to salvation.
Your power moves in the waters of the womb to hold and protect us.
Bless this baby [name] in your love. Amen.

We bathe this child in the love of God. We bathe this child in the tears of her parents. We know the power of water to permeate life and hold this child. The water of the womb sustained this child as the water of the universe and the power of God will hold her now. Amen.

—Adapted and used with permission from
Sister Mary Claire VanOrsdal, OSU

This ritual can be combined with the naming of the baby, usually by asking the parents, "What name have you given your child?" and can be as powerful and comforting as baptism. The feeling of commitment to the baby can be especially strong if a naming certificate is completed and handed to the parents at the close of the service. Sister Jane Marie Lamb has established the custom of using a small seashell to hold water for blessing or baptizing a baby. When the ceremony is finished, the member of the clergy gives the seashell to the parents as a cherished keepsake.

RESPONSIVE READING

Responsive reading is a powerful form of prayer that includes everyone who attends the service. A litany in which the "leader" pleas for God's mercy followed by the group's unison recitation of a reply, such as "God, hear our prayer," can evoke the sense of community so important in saying good-bye to your baby. The following responsive readings can be adapted to suit the needs of each bereaved family. Christians may say "Jesus" for "God."

Responsive Reading after a Pregnancy Loss

Choose one of the following responses:

God, hear us
Be with us, God
God, grant us healing and strength
Hear us, Mother [or Father] God

LEADER:

For the time of unending tears, pain and struggle;
times of not being understood by family, friends,
times of longing and emptiness,
times of not being in control,
times of searching within and without.
We pray . . .
Response

LEADER:

For all the memories of our baby;
for any brief moment of being with our baby,
for those who walked the journey of mourning with us,
for each time of remembering.
We pray . . .
Response

LEADER:

For the times of letting go,
for the times of reaching out,
for each new day and each ray of hope,
for the gifts our baby left us:
    in giving us new eyes with which to see,
    new ears to help us hear others,
    a new heart to love more deeply,
    and for new values in our lives.
We pray . . .
Response

—Adapted with permission from *Bittersweet*
. . . *hellogoodbye,* by Sister Jane Marie Lamb

PRAYERS
Prayer following Pregnancy Loss

May the Holy One who blessed our mothers
Sarah, Rebeccah, Rachel, and Leah,
bless and protect [name of mother].
May the wounds she has suffered,
both physical and emotional,
soon be healed.
May she find comfort in knowing
that You, O God, weep with her.
May the Source of Life,

the Creator of all flesh,
restore her body to its rhythms
and her soul to its songs of joy.
As she and [baby's father's name] stand before You
help them to move forward
to feel the pain,
acknowledge the loss
and move forward.
May all of us here be committed to living
always aware that we are created in Your image,
by caring, supporting, and loving one another
in times of pain as well as in times of joy.
As we have wept together,
so may we soon gather to rejoice together.
And let us all say
Amen.

—by Rabbi Diane Cohen, used with permission

A Prayer for Mothers

Mothers may not feel up to reading during their baby's funeral or memorial service, so this prayer is written to be read by someone else. If a mother did wish to read the prayer, it could be adapted by replacing all the personal pronouns with *me* or *my.*

O God of love, source of life,
Hear our prayers for [name of mother]
Her baby died before it ever came to birth.
The blessing of your love was torn from her body, leaving her
    empty and devastated.
Comfort her in her sorrow.
Restore her hope for a child to come.
Give her courage and new delight in the days ahead.
In good time, grant her a new life that her soul may rejoice and
    her body give birth.
Amen.

—Reprinted from *Prayers of Our Hearts,* copyright © 1991 by Vienna Cobb Anderson, with the permission of The Crossroad Publishing Company, New York

A Prayer for Fathers

Fathers have their own special grief, which may be overlooked in rituals. Be sure to include the father's thoughts, prayers or poems. Here is a prayer fathers may recite during the service:

God, my child has died! I want to scream that at you, as if you did not already know. I hurt so badly inside that somehow it seems easier to endure if I scream at someone or at some power. My grief is two-sided, God. I grieve for the life that will never be, the life that lived only for a while in its mother's womb. We wanted that life, God, we wanted it desperately. It is over now, and it has produced a grief that seems unendurable.

The other side of my grief comes from my dreams and fantasies that have also died and been buried. I was going to be such a good father. My child would have known the joy of being loved and cherished. We would have walked through scented woods, touched the sky on lofty mountaintops, had fantasies of walking on the stars, whirled dizzily and screamed uninhibitedly on some fast-moving ride, held warm puppies, stared in wonder at an intricate spider's web, and we would have dreamed together. Now my dreams are gone, and I cannot seem to revive them. God, let me dream again dreams of hope. Let me know happiness once again. Revive my dreams, God, they are so far from me now.
Amen.

—Adapted and reprinted with permission from
Comfort Us, Lord—Our Baby Died,
by Norman E. Hagley

READING FOR A MISCARRIED BABY

Today we come together in sorrow over the death of [name of mother] and [name of father]'s baby. Their child, created in love and eagerly wished for, has died—never to be nestled securely in their arms in this lifetime. To these parents, the pain and the disappointment are great, and their loss will be carried heavily in their hearts in the weeks and months ahead. They will miss their child terribly and will be in need of love, compassion, time, and understanding from all of us.

Each life comes into this world with a mission. Sometimes the mission or purpose is clear; sometimes it is vague and shrouded in misunderstandings. In time, we will see what this baby's mission was on earth. Could it have been just to add a little flicker of love that otherwise may never have been lit? Was it to soften our hearts so that we may in turn comfort others? Could it have been to bring us closer to our God and each other?

This child's life was short, yet the death has left a huge void in all of our hearts and lives. Let us remember today and for always the tiny baby who will never see childhood or adulthood, but will remain our tiny baby forever.

—Susan Erling; reprinted with permission
from *Planning a Precious Goodbye,*
by Sherokee Ilse and Susan Erling,
published by Wintergreen Press

RITUAL FOR PREGNANCY LOSS

This ecumenical ritual can be combined with musical selections and may be adapted for early or full-term losses. Christian references have been placed in parentheses and can be added as needed.

LEADER: God, you are our refuge and our fortress.

MOTHER: I am so overwhelmed with sorrow, words do not express how I feel now. My dreams have been shattered, yet will I trust God.

FATHER: We can continue to trust God. We can lay our plans for the future and our new dreams can fill us with hope.

MOTHER [Scripture reading: Psalm 139:13-16 from *The Living Bible*, paraphrase translation]: You made, O God, all of the delicate parts of my body and knit them together in my mother's womb. Thank you for making me so wonderfully complex. It is amazing to think about. Your workmanship is marvelous and how well I know it. You were there while I was being formed in utter seclusion. You saw me before I was born and scheduled each day of my life before I began to breathe. Every day was recorded in your book.

PEOPLE: God speaks to us in many ways,
And often through our days,
We find God's love so near at hand,
Yet often we fail to understand.

MOTHER: Oh, how we longed to share life with you, our baby; to hold you in our arms, to look into your eyes, to see your first steps, to hear your first words, to feel your hands clinging to ours, to watch you gather seashells in your pail along the sandy beach, to read books to you at bedtime, and to observe you grow in wisdom, in stature, and in favor with God and humankind.

PEOPLE: O God, comfort your children whose hearts are now sad and heavy with bereavement.

LEADER: Merciful God, we thank you for your promises to sustain and comfort us, even when we lack understanding of why you would have given life and taken it away again so quickly. Through our tears, enable us to see the consolation you intend for us.

MOTHER: Although my dreams have crumbled into dust, I shall dare to have faith in God. God has not planned a sorrow for me that cannot be healed. I am grateful for all the blessings God has bestowed upon me, my partner, my family and friends, including the strength to rise and face the future.

PEOPLE: (Blessed are they that mourn, for they shall be comforted.) We are here because we love you and would share in your sorrow.

FATHER [*Turning toward mother*]: I am confident that God (and the Holy Mother Mary) will care for our unborn child and love [him/her; name of baby, or "our baby"] forever. God accepts that no matter how short our child's life was, it was still the pure embodiment of the love we shared for life and for each other. As we commit our child unto the arms of God, I give you this rose. Long after it has faded we shall remember its beauty and our child. *[He gives her the rose and bends over and kisses her.]*

MOTHER: How grateful we are for God's love that binds us together in joy, in sorrow, in life, and in death.

LEADER: ("Suffer little children to come unto me and forbid them not, for of such is the kingdom of heaven.") O God, comfort and strengthen us in the assurance that the ties which are broken here are still preserved in the love that made them ours.

PEOPLE: We who are here share your sorrow,
> Yet we behold another tomorrow,
> Another day that God doth give,
> Now, let us love and continue to live.

LEADER: May God bless you and keep you and may your troubled minds and hearts find peace in God's everlasting love. *[People rise and hug and kiss each other and depart.]*

> —Created by the Reverend Walton Denson Moffitt;
> used with permission

ANNIVERSARY RITUAL

Many bereaved parents recognize the need to acknowledge their loss not only in the moment, but also as the sorrow becomes integrated into their lives. The following prayer could be read privately or in front of others, perhaps once a week in the beginning and then once a year:

Hear my prayer, O God of love.
Give me the courage to face life again, to make new friendships, new commitments, and to risk loving and losing love. Embolden me to reach out to others and to try new things. Let the love that I have known for my baby be my surety that you will always be with me until my life's end. Bless my child with your eternal love. In the name of God, Amen.

> —Adapted from *Prayers of Our Hearts,* copyright © 1991 by
> Vienna Cobb Anderson. Reprinted with the permission of
> The Crossroad Publishing Company, New York

RITUAL FOR A SUBSEQUENT PREGNANCY

Some parents may wish to acknowledge the passing of each week as the pregnancy progresses; others may prefer to mark only the conception and the birth. Rabbi Nina Beth Cardin developed a weekly ritual when she discovered she was pregnant following her own losses. She gathered her family together for the weekly lighting of the Sabbath candles, lighting one for each member of her family. She then added one extra candle, which remained unlit during each week that followed the confirmation of her pregnancy. As she explained:

> The candle was there marking the start of life, whose significance wouldn't be lost if it ended, even if it was only a brief existence. When the baby was eventually born, we gathered around that first Friday night after the birth and finally lit the candle that had remained unlit for nine months.

The following prayer may be read during the ritual:

Prayer for a Safe Pregnancy

This life you have given us
is so tiny, fragile, and vulnerable,
safe in the womb of flesh and hope,
yet subject to danger and death.
O God of love, creator of life, hear our prayer.
We want this baby so much.
Please grant this child of ours
a full term of nurture,
the joy and mystery of life,
and the blessing of your love.
Grant us the fulfillment of our dreams,
a baby to cherish and protect, a child to teach and guide,
a blessing to our family;
in the name of God (of your chosen child, Jesus Christ),
we pray.
Amen.

—Reprinted from *Prayers of Our Hearts,* copyright © 1991 by Vienna Cobb Anderson. Reprinted with the permission of The Crossroad Publishing Company, New York

RITUALS FOR ENDING A PREGNANCY

Parents who decide to end a pregnancy may want to set aside some private moments to say good-bye to their baby, either before or after the procedure, to express their love and the deep sorrow they feel that the baby could not survive or would have lived with a diminished quality of life.

Ritual for Ending a Pregnancy

LEADER: *God, Mother of us all, we ask Your blessing upon [parents' names] and all who face this difficult choice. Thank You for granting them the wisdom to make their choice and the courage to act upon it, all while embracing the knowledge of*

Your love. Grant unto all women the support and love we offer unto [parents' names] this day and always. Bind us close in Your love and keep us faithful in our friendships. Hear our prayer, O God, our Mother and grant us mercy and forgiveness upon all our lives.
Amen.

The mother may wish to read the following prayer:

The choice has been made.
One of the hardest of my life.
Bless me as I go forth.
Help me to face the guilt I feel
so that I may not run away from the truth.
Empower me to own the fear in my heart
that I may have compassion
for others who share my pain.
Bless all who support me
with the strength of their love;
In the name of God (Jesus Christ).
Amen.

The mother and father may wish to make an "act of dedication," individually or jointly in the name of their child, and ask for friends' support to keep their vow. The promise should be personal, specific and attainable, such as "In the name of our child, we promise to give $ _____ every month for the coming year to support a homeless child" or "In the name of our child, we promise we will plant a garden on the street where all who pass by may see the abundance of God's grace."

Prayer [*as water is poured from a pitcher into a bowl placed in front of the woman*]:

LEADER: We pour this water as a symbol of the tears of mourning, the forgiveness of guilt, and the beginning of a new life for you. We beseech God to uphold you and to fill you with grace, that you may know the healing power of God's divine love. We give you our love, promising to stand by you now and through the days to come. Amen.
[*At the end, friends greet one another with hugs, the sign of friendship and peace.*]

—Adapted from *Prayers of Our Hearts,* copyright © 1991 by Vienna Cobb Anderson. Reprinted with the permission of The Crossroad Publishing Company, New York

Appendix C

Pregnancy Loss and the Environment

As we learn to accept the emotional needs of bereaved parents, we must also learn to understand the larger issues that impact on pregnancy loss. Pregnancy outcome can be affected by numerous factors, from exposures to certain toxic substances to the grinding poverty that denies many pregnant women good prenatal care.

To protect our future children, we must think beyond what a mother eats for nine months or which diseases she might contract during pregnancy. We must consider the quality of the air she breathes, the pollutants her baby's father may have been exposed to at work and what prenatal medical care her dollars can buy.

It is incumbent upon us to halt increased damage to our environment and, ultimately, ourselves. We must become educated and vocal opponents of policies that allow reckless and hazardous exposure to occur or that leave vast members of the human race without access to good medical care. We should support efforts to regulate harmful substances, not just in our own backyards but worldwide. We must become advocates for a cleaner, safer, more ethically managed, environmentally equitable planet so that we will give all unborn babies a better chance in life.

THE MECHANISM OF EXPOSURE

Harmful substances can enter the body by being inhaled, ingested or absorbed through the skin or mucous membranes. Some types of radiation can penetrate human tissues, and most toxins can cross the placenta. Harmful agents can have an impact on the mother, father or developing baby in one of several ways: (1) by damaging the structure of sperm, ova or embryonic cells, so they do not grow properly; (2) by altering the number or pairing of chromosomes within a cell; (3) by affecting the genetic material within the chromosomes; or (4) by compromising some bodily function in the baby or the mother, including the placenta.

240

Once a hazardous agent does its damage, the baby may stop growing properly, triggering a miscarriage, or the unborn baby may develop a disorder that could lead to abnormalities or stillbirth. Risk assessment of potentially harmful exposures covers a much longer time frame than was previously recognized. Some exposures may occur after birth through the mother's breast milk; others, such as DES, may not become evident until the child reaches sexual maturity.

Cause and effect cannot be determined from case reports or "clusters" of incidences. Controlled scientific studies are always necessary. Although clusters may alert scientists to a serious problem, as they did with the drugs thalidomide and DES, they are never the final word. Even large doses of substances given to pregnant animals in controlled laboratory tests do not necessarily correspond to most human exposures.

If you are pregnant or plan on becoming pregnant, you should consult your doctor about avoiding any potential hazards.

EXPOSURES WITH KNOWN RISKS

Many substances are regulated because they have an established detrimental effect on health, but only four are restricted in the workplace because of their known reproductive hazards: ionizing radiation, lead, a pesticide called DBCP, and ethylene oxide, a sterilizing compound used on medical equipment and in some food processing. Products available for home use may contain harmful substances, but it is up to the consumer to read the warning labels and take precautions.

In addition to DBCP and ethylene oxide, the following substances are known to have a harmful effect on pregnancy outcome based on current, conclusive scientific documentation:

Alcohol definitely has an effect on pregnancy, but it varies with the frequency and amount ingested and at the point during pregnancy it is consumed. No clear, safe level of alcohol has been established during pregnancy. Pregnant women who drink run an increased risk of miscarrying or giving birth to babies with growth and mental abnormalities associated with fetal alcohol syndrome. If you are having trouble giving up alcohol, seek help from Alcoholics Anonymous or an alcoholism referral organization.

Chemotherapy treatments are designed to interfere with the rapid division of cells, so there is concern about using chemotherapy on a pregnant patient. The effect on pregnant medical staff who work with these drugs has not been thoroughly examined, but one study indicated that pregnant health care professionals who handled chemotherapy medications in the first trimester had a statistically significant increase in miscarriage rates. Patients can have healthy pregnancies following certain chemotherapy treatments.

Lead is a toxic metal that accumulates in the body primarily through exposure to industrial waste and contact with old paint and plumbing. Its adverse effect on pregnancy is not known at low levels but is confirmed at high levels of exposure. The Environmental Protection Agency (EPA) has banned and phased out lead in gasoline, motor oil, paints and plumbing.

Smoking tobacco has long been implicated in heart disease, lung disease and cancer, but recent studies have also shown a correlation between smoking and an increase in miscarriage rates, stillbirth, placental separation, newborn death and birth defects. Men who smoke tend to have lower sperm counts and a higher incidence of damaged sperm, which could lead to additional reproductive problems and loss. More research is needed to assess the relationship between inhaling secondary smoke and the health of unborn children, but the risks to the mother are so clear that a pregnant woman should not smoke or be around smokers. If you are having trouble quitting, contact your local chapter of the American Lung Association or the American Cancer Society about programs they recommend for breaking the habit.

X rays should be used with caution during pregnancy. In some medical situations, X rays are the best diagnostic tool. A pregnant woman should feel safe having the examination as long as proper precautions are taken by a knowledgeable physician. A woman who did not realize she was pregnant when she had a diagnostic X ray should not end her pregnancy without consulting a specialist, since it is unlikely that low doses would harm the developing baby.

EXPOSURES SUSPECTED OF RISKS

Some substances have been subjected to studies, but the results have been flawed, contradictory or inconclusive. Because genuine concerns remain, these agents should be avoided until further study:

Caffeine is a stimulant that is a major ingredient in a number of foods, beverages and over-the-counter medicines, which by law must specify the drug on the package. Some studies have linked caffeine consumption to a greater risk of miscarriage, stillbirth and premature birth, but the strong association between caffeine and cigarette smoking, which has definitely been proved harmful, may have skewed the results.

Cocaine is an illegal stimulant that can produce an intense euphoria or "high." It constricts the mother's blood vessels, increases her heart rate and causes a rise in blood pressure, all of which may affect the incidence of preterm delivery and placental abruption. The outcomes of some studies may be clouded by such factors as the incidence of poor nutrition and other drug use among cocaine users.

Glycol-ethers are a group of chemicals widely used in a number of products such as varnishes, spray lacquers and metal-cleaning formulas. Animal tests indicate glycol-ethers may have a potent effect on both male and female reproduction, but no extensive studies have been done in humans.

Mercury accumulates in the body from environmental exposures and has been implicated in birth defects. Inorganic mercury enters the water supply primarily through industrial wastes. Fish absorb the mercury and transform it into an organic form that is extremely toxic to people who eat the fish. Accidental exposure to inorganic mercury by breaking a thermometer is not serious. There are no reliable studies on the risks of exposure to inorganic mercury, a common amalgam used in dentistry.

Power plants vary in hazards according to the source of power. Coal-burning plants are the most dangerous, since they spew harmful emissions, including some radioactive material. Nuclear power plants are highly regulated, and the radioactive emissions are lower than those of coal plants, but the danger comes from catastrophic accidents, such as the one in Chernobyl, and from the leakage of stored radioactive waste products.

EXPOSURES WHOSE RISKS ARE UNKNOWN

Some exposures have been questioned because "cluster" incidences of miscarriages have been noticed. In other situations, exposure to a hazardous agent is known, but increased risk of pregnancy loss has not been demonstrated. Further scientific study is needed in the following areas: the nonionizing electromagnetic radiation emitted by electrical appliances, video display terminals, radio towers and high-tension wires; exposure to additional radiation levels during extended air travel at high altitudes; the chemicals in hair and nail care products; and exposure to radon, a radioactive gas that can enter homes from the soil beneath them.

Always consult your doctor to avoid as many potential risks as possible during your pregnancy.

Appendix D

Resources

RESOURCES FOR PREGNANCY LOSS

The following alphabetically listed organizations supply a variety of materials and services, including parent newsletters, books, hospital bereavement protocols and pamphlets on pregnancy loss. Several offer bereavement workshops and guidance on starting a pregnancy loss support group in your own community. Others maintain Internet chat rooms and support networks for bereaved parents. Asterisked organizations carry special items such as announcement cards, certificates of life, baby memory books, burial cradles and baby bunting burial gowns for even the tiniest infants. Contact the individual organization and request information on the services and materials it provides. Some may require a membership fee for their services.

AMEND (Aiding a Mother Experiencing Neonatal Death)
4324 Berrywick Terrace
St. Louis, MO 63128
   Phone: 314-487-7582
   Toll-free: none
   Fax: none
   E-mail: none
   Web site: none

Association for Recognition of Life of Stillbirths
11128 West Front Avenue
Littleton, CO 80127
   Phone: 303-978-9517
   Toll-free: none
   Fax: none
   E-mail: linpav@aol.com
   Web site: none

* Bereavement Services (formerly "Resolve Through Sharing")
  La Crosse Lutheran Hospital
  1910 South Avenue
  La Crosse, WI 54601
      Phone: 608-791-4747
      Toll-free: 800-362-9567 ext. 4747
      Fax: 608-791-5137
      E-mail: berservs@gundluth.org
      Web site: www.gundluth.org/bereave

* Bonnie Babies
  Jean Morrisey, President
  15 Clelland Road
  Lexington, MA 02421-4120
      Phone: 781-674-0071
      Toll-free: none
      Fax: none
      E-mail: DSAngelMom@aol.com
      Web site: none

* Centering Corporation
  1531 North Saddle Creek Road
  Omaha, NE 68104
      Phone: 402-553-1200
      Toll-free: none
      Fax: 402-553-0507
      E-mail: jl200@aol.com
      Web site: none

  Compassion Books (formerly The Rainbow Connection)
  477 Hannah Branch Road
  Burnsville, NC 28714
      Phone: 828-675-5909
      Toll-free: none
      Fax: 828-675-9687
      E-mail: Heal2grow@aol.com
      Website: none

The Compassionate Friends, Inc.
National Office
P.O. Box 3696
Oak Brook, IL 60522-3696
    Phone: 630-990-0010
    Toll-free: none
    Fax: 630-990-0246
    E-mail: TCF_National@prodigy.com
    Web site: www.compassionatefriends.org

Jewish Family Service of San Diego
3715 Sixth Avenue
San Diego, CA 92103-5703
    Phone: 619-291-0473
    Toll-free: none
    Fax: 619-291-2419
    E-mail: none
    Web site: none

National SIDS Alliance
1314 Bedford Avenue, Suite 210
Baltimore, MD 21208
    Phone: use toll-free number
    Toll-free: 800-221-SIDS
    Fax: none
    E-mail: sidshg@charm.net
    Web site: www.sidsalliance.org

National SIDS Resource Center
2070 Chain Bridge Road, Suite 450
Vienna, VA 22182
    Phone: 703-821-8955
    Toll-free: none
    Fax: 703-821-2098
    E-mail: sids@circsol.com
    Web site: www.circsol.com/sids

Pen-Parents, Inc.
P.O. Box 8738
Reno, NV 89507-8738
    Phone: 775-826-7332
    Toll-free: none
    Fax: 775-337-0866
    E-mail: penparents@aol.com
    Web site: www.penparents.org

* Perinatal Loss Project
  2116 N.E. 18th Avenue
  Portland, OR 97212-2621
  Phone: 503-284-7426
  Toll-free: none
  Fax: 503-282-8985
  E-mail: grieving@teleport.com
  Web site: www.teleport.com/~grieving

* A Place to Remember
  deRuyter-Nelson Publications, Inc.
  1885 University Avenue, Suite 110
  Saint Paul, MN 55104
  Phone: 612-645-7045
  Toll-free: 800-631-0973
  Fax: 612-645-4780
  E-mail: APTR@aplacetoremember.com
  Web site: www.aplacetoremember.com

* Pregnancy and Infant Loss Center
  1421 East Wayzata Boulevard, Suite 70
  Wayzata, MN 55391
  Phone: 612-473-9372
  Toll-free: none
  Fax: 612-473-8978
  E-mail: none
  Web site: none

  Pregnancy Loss Support Program
  National Council of Jewish Women, New York Section
  9 East 69th Street
  New York, NY 10021
  Phone: 212-535-5900 ext. 40
  Toll-free: none
  Fax: 212-535-5909
  E-mail: plspncjw@aol.com
  Web site: none

* SHARE
Pregnancy and Infant Loss Support, Inc.
St. Joseph Health Center
300 First Capitol Drive
St. Charles, MO 63301
    Phone: 314-947-6164
    Toll-free: 800-821-6819
    Fax: 314-947-7486
    E-mail: share@nationalshareoffice.com
    Web site: www.nationalshareoffice.com

SIDELINES
(a national support network for women facing high-risk pregnancies)
P.O. Box 1808
Laguna Beach, CA 92652-1808
    Phone: 949-497-2265
    Toll-free: none
    Fax: none
    E-mail: none
    Web site: www.sidelines.org

SIDS (see National SIDS Alliance and National SIDS Resource Center)

* Wintergreen Press
3630 Eileen Street
Maple Plain, MN 55359
Phone: 612-476-1303
    Toll-free: none
    Fax: use phone number 612-476-1303
    E-mail: none
    Web site: none

RESOURCES FOR LOSS IN MULTIPLE GESTATIONS

Center for Loss in Multiple Births (CLIMB)
P.O. Box 1064
Palmer, AK 99645
    Phone: 907-746-6123
    Toll-free: none
    Fax: none
    E-mail: climb@poboxalaska.net
    Web site: none

The Triplet Connection
P.O. Box 99571
Stockton, CA 95209
  Phone: 209-474-0885
  Toll-free: none
  Fax: 209-474-2233
  E-mail: tc@tripletconnection.org
  Web site: www.tripletconnection.org

The Twin to Twin Transfusion Syndrome Foundation
411 Longbeach Parkway
Bay Village, OH 44140
  Phone: 440-899-TTTS
  Toll-free: none
  Fax: 440-366-6148
  E-mail: tttsfound@aol.com
  Web site: www.tttsfoundation.org

RESOURCES ONLINE

Many of the pregnancy loss and other resource organizations listed in this appendix maintain their own Websites through the online addresses we have provided. The following are a sample of a few Web sites that exist as online services only. There are many chat rooms and other informational resources that can be accessed through the internet by entering key words, such as "miscarriage," "stillbirth," "ectopic pregnancy" and many other topics. Beware that some Web sites may be affiliated with political or religious organizations that do not support the views expressed in this book. Others may have ties to businesses that may influence the services and products they recommend.

  Hygeia: An Online Journal for Pregnancy and Neonatal Loss
    E-mail: hygeia@connix.com
    Web site: www.connix.com/~hygeia
  StorkNet: Pregnancy/Infant Loss Links
    Web site: www.storknet.org/links/pil.htm
  Women's Health: Loss and Bereavement
    Web site: www.obgyn.net/women/loss'loss.htm
  International Council on Infertility Information Dissemination: The Miscarriage Manual
    Web site: www.inclid.org/mismanl.html

RESOURCES FOR PSYCHOTHERAPY

When selecting a psychotherapist following a pregnancy loss, you may want to choose a licensed or board-certified mental health professional or an accredited agency. It is also important to locate a counselor experienced in bereavement and pregnancy loss. Because of their expertise, these specially trained caregivers can provide validation and support after your loss that will help you receive the maximum benefit from psychotherapy. You may want to obtain a recommendation or referral from a local pregnancy loss support program, your hospital social work department or obstetrical nursing department or your obstetrician or midwife.

Three national organizations with affiliated agencies of professionals throughout the United States and Canada are listed below. Again, consider requesting a psychotherapist with expertise in bereavement and pregnancy loss.

Alliance for Children and Families
(formerly Family Service America)
11700 West Lake Park Drive
Milwaukee, WI 53224
Phone: 414-359-1040
Toll-free: 800-221-2681
Fax: 414-359-1074
E-mail: none
Web site: www.alliancel.org

Association of Jewish Family and Children's Agencies
(nondenominational referrals)
3084 State Highway 27, Suite 1
P.O. Box 248
Kendall Park, NJ 08824-0248
    Phone: 732-821-0909
    Toll-free: 800-634-7346
    Fax: 732-821-0493
    E-mail: ajsca@aol.com
    Web site: www.ajsca.com

American Association for Marriage and Family Therapy
1133 15th Street, NW, Suite 300
Washington, DC 20005-2710
    Phone: 202-452-0109
    Toll-free: none
    Fax: 202-223-2329
    E-mail: central@aamft.org
    Web site: www.aamft.org

RESOURCES FOR GENETICS INFORMATION AND FOR ENDING A PREGNANCY

Alliance of Genetic Support Groups
4301 Connecticut Avenue, NW, Suite 404
Washington, DC 20008-2304
  Phone: 202-566-5557
  Toll-free: 800-336-GENE
  Fax: 202-966-8553
  E-mail: info@geneticalliance.org
  Web site: www.geneticalliance.org

March of Dimes Birth Defects Foundation
1275 Mamaroneck Avenue
White Plains, NY 10605
  Phone: 914-428-7100
  Toll-free: 888-MODIMES
  Fax: 914-428-8203
  E-mail: use the Web site
  Web site: www.modimes.org

National Abortion Federation
1755 Massachusetts Avenue, NW, Suite 600
Washington, DC 20036
  Phone: 202-667-5881
  Toll-free: 800-772-9100
  Fax: 202-667-5890
  E-mail: naf@prochoice.org
  Web site: www.prochoice.org

National Abortion and Reproductive Rights Action League
1101 14th Street, NW, Suite 500
Washington, DC 20005
  Phone: 202-973-3000
  Toll-free: none
  Fax: 202-973-3096
  E-mail: naral@naral.org
  Web site: www.naral.org

National Organization of Rare Disorders (NORD)
P.O. Box 8923
New Fairfield, CT 06812-8923
    Phone: 203-746-6518
    Toll-free: none
    Fax: 203-746-6481
    E-mail: orphan@rarediseases.org
    Web site: www.rarediseases.org

Pineapple Press
(newsletter: A Heartbreaking Choice)
P.O. Box 312
St. Johns, MI 48879
    Phone: 517-224-1881
    Toll-free: none
    Fax: 517-224-0058
    E-mail: none
    Web site: none

Planned Parenthood Federation of America
810 Seventh Avenue
New York, NY 10019
    Phone: 212-541-7800
    Toll-free: 800-230-7526
    Fax: 212-245-1845
    E-mail: none
    Web site: www.plannedparenthood.org

Project Rachel
National Office of Post Abortion Reconciliation and Healing
Support (A Catholic Ministry)
3501 South Lake Drive
P.O. Box 07477
Milwaukee, WI 53207-0477
    Phone: 414-483-4141
    Toll-free: 800-5WE-CARE
    Fax: 414-483-7376
    E-mail: noparh@juno.com
    Web site:www.marquette.edu/rachel

RESOURCES FOR INFERTILITY

The American Society for Reproductive Medicine
1209 Montgomery Highway
Birmingham, AL 35216-2809
  Phone: 205-978-5000
  Toll-free: none
  Fax: 205-978-5005
  E-mail: asrm@asrm.org
  Web site: www.asrm.org

Endometriosis Association
P.O. Box 92187
8585 North 76th Place
Milwaukee, WI 53223
  Phone: 414-355-2200
  Toll-free: 800-992-3636 (information only)
  Fax: 414-355-6065
  E-mail: endo@endometriosisassn.org
  Web site: www.endometriosisassn.org

RESOLVE, Inc.
1310 Broadway
Somerville, MA 02144-1731
  Phone: 617-623-0744
  Toll-free: none
  Fax: 617-623-0252
  E-mail: resolveinc@aol.com
  Web site: www.resolve.org

RESOURCES FOR CHILDBIRTH

American College of Obstetricians and Gynecologists (ACOG)
409 12th Street, SW
Washington, DC 20024
  Phone: 202-638-5577
  Toll-free: 800-673-8444
  Fax: 202-484-5107
  E-mail: none
  Web site: www.acog.org

C/SEC, Inc.
(cesarean section)
22 Forest Road
Framingham, MA 01701
    Phone: 508-877-8266
    Toll-free: none
    Fax: none
    E-mail: none
    Web site: none

International Childbirth Education Association (ICEA)
P.O. Box 20048
Minneapolis, MN 55420
    Phone: 612-854-8660
    Toll-free: 800-624-4934 (book orders)
    Fax: 612-854-8772
    E-mail: info@icea.org
    Web site: www.icea.org

La Leche League International
1400 North Meacham Road
Schaumburg, IL 60173
    Phone: 847-519-7730
    Toll-free: 800-525-3243
    Fax: 847-519-0035
    E-mail: LLLhq@LLLinternational.org
    Web site: www.lalecheleague.org

National Association for Parents and Professionals for Safe
Alternatives in Childbirth (NAPSAC)
Route 4, Box 646
Marble Hill, MO 63764
    Phone: 573-238-2010
    Toll-free: none
    Fax: 573-238-2010
    E-mail: napsac@clas.net
    Web site: none

National Perinatal Association
3500 East Fletcher Avenue, Suite 525
Tampa, FL 33613
    Phone: 813-971-1008
    Toll-free: none
    Fax: 813-971-9306
    E-mail: npaonline@aol.com
    Web site: www.nationalperinatal.org

RESOURCES FOR ADOPTION

AASK (Aid to Adoption of Special Kids)
3530 Grand Avenue
Oakland, CA 94610
    Phone: 510-451-1748
    Toll-free: 888-680-7349
    Fax: 510-451-2023
    E-mail: none
    Web site: www.adoptaspecial kid.org

Adoptive Families of America
2309 Como Avenue
St. Paul, MN 55108
    Phone: 612-535-4829
    Toll-free: 800-372-3300
    Fax: 651-645-0055
    E-mail: pharder@usinternet.com
    Web site: www.adoptivefam.org

National Adoption Foundation
(provides financial assistance programs for the adopting community)
100 Mill Plain Road
Danbury, CT 06811
    Phone: 203-791-3811
    Toll-free: none
    Fax: 203-791-3801
    E-Mail: none
    Web site: none

National Adoption Information Clearinghouse
11426 Rockville Pike, Suite 410
Rockville, MD 20852
   Phone: 301-231-6512
   Toll-free: none
   Fax: none
   E-mail: none
   Web site: none

RESOURCES ON HEALTH AND PREGNANCY

The Coalition for Positive Outcomes in Pregnancy
507 Capitol Court, NE, Suite 200
Washington, DC 20002
   Phone: 202-544-7499
   Toll-free: none
   Fax: 202-546-7105
   E-mail: none
   Web site: none

DES Action USA
1650 Broadway
Oakland, CA 94612
   Phone: 510-465-4011
   Toll-free: 800-DES-9288
   Fax: 510-465-4815
   E-mail: desact@well.com
   Web site: www.desaction.org

National Women's Health Network
514 10th Street, NW, Suite 400
Washington, DC 20004
   Phone: 202-347-1140 or information clearinghouse: 202-628-7814
   Toll-free: none
   Fax: 202-347-1168
   E-mail: none
   Web site: none

The Organization of Teratology Information Services (OTIS)
(a referral-only service to local resources that provide information
about fetal effects of maternal exposure to drugs, chemicals and
infections before and during pregnancy)
P.O. Box 142106
Salt Lake City, UT 84114-2106
    Phone: 801-328-2229
    Toll-free: none
    Fax: 801-538-9448
    E-mail: none
    Web site: none

Glossary

abortion, elective, therapeutic or voluntary: these terms describe a deliberate ending of a pregnancy by medical intervention.

abortion, spontaneous: see miscarriage.

abruption, placental: separation of the placenta from the uterine wall.

adhesions: the scar tissue that binds together two surfaces that are usually apart.

AIDS (acquired immune deficiency syndrome): a disease that affects the immune system and that can be transmitted through the exchange of blood, semen or other bodily fluids.

alpha-fetoprotein: protein produced by the fetus that can be measured prenatally to identify possible neural tube disorders.

amniocentesis: the removal of a sample of amniotic fluid by means of a needle inserted through the mother's abdominal wall; used for genetic and biochemical analysis of the fetus.

amniotic fluid: the liquid surrounding and protecting the baby within the amniotic sac during pregnancy.

amniotic sac: the membrane within the uterus that contains the baby and the amniotic fluid during pregnancy.

anencephaly: a fatal congenital condition in which most of the brain and skull are absent.

anesthesia: a gas or drug that causes partial or complete loss of sensation either in one part of the body (local) or with loss of consciousness (general).

anniversary reaction: the resurgence of grief feelings and symptoms around a significant date following a loss. For a pregnancy loss this might be a due date or a delivery date.

anomaly: a physical malformation or abnormality.

antibiotics: medication that can eradicate or stop the growth of bacteria that attack humans.

antibody: a substance produced in the body that attacks bacteria and viruses.

Asherman's syndrome: uterine adhesions produced by infection or overly vigorous curettage of the uterus.

258

autoimmune disease: the process in which the body's defense system acts against its own tissues, causing damage.

bacteria: one-celled microorganisms. Some bacteria live in harmony with the human body, while others cause disease.

bereavement (grief, mourning): the emotional state that accompanies a significant loss.

bereavement, chronic or inhibited: the emotional state in which feelings of loss are not released and are pushed from consciousness, resulting in physical and psychological symptoms.

beta subunit of HCG: see HCG.

biopsy: the surgical removal of a small amount of tissue for microscopic analysis and diagnosis.

birth control: the act of preventing conception through various methods.

blighted ovum: see miscarriage.

board-certified: a physician who has passed the qualifying examinations required by a particular specialty.

bonding: the emotional attachment of parents to their child, which can begin from confirmation of the pregnancy.

bris: the Jewish ritual circumcision.

catheter: a slim tube used for removing or injecting fluids.

cerclage: a surgical method for closing an incompetent cervix during pregnancy to prevent premature delivery.

cervical incompetence: the condition in which a weakened cervix opens prematurely during pregnancy, sometimes resulting in pregnancy loss.

cervix: the neck of the uterus leading to the vagina that opens during labor.

cesarean section: the surgical removal of an unborn baby by means of an incision through the abdominal wall and the uterus.

chorionic villus sampling: a prenatal test in which a soft, thin tube is inserted through the cervix, or a needle through the abdomen, to the chorionic villi, the embryonic tissue that forms the placenta, to withdraw a tissue sample for chromosomal and genetic analysis.

chromosomal abnormality: a birth defect resulting from accidental anomalies of the chromosomes, as in Down syndrome.

chromosomes: structures found in human cells that contain genes, the material responsible for the transmission of hereditary information.

climax: see orgasm.

Clomid: the brand name for clomiphene citrate, a synthetic hormone that stimulates the pituitary gland and ovulation.

clomiphene challenge test: an analysis of the woman's response to doses of Clomid, which may be an indicator of her closeness to the onset of menopause and her ability to sustain a pregnancy.

conception (becoming pregnant): the fertilization or union of egg and sperm to create a new life.

cone biopsy: the surgical removal of a cone-shaped wedge of tissue from the cervix for microscopic analysis.

congenital defect: a condition or abnormality that is present at birth, which may or may not be hereditary.

contraception: see birth control.

contraction stress test: the intravenous stimulation of the uterus with the hormone oxytocin, creating mild uterine contractions. If the baby's heart rate drops during or following one of these contractions, it may mean the placenta is not functioning correctly.

crisis pregnancy: a pregnancy that requires medical intervention including surgery, bed rest, induction of labor or other treatments.

culdocentesis: the insertion of a needle through the vaginal wall into the abdominal cavity behind the uterus to see if blood is present, indicating internal bleeding.

D&C (dilatation and curettage): expansion of the cervix and suctioning to remove most of the products of conception, followed by gentle scraping of the uterine lining using a surgical instrument (curette) with an open, spoon-shaped tip, usually performed between conception and twelve weeks.

D&E (dilatation and evacuation): a procedure performed usually between the fourteenth and twentieth weeks of pregnancy in which the cervix is opened and the uterine contents removed by a suction device or by curettage.

DES (diethylstilbestrol): a synthetic form of estrogen used from 1945 until the early 1970s and previously believed to prevent potential miscarriages. DES did not forestall miscarriages and caused medical problems in the offspring of mothers who took this hormone while pregnant.

DNA (deoxyribonucleic acid): a chemical compound within the gene that contains the genetic code.

Doppler instrument: a listening device that makes the fetal heartbeat audible.

doula: a specially trained labor assistant.

Down syndrome: a chromosomal birth abnormality with characteristic facial and other physical traits and differing levels of mental retardation.

ectopic pregnancy: the implantation of a fertilized egg outside the uterus.

efface, effacement: the thinning of the cervix during labor.

embryo: the term used to describe a pregnancy from the fourth to the ninth week after conception.

embryonic sac: the membrane within the uterus that contains the embryo.

endocrine: the system of glands that secretes hormones.

endometrial biopsy: the removal of a small sample of uterine lining, or endometrium, through the cervix, done for laboratory analysis.

endometriosis: a condition in which pieces of the endometrium, or uterine lining, are located outside the uterus.

endometrium: the lining of the inner surface of the uterus.

episiotomy: a surgical incision made during delivery that enlarges the external vaginal opening.

estrogen: the principle female sex hormone that stimulates the reproductive cycle.

fallopian tube: the thin, hollow conduit that carries the ovum, or egg, from the ovary to the uterus; named after the Italian anatomist Fallopius.

fertilization: the penetration of the sperm into the ovum, or egg, to create a new life.

fetal heart monitor: a small device that can be strapped to a pregnant woman's abdomen to evaluate the baby's heart rate.

fetus: the term applied to a developing baby from nine weeks until birth.

fibroid tumors (myomas): nonmalignant growths within the wall of the uterus that may expand during pregnancy.

folic acid: a B vitamin, which, if present in the diet of childbearing-age women, can help reduce the risk of neural tube defects and premature birth.

gene: the biological unit of a chromosome that carries inherited traits.

genetic abnormality: a disorder resulting from an anomaly in the gene structure that is hereditary or that can occur as a spontaneous mutation.

genetic counseling: the advice offered by experts in genetics on the detection, consequences and risk of recurrence of chromosomal and genetic disorders.

gestation: the period of fetal development in the womb from implantation to birth.

gestational trophoblastic neoplasia: a rare and highly treatable form of cancer that develops from placental tissue in about 15 percent of molar pregnancies.

grief: see bereavement.

gynecologist: a physician who specializes in the care of the female reproductive tract. The field is called gynecology.

habitual abortion: see miscarriage, habitual miscarrier.

HCG (human chorionic gonadotropin): a hormone produced by the placenta early in pregnancy and necessary for the maintenance of normal gestation. The blood test called beta subunit of HCG is used to diagnose pregnancy.

hemophilia: a genetic blood disorder, usually hereditary, characterized by failure of the blood to clot and the occurrence of abnormal bleeding.

hemorrhage: profuse bleeding.

hereditary: transmitted from generation to generation by way of genes within the chromosomes of the fertilizing sperm and ovum.

herpes simplex: a virus that can cause blisterlike eruptions of mucous membranes such as in the mouth, eyes and genitals.

high-risk pregnancy: a pregnancy that is at greater than average risk for an adverse outcome.

hormone: a chemical produced and secreted into the blood by the endocrine glands and some organs and that has an effect on other bodily functions, including reproduction.

human chorionic gonadotropin: see HCG.

hydatidiform mole: see molar pregnancy.

hysterosalpingogram: a procedure in which a dye is introduced into the uterine cavity and coursed through the uterus and fallopian tubes while X-ray pictures are taken to identify scarring, blockages or other reproductive problems.

hysteroscopy: a procedure in which a small optical instrument is introduced into the cervix so the doctor can visualize the lining and contour of the uterus, including any fibroid tumors or uterine malformations.

immunological: that which pertains to the body's natural defenses, or immunity, against disease.

impaired pregnancy: a pregnancy that is abnormal due to environmental, genetic, chromosomal or other causes.

implantation: the process by which the fertilized egg attaches to the uterine lining.

incompetent cervix: see cervical incompetence.

incongruent grief: the differing intensity and duration of grief a father and mother may experience.

induction of labor: the use of artificial means to stimulate the onset of labor.

infection: the contamination resulting from harmful bacteria or viruses.

infertility: the inability to conceive after one year of unprotected intercourse. Repeated consecutive pregnancy losses, without a live birth, may also be referred to as infertility.

inflammation: a bodily response to irritation or infection involving increased redness, swelling or pain.

in vitro fertilization (IVF): a procedure in which eggs are surgically removed from a woman and mixed with sperm in a petri dish, after which the fertilized eggs are inserted into a woman's uterus in an effort to obtain a viable pregnancy.

isolette: an incubator for infants that provides a controlled temperature and oxygen supply.

karyotype: an analysis of human chromosomes for genetic evaluation.

laminaria sticks: stems of dried seaweed that absorb moisture, inserted into the cervix to aid dilatation.

laparoscopy: a procedure performed under general anesthesia in which an optical instrument, the laparoscope, is inserted through a small incision in the abdominal wall, enabling the physician to see the fallopian tubes, uterus and ovaries directly.

low birth weight: a baby's weight at birth if it is under 2,500 grams (5 1/2 pounds).

luteal phase defect (LPD): a condition in which too little progesterone is produced following ovulation, affecting the menstrual cycle and the ability to sustain a pregnancy.

maternal serum alpha-fetoprotein (MSAFP): a test of the mother's blood that checks for neural tube defects in the unborn baby.

menstruation (period): the monthly uterine bleeding in which the lining of the womb is expelled from the woman's body if she does not conceive.

microsurgery: operations in which special techniques and magnifying instruments are used to correct delicate organs and tissues.

midwife: a health care practitioner, usually a nurse, who has special training to help manage pregnancies and births and may function independently from a physician.

miscarriage: a lay term describing early spontaneous loss within the first twenty weeks of pregnancy. The correct medical term is *abortion,* but many bereaved couples prefer the word *miscarriage.* There are several types of early miscarriage:

blighted ovum: an early loss in which the egg was fertilized but no fetus developed.

complete miscarriage: an early loss in which all the products of the conception, including the fetus, the sac, and the forming placenta, are expelled from the uterus.

habitual miscarrier: a woman who has suffered three or more consecutive miscarriages.

incomplete miscarriage: an early loss in which some products of the pregnancy still remain inside the uterus.

inevitable miscarriage: an early loss in progress that cannot be stopped.

missed miscarriage: an early loss in which the fetus has died but remains in the uterus, along with the placenta and other elements of conception, without being expelled.

preclinical pregnancy: an early loss that ends before the woman's next period is due. There are usually no pregnancy symptoms, but a blood test can reveal small amounts of the pregnancy hormone HCG.

septic miscarriage: an early loss complicated by uterine infection, usually from an incomplete miscarriage.

spontaneous miscarriage: any unplanned termination of a pregnancy in the first twenty weeks.

threatened miscarriage: an incidence in which certain symptoms such as vaginal bleeding or severe cramping occur during pregnancy. The symptoms may stop or may progress to a miscarriage.

molar pregnancy: the fertilization of an ovum without a nucleus. There is no fetus present, and the placenta develops into a nonmalignant tumor called a hydatidiform mole.

mycoplasma (T-strain mycoplasma): a microscopic organism thought to be responsible for pregnancy loss.

myoma: see fibroid tumor.

neural tube defect: an abnormality of the brain and/or the spinal cord.

neonatal: the first twenty-eight days of a baby's life after birth.

neonatal death: see newborn death.

neonatal intensive care unit: a special-care nursery for critically ill newborns, often located in regional medical centers.

neonatologist: a pediatrician with specialized training in the care of newborn infants.

newborn death: the death of a baby within twenty-eight days of a live birth.

nonstress test (NST): an examination to detect the health of the baby, in which the woman is hooked up to a fetal monitor and is asked to press a button whenever she feels fetal movement. A healthy baby's heart rate usually increases following fetal movement.

obstetrician: a physician who specializes in pregnancy and delivery. The field of specialty is called obstetrics.

orgasm: the peak state of sexual arousal in which the male ejaculates sperm and the woman achieves satisfaction.

ova: see ovum.

ovary: the female organs that produce sex hormones and ova, or eggs.

ovulation: the release of a mature, unfertilized egg from the ovary.

ovum: the reproductive cell, or egg, of the female. Plural: ova.

pelvic inflammatory disease (PID): infection and inflammation of the woman's pelvic organs.

pelvic or internal examination: a medical examination of the vagina, cervix, uterus and fallopian tubes.

perinatal: the period of time from the twentieth week of pregnancy through the twenty-eighth day after birth.

Pergonal: the brand name of a medication used in fertility treatments to stimulate the ovaries to produce additional eggs in one menstrual cycle.

period: see menstruation.

PID: see pelvic inflammatory disease.

placenta: the spongy, vascular organ that supplies the fetus with nutrients through the umbilical cord.

placenta previa: a condition in which the placenta is located over the cervix, creating a risk of hemorrhage during labor and delivery.

postmature: a baby born after forty-two weeks' gestation.

preeclampsia: see toxemia.

pregnancy reduction: a medical procedure for reducing the number of fetuses in a multiple pregnancy.

premature: a baby born before thirty-seven weeks' gestation.

premature rupture of the membranes (PROM): a break in the amniotic sac, resulting in loss of amniotic fluid, before the onset of labor.

prenatal: the period before birth and after conception.

prenatal diagnosis: the testing of a baby prior to birth.

preterm labor: the early onset of uterine contractions, generally at least six to eight per hour, accompanied by progressive cervical dilation and effacement between the twentieth and thirty-seventh weeks of pregnancy.

progesterone: a female hormone important during pregnancy and menstruation.

prolapsed cord: the expulsion of a portion of the umbilical cord after the membranes have ruptured but before delivery. Pressure on the cord from labor and delivery cuts off the baby's supply of blood and oxygen.

prostaglandin: a hormone produced by the body that may be administered to induce labor.

psychotherapist: a health care professional who treats emotional problems.

Rh-incompatibility disease: a serious medical complication during pregnancy in which harmful antibodies in the mother's blood attack her developing baby.

rubella (German measles): a viral disease characterized by headache, fever, rash and inflammation of the throat. Infection in a pregnant mother can damage the fetus.

saline: a salt solution used for medical procedures.

secondary infertility: the inability of a couple to conceive after a previous pregnancy.

semen: the fluid that contains male reproductive cells (sperm).

septum, uterine: a wall of tissue that divides the uterus in two parts.

sonogram: a visualization of a woman's reproductive organs achieved by bouncing sound waves into her abdomen. The technique is called sonography or ultrasound.

sonographer: a technician or doctor trained in the techniques of administering and evaluating sonograms.

specialist, medical: a physician who has received advanced training in a specific area of medical care.

sperm: the male reproductive cells.

spina bifida: an abnormality in the development of the spine that can cause severe neurological impairment and paralysis.

stillbirth: the death of a baby of at least twenty weeks' gestation prior to delivery.

term: forty weeks' gestation, the normal duration of a pregnancy.

termination (therapeutic or elective abortion): the ending of a pregnancy by choice.

tocolytics: drugs used to curb uterine contractions after the twentieth week of pregnancy.

toxemia (preeclampsia): an abnormal condition of late pregnancy characterized by high blood pressure, protein in the urine and swelling.

Trendelenburg position: the position in which the patient lies on her back with the bed tilted, so that the knees and hips are higher than the head.

trimester: the term used to define each three-month segment of pregnancy.

triple test: an analysis of three substances in maternal blood to screen for certain fetal defects.

T-strain mycoplasma: see mycoplasma.

twin-to-twin transfusion syndrome: an anomaly in identical twins in which a blood vessel in the placenta connects the circulatory system of both babies.

ultrasound: see sonogram.

umbilical cord: the blood vessels that connect the baby to the placenta.

uterus (womb): the female reproductive organ that contains the developing baby.

vagina (birth canal): the organ of the female that forms a passageway between the uterus and the external genitals.

vanishing twin syndrome: the spontaneous disappearance of a previously detected fetus in a multiple pregnancy.

viability: the ability of an infant to survive outside the uterus.

virus: a microscopic organism that can cause disease in humans. It differs from bacteria in that it cannot live on its own but must reside inside the cell of another organism.

womb: see uterus.

Bibliography

The bibliography has changed with this revised edition of A Silent Sorrow. We added new sources to support new research, but we still preferred to acknowledge the texts that were significant in the creation of the first edition. Some of the books we consulted earlier are no longer in print, but they were important to our initial research and we have retained them in the bibliography. Online bookstores, such as Amazon.com, have out-of-print book search services if you wish to find titles that are no longer available. For sources of current books about grief, pregnancy loss and related issues, please see Appendix D: Resources.

SECTION I: THE GRIEF OF PREGNANCY LOSS

Chapter 1: When an Unborn or Newborn Baby Dies

Benfield, Gary D., M.D., et al. "Grief Response of Parents to Neonatal Death and Parent Participation in Deciding Care." *Pediatrics* 62, no. 2 (August 1978): 171–77.

Bourne, Stanford, et al. "Delayed Psychological Effects of Perinatal Death: The Next Pregnancy and the Next Generation." *British Medical Journal* 289 (July 21, 1984): 147–48.

Bowlby, John, M.D. "Processes of Mourning." *The International Journal of Psychoanalysis* 42 (1961): 317–40.

Bugen, Larry A., Ph.D. "Human Grief: A Model for Prediction and Intervention." *American Journal of Orthopsychiatry* 47, no. 2 (April 1977): 196–206.

De Lia, Julian E., M.D., M.B.A., et al. "Fetoscopic Laser Treatment of Twin-Twin Transfusion Syndrome: Expectations and Results Post Learning Curve." *Fetal Diagnosis Therapy* 13 (1998): 126.

Ewy, Donna, and Roger Ewy. *Death of a Dream*. New York: E. P. Dutton, 1984.

Fletcher, John C., Ph.D. "Maternal Bonding in Early Fetal Ultrasound Examinations." *The New England Journal of Medicine* 308 (February 17, 1983): 392–93.

Friedman, Rochelle, and Bonnie Gradstein. *Surviving Pregnancy Loss*. Boston: Little, Brown, 1992.

Furlong, Regina, M.S.W., and John Hobbins, M.D. "Grief in the Perinatal Period." *Obstetrics and Gynecology* 61, no. 4 (April 1983): 497–500.

Heiman, J., et al. "Grief Support Programs: Patient's Use of Services Following the Loss of a Desired Pregnancy and Degree of Implementation in Academic Centers." *American Journal of Perinatology* (1997): 14, 587–91.

Hettie, J. E. M., et al. "Controlled Prospective Study on the Mental Health of Women Following Pregnancy Loss." *American Journal of Psychiatry* (February 1996): 153:226–30.

Ilse, Sherokee. *Empty Arms: Coping with Miscarriage, Stillbirth and Infant Death*. Maple Plain, MN: Wintergreen Press, 1995.

Janssen, H., et al. "A Prospective Study of Risk Factors Predicting Grief Intensity Following Pregnancy Loss." *Archives of General Psychiatry* (1997): 54, 56–61.

Kellner, Kenneth, M.D., and Marian Lake. "Grief Counseling." In *High-Risk Pregnancy: A Team Approach,* ed. Robert A. Knuppel and Joan E. Drukker. Philadelphia: W. B. Saunders Company, 1986, pp. 561–74.

Kellner, Kenneth, M.D., et al. "Parental Behavior After Perinatal Death: Lack of Predictive Demographic and Obstetric Variables." *Obstetrics and Gynecology* 63, no. 6 (June 1984): 809–14.

———. "Perinatal Mortality Counseling Program for Families Who Experience a Stillbirth." *Death Education* 5 (1981): 29–35.

Kennell, John, M.D., Howard Sinter, and Marshall Klaus, M.D. "The Mourning Response of Parents to the Death of a Newborn Infant." *The New England Journal of Medicine* 283, no. 7 (August 13, 1970): 344–49.

Klaus, Marshall H., and John H. Kennell. *Parent-Infant Bonding,* 2nd ed., St. Louis: C. V. Mosby Company, 1981.

Kowalski, Karren, R.N., M.S. "Managing Perinatal Loss." *Clinical Obstetrics and Gynecology* 23, no. 4 (December 1980): 1113–23.

Kübler-Ross, Elisabeth, M.D. *On Death and Dying*. New York: Macmillan Publishing Company, 1969.

Lewis, Emanuel, M.D. "Inhibition of Mourning by Pregnancy: Psychopathology and Management." *British Medical Journal* 2 (July 7, 1979): 27–28.

———. "Mourning by the Family After a Stillbirth or Neonatal Death." *Archives of Diseases in Childhood* 54 (1979): 303–6.

Lewis, Thomas, M.D. "A Culturally Patterned Depression in a Mother After Loss of a Child." *Psychiatry* 38 (February 1975): 92–95.

Limbo, Rana K., and Sara Rich Wheeler. *When a Baby Dies: A Handbook for Healing and Helping.* La Crosse, WI: Bereavement Services, 1998.

Lindemann, Erich. "Symptomatology and Management of Acute Grief." *American Journal of Psychiatry* 101 (September 1944): 141–48.

Morris, D. "Management of Perinatal Bereavement." *Archives of Diseases in Childhood* 63 (1988): 870–72.

Nicolini, Umberto, M.D., et al. "Serial Amniocenteses in the Management of Twin-Twin Transfusion Syndrome: When Is It Valuable?" *Fetal Diagnosis Therapy* (1997): 12, 15–20.

Peppers, Larry, and Ronald Knapp. *How to Go on Living After the Death of a Baby.* Atlanta: Peachtree Publishers, 1985.

Pollock, George H. "Anniversary Reactions, Trauma, and Mourning." *The Psychoanalytic Quarterly* 39 (July 1970): 347–71.

Prend, Ashley Davis. *Transcending Loss: Understanding the Lifelong Impact of Grief and How to Make It Meaningful.* New York: Berkley Books, 1997.

Rando, Therese, ed. *Parental Loss of a Child.* Champaign, IL: Research Press, 1986.

Scheper-Hughes, Nancy. *Death Without Weeping.* Berkeley, CA: University of California Press, 1992.

Schwiebert, Pat, R.N., and Paul Kirk, M.D. *When Hello Means Goodbye.* Portland, OR: Perinatal Loss, 1985.

Swanson-Kauffman, Kristen, Ph.D., R.N. "There Should Have Been Two: Nursing Care of Parents Experiencing the Perinatal Death of a Twin." *Journal of Perinatal Neonatal Nursing* 2, no. 2 (1988): 78–86.

Tom-Johnson, Christina. "Talking Through Grief." *Nursing Times* 86, no. 1 (January 3, 1990): 44–46.

Ward, Kenneth, M.D. "Promising News About Twin-Twin Transfusion Syndrome." *Twins* (March/April 1996): 52, 57.

Woods, James R., Jr., M.D., and Jenifer L. Esposito. *Pregnancy Loss: Medical Therapeutics and Practical Considerations.* Baltimore: Williams and Wilkins, 1987.

——— and Jenifer L. Esposito Woods. *Loss During Pregnancy or in the Newborn Period: Principles of Care with Clinical Cases and Analyses.* Pitman, NJ: Jannetti Publications, 1997.

Worden, J. W. *Grief Counseling and Grief Therapy: A Handbook for the Mental Health Practitioner.* New York: Springer, 1982.

Zahourek, Rothlyn. "Grieving and the Newborn." *American Journal of Nursing* 73 (May 1973): 836–39.

Chapter 2: The Mother's Experience

Chapter 3: The Father's Experience

Chapter 4: Pregnancy Loss and Your Relationship

Berk, Aliza, and Jerrold Lee Shapiro. "Some Implications of Infertility on Marital Therapy." *Family Therapy* 11, no. 1 (1984): 37–47.

Boyle, F., et al. "The Mental Health Impact of Stillbirth, Neonatal Death or SIDS: Prevalence and Patterns of Distress Among Mothers." *Social Science Medicine* (1996): 43, 1273–82.

Chernus, Linda. "Marital Treatment Following Early Infant Death." *Clinical Social Work Journal* 10, no. 1 (Spring 1982): 28–38.

Condon, John T. "Management of Established Pathological Grief Reaction After Stillbirth." *American Journal of Psychiatry* 143, no. 8 (August 1986): 987–92.

———. "The Parental-Foetal Relationship—A Comparison of Male and Female Expectant Parents." *Journal of Psychosomatic Obstetrics and Gynecology* 4 (1985): 271–84.

Feeley, Nancy N., and Laurie N. Gottlieb. "Parents' Coping and Communication Following Their Infant's Death." *Omega* 19, no. 1 (1988–89): 51–67.

Hardin, Sally Brosz, and Patricia Urbanus. "Reflections on a Miscarriage." *Maternal Child Nursing Journal* 15, no. 1 (Spring 1986): 23–30.

Helmrath, Thomas A., and Elaine M. Steinitz. "Death of an Infant: Parental Grieving and the Failure of Social Support." *The Journal of Family Practice* 6, no. 4 (1978): 785–90.

Herz, Elisabeth. "Psychological Repercussions of Pregnancy Loss." *Psychiatric Annals* 14, no. 6 (June 1984): 454–57.

Hunfield, J., and M. Mourik. "Do Couples Grieve Differently Following Pregnancy Loss?" *Psychology Reports* (1996): 79, 407–10.

Jeter, Kris. "Analytic Essay: Family Stress and Bereavement." *Marriage and Family Review* 6, nos. 1–2 (Spring–Summer 1983): 219–25.

LaRoche, C., et al. "Grief Reactions to Perinatal Death: A Follow-up Study." *Canadian Journal of Psychiatry* 29 (1984): 14–19.

Lovell, Alice. "Some Questions of Identity: Late Miscarriage, Stillbirth and Perinatal Loss." *Social Science and Medicine* 17 (1983): 755–61.

McCracken, Anne, and Mary Semel. *A Broken Heart Still Beats After Your Child Dies.* Center City, MN: Hazelden Information and Educational Services, 1998.

Moriarity, H., et al. "Differences in Bereavement Reactions Within Couples Following the Death of a Child." *Research in Nursing and Health* (1996): 19, 461–69.

Nelson, Tim. *A Father's Story.* St. Paul, MN: A Place to Remember, 1994.

Page, Tim. "Life Miscarried." *The New York Times Magazine,* January 27, 1985.

Reed, Karen. "Involuntary Pregnancy Loss Research and Implications for Nursing." *Issues in Mental Health Nursing* 6, nos. 3–4 (1984): 209–17.

Schatz, William H. *Healing a Father's Grief.* Redmond, WA: Medic Publishing, 1984.

Schiff, Harriet Sarnoff. *The Bereaved Parent.* New York: Crown, 1977.

———. *Living Through Mourning: Finding Comfort and Hope When a Loved One Has Died.* New York: Penguin Books, 1987.

Stack, Jack M. "The Psychodynamics of Spontaneous Abortion." *American Journal of Orthopsychiatry* 54, no. 1 (January 1984): 162–67.

———. "Reproductive Casualties: Effects on Families and Professional Caregivers." *Seminars in Family Medicine* 3, no. 2 (May 1982): 98–104.

Staudacher, Carol. *Men and Grief.* Oakland, CA: New Harbinger Publications, 1991.

Tadmor, Ciporah S. "A Crisis Intervention Model for a Population of Mothers Who Encounter Neonatal Death." *Journal of Primary Prevention* 7, no. 1 (Fall 1986): 17–26.

Theut, Susan K., M.D., et al. "Perinatal Loss and Parental Bereavement." *American Journal of Psychiatry* 146, no. 5 (May 1989): 635–39.

SECTION II: PREGNANCY LOSS EXAMINED

American Academy of Obstetricians and Gynecologists. *Planning for Pregnancy, Birth, and Beyond.* New York: Dutton, 1992.

Burrow, Gerald N., M.D., and Thomas F. Ferris, M.D. *Medical Complications During Pregnancy.* Philadelphia: W. B. Saunders Company, 1988.

Droegumueller, William, M.D., et al. *Comprehensive Gynecology.* St. Louis: C. V. Mosby Company, 1987.

Gabbe, Steven G., M.D., et al. *Obstetrics: Normal and Problem Pregnancies.* New York: Churchill Livingstone, 1986.

Johnson, Robert V., M.D., ed. *Mayo Clinic Complete Book of Pregnancy and Baby's First Year.* New York: William Morrow, 1994.

Semchyshyn, Stefan, M.D., and Carol Colman. *How to Prevent Miscarriage and Other Crises in Pregnancy.* New York: Macmillan Publishing Company, 1989.

Woods, James R., Jr., M.D. and Jenifer L. Esposito. *Pregnancy Loss: Medical Therapeutics and Practical Considerations.* Baltimore: Williams and Wilkins, 1987.

Woods, James R., Jr., M.D., and Jenifer L. Esposito Woods. *Loss During Pregnancy or in the Newborn Period: Principles of Care with Clinical Cases and Analyses.* Pitman, NJ: Jannetti Publications, 1997.

Chapter 5: Early Losses

Achiron, R., et al. "Heart Rate as a Predictor of First-Trimester Spontaneous Abortion after Ultrasound Viability." *Obstetrics and Gynecology* 78, no. 3 (part 1) (September 1991): 330–34.

Adler, Jerry, et al. "Learning from the Loss." *Newsweek*, March 24, 1986: 66–67.

Altman, Lawrence K. "Pregnancy Problems Linked to Hormone." *The New York Times*, November 13, 1990.

Beck, Melinda. "The Bacteria That Hates Women." *Ladies' Home Journal*, August 1989: pp. 119, 163–66.

Beck, Melinda, et al. "A Medical Mystery." *Newsweek*, August 15, 1988: 49–52.

Blakeslee, Sandra. "Research on Birth Defects Shifts to Flaws in Sperm." *The New York Times*, January 1, 1991.

The Boston Women's Health Collective. *Our Bodies, Ourselves for the New Century.* New York: Simon and Schuster, 1998.

Brody, Jane E. "Ectopic Pregnancy: Increasing Hazard." *The New York Times*, May 9, 1984.

Clark, B. A., et al. "Pregnancy Loss in a Small Chorionic Villus Sampling Series." *American Journal of Obstetrics and Gynecology* 161, no. 2 (August 1989): 301–2.

Cole, Diane. "It Might Have Been: Mourning the Unborn." *Psychology Today*, July 1987, 21: 64–65.

Crowley, Mary. "Miscarriage: What Happens When a Pregnancy Can't Last, and Why." *Glamour*, October 1998, pp. 64, 70–72.

"Ectopic Pregnancies Reported on the Rise." *The New York Times*, January 27, 1995.

Fine, C., et al. "Sonographic Diagnosis of Partial Hydatidiform Mole." *Obstetrics and Gynecology* 73, no. 3 (part 1) (March 1989): 111–18.

Frisch, Melvin J., M.D., and Gayle Rapoport. *Getting Pregnant.* Tucson, AZ: The Body Press, 1987.

Gindoff, Paul, and Raphael Jewelewicz. "Reproductive Potential in the Older Woman." *Fertility and Sterility* 46, no. 6 (December 1986): 989–1001.

Harkness, Carla. *The Infertility Book.* San Francisco: Volcano Press, 1987.

Hudson, Richard L. "Scientists Discover Test that Predicts Miscarriage Risk." *Wall Street Journal*, November 12, 1990.

Ilse, Sherokee. *Unsupported Losses: Blighted Ovum, Ectopic Pregnancy and Molar Pregnancies.* Maple Plain, MN: Wintergreen Press, 1994.

Ilse, Sherokee, and Linda Hammer Burns. *Miscarriage: A Shattered Dream.* Maple Plain, MN: Wintergreen Press, 1985.

Jones, Walter B. "Gestational Trophoblastic Disease: What We Have Learned in the Past Decade." *American Journal of Obstetrics and Gynecology* 162, no. 5 (May 1990): 1286–95.

Kolata, Gina. "New Treatments May Aid Women Who Have Repeated Miscarriages." *The New York Times,* January 5, 1988.

Kutteh, W.H., M.D. "Antiphospholipid Antibody-Associated Recurrent Pregnancy Loss: Treatment with Heparin and Low-Dose Aspirin Is Superior to Low-Dose Aspirin Alone." *American Journal of Obstetrics and Gynecology* 174, no. 5 (May 1996): 1584–89.

McBride, W. Z. "Spontaneous Abortion." *American Family Physician* 13, no. 1 (January 1991): 175–82.

Moffitt, Perry-Lynn. "Miscarriage: The Most Silent of Sorrows." *SHARE: Caring Notes* 4, no. 2 (Second Quarter, 1998): 1–3.

Morgan, Brian L. G., and Roberta Morgan. *Hormones.* Los Angeles: The Body Press, 1989.

Nager, C. W., and A. A. Murphy. "Ectopic Pregnancy." *Clinical Obstetrics and Gynecology* 31, no. 2 (June 1991): 103–11.

Scher, Jonathan, M.D. *Preventing Miscarriage: The Good News.* New York: Harper and Row, 1990.

Schwan, Kassie. *The Infertility Maze.* Chicago: Contemporary Books, 1988.

Seifer, D. B., et al. "Persistent Ectopic Pregnancy." *Obstetrics and Gynecology* 76, no. 6 (December 1990): 1121–25.

Shaw, Clayton T. "Grief over Fetal Loss." *Family Practice Recertification* 5, no. 9 (September 1983): 129–38.

Simpson, J., et al. "Low Fetal Loss Rates after Ultrasound-Proved Viability in Early Pregnancy." *Journal of the American Medical Association* 258, no. 19 (November 13, 1987): 2555–57.

Stovall, T. G., et al. "Nonsurgical Diagnosis and Treatment of Tubal Pregnancy." *Fertility and Sterility* 51, no. 3 (September 1990): 537–38.

Wilcox, Allen J., M.D., et al. "Incidence of Early Loss of Pregnancy." *New England Medical Journal* 319, no. 4 (July 1988): 189–91.

Yuen, Basil Ho, and Patti B. Callegari. "Occurrence of Molar Pregnancy in Patients Undergoing Elective Abortion." *American Journal of Obstetrics and Gynecology* 154, no. 1 (February 1986): 273–76.

Zerifin, Israel. "Ovarian Pregnancy." *American Journal of Obstetrics and Gynecology* 163, no. 1 (part 1) (October 1990): 1182–85.

Chapter 6: Crisis Pregnancies and Loss

Altman, Lawrence K. "Electronic Monitoring Doesn't Help in Premature Births." *The New York Times,* March 1, 1990.

Anderson, Frank, M.D., et al. "Predictions of Risk for Preterm Delivery by Ultrasonographic Measurement of Cervical Length." *American Journal of Obstetrics and
   Gynecology* 163, no. 3 (September 1990): 859–67.

Berkow, Robert, M.D., ed. *The Merck Manual of Diagnosis and Therapy.* Rahway, NJ:
   1992.

Campbell, B. A., et al. "Uterine Activity after Preterm Labor and Premature Rupture of the Membranes." *American Journal of Obstetrics and Gynecology* 165, no. 2
   (August 1991): 422–25.

Iams, J. D., et al. "The Length of the Cervix and the Risk of Spontaneous
   Premature Delivery." *New England Journal of Medicine* 334 (1996): 567–72.

———. "Cervical Competence as a Continuum: A Study of Ultrasonographic
   Cervical Length and Obstetric Performance." *American Journal of Obstetrics and
   Gynecology* 172 (1995): 1097–106.

Levine, Cheryl Driver. "Premature Rupture of the Membranes and Sepsis in
   Preterm Neonates." *Nursing Research* 10, no. 1 (January–February 1991): 36–41.

McGregor, James A., M.D., et al. "Antimicrobial Therapy in Preterm Premature
   Rupture of the Membranes." *American Journal of Obstetrics and Gynecology* 165,
   no. 3 (September 1991): 632–40.

———. "Cervicovaginal Microflora and Pregnancy Outcome." *American Journal of
   Obstetrics and Gynecology* 163, no. 5 (part 1) (November 1990): 1580–91.

Parisi, Valerie M., M.D. "Cervical Incompetence and Preterm Labor." *Clinical
   Obstetrics and Gynecology* 31, no. 3 (September 1988): 585–98.

Physician's Desk Reference. Montvale, NJ: Medical Economics Company, 1998.

Robertson, Patricia Anne, M.D., and Peggy Henning Berlin. *The Premature Labor
   Handbook.* Garden City, NY: Doubleday and Company, 1986.

Savitz, David A., et al. "Epidemiologic Characteristics of Preterm Delivery."
   American Journal of Obstetrics and Gynecology 161, no. 2 (February 1991): 467–71.

Shortle, B., and R. Jewelewicz. "Cervical Incompetence." *Fertility and Sterility* 52,
   no. 2 (August 1989): 181–88.

Treadwell, Marjorie, M.D., et al. "Prognostic Factors and Complication Rates for
   Cervical Cerclage." *American Journal of Obstetrics and Gynecology* 165, no. 3
   (September 1991): 555–58.

Whitehead, Keith D., M.D., et al. "Retrospective Analysis of Cervical Cerclage
   Procedures at the Louisiana State University." *Southern Medical Journal* 83, no. 1
   (February 1990): 159–60.

Wilkins, I. A., M.D. et al. "Efficacy and Side Effects of Magnesium Sulfate and
   Ritodrine as Tocolytic Agents." *American Journal of Obstetrics and Gynecology* 159
   (1988): 685–89.

Chapter 7: Stillbirth and Newborn Death

Atkinson, Melissa. "No Heartbeat." *Parents Magazine,* April 1987: 134–35.

Beckendorf, Judith L., M.S. "Grieving and Believing: Helping Parents Through Imperfect Beginnings." *Birth Defects* 23, no. 6 (1987): 25–36.

Bloom, Beth-Ann, M.S. "Support for Families with Unsuccessful Pregnancies." *Birth Defects* 23, no. 6 (1987): 45–51.

Brody, Jane E. "Helping Parents to Cope with Tragedy, the Death of a Child." *The New York Times,* February 16, 1983.

Davis, Deborah L. *Empty Cradle, Broken Heart.* Golden, CO: Fulcrum Publishing, 1996.

Harrison, Helen. *The Premature Baby Book: A Parents' Guide.* New York: St. Martin's Press, 1983.

Jason, Janine, M.D., and Antonia Van der Meer. *Parenting Your Premature Baby.* New York: Dell Publishing, 1990.

Johnson, Joy, and Marvin Johnson. *Newborn Death.* Omaha, NE: Centering Corporation, 1987.

Kolata, Gina. "Fatal Syndrome in Infants Raises Painful Questions for Doctors." *The New York Times,* August 11, 1988.

———. "Survival of the Fetus: A Barrier Is Reached." *The New York Times,* April 18, 1989.

———. "When the Baby Is Late: Obstetricians Search for the Safest Approach." *The New York Times,* May 10, 1988.

Lyon, Jeff. *Playing God in the Nursery.* New York: W. W. Norton and Company, 1985.

Mackler, Ellen. "Messages from Our Baby." *The New York Times,* August 13, 1989.

Nance, Sherri, et al. *Premature Babies.* New York: Priam Books, 1982.

Stringham, Jean G., et al. "Silent Birth: Mourning a Stillborn Baby." *Social Work* (July 1982): 322–27.

Toder, Francine, Ph.D. *When Your Child Is Gone: Learning to Live Again.* New York: Fawcett Crest, 1986.

Trout, Michael David, M.A. "Birth of a Sick or Handicapped Infant: Impact on the Family." *Child Welfare* 62, no. 4 (July–August 1983): 337–48.

Vance, J., et al. "Psychological Changes in Parents Eight Months After the Loss of an Infant from Stillbirth, Neonatal Death, or Sudden Infant Death Syndrome— A Longitudinal Study." *Pediatrics* 96 (1995): 933–38.

Wilkins, I. A., M.D. and L. Hudon. "Evaluation and Management of the Patient with a Stillborn Fetus." In *Obstetics and Gynecology: Principles for Practice,* by Frank W. Ling, M.D. and Patrick Duff, M.D. Stanford, CT: Appleton & Lang, 2000.

Winik, Marion. "The Baby Who Never Came Home." *Parenting*, September 1990: 94–98.

Woods, James R., Jr., M.D. "Stillbirth." In *Pregnancy Loss: Medical Therapeutics and Practical Considerations*. Baltimore: Williams and Wilkins, 1987: 51–74.

———. "Death of a Newborn: Merging Parental Expectation and Medical Reality." *Pregnancy Loss: Medical Therapeutics and Practical Considerations*. Baltimore: Williams and Wilkins, 1987: 75–106.

Woods, James R., Jr., M.D., and Jenifer L. Esposito Woods. *Loss During Pregnancy or in the Newborn Period: Principles of Care with Clinical Cases and Analyses*. Pitman, NJ: Jannetti Publications, 1997.

Chapter 8: Prenatal Diagnosis and the Burden of Choice

Abramson, Marcia, and Rita Beck Black. "Extending the Boundaries of Life: Implications for Practice." *Health and Social Work* 10, no. 3 (Summer 1985): 165–73.

Apgar, Virginia, M.D., and Gabriel Stickle. "Birth Defects." *Journal of the American Medical Association* 204, no. 5 (April 29, 1968).

Baruch, D'Adamo, Jr., et al, eds. *Embryos, Ethics and Women's Rights: Exploring the New Reproductive Technologies*. New York: Haworth Press, 1988.

Berkow, Robert, M.D., ed. *The Merck Manual of Diagnosis and Therapy*. Rahway, NJ: 1992.

Black, Rita Beck. "Risk-Taking Behavior: Decision-Making in the Face of Genetic Uncertainty." *Social Work in Health Care* 7, no. 1 (Fall 1981): 11–25.

———, and Regina Furlong. "Impact of Prenatal Diagnosis in Families." *Social Work in Health Care* 9, no. 3 (Spring 1984): 37–50.

Blumberg, Bruce D., M.D. "The Psychological Sequelae of Abortion Performed for a Genetic Indication." *American Journal of Obstetrics and Gynecology* 122, no. 7 (August 1, 1975): 799–808.

Brown, Judy, M.D. "The Choice." *Journal of the American Medical Association* 262, no. 19 (November 17, 1989): 2735.

Coyle, Catherine T., and Robert D. Enright. "Forgiveness Intervention with Postabortion Men." *Journal of Consulting and Clinical Psychology* 65, no. 6 (1997): 1042–46.

Cuckle, H. "Biochemical and Ultrasound Screening for Down Syndrome: Rivals or Partners?" *Ultrasound Obstetrics and Gynecology* 7 (1996): 236–38.

Daniels, Ken R., M.A. "New Birth Technologies: A Social Work Approach to Researching the Psychosocial Factors." *Social Work in Health Care* 11, no. 4 (Summer 1986): 49–60.

Donnai, Paul, M.D., et al. "Attitudes of Patients after 'Genetic' Termination of Pregnancy." *British Medical Journal* 282 (February 21, 1981): 621–22.

Downe, Soo. "The Price of Progress." *Nursing Times* 86, no. 8 (February 21, 1990): 26–27.

Edwards, Janice, M.D. "Elective Termination of Chromosomally Abnormal Pregnancies: Psychosocial Effects and Experience in Genetic Counseling." *Loss, Grief and Care* 3, nos. 3–4 (1989): 21– 36.

Faulkner, Annie. "Forgotten Mothers." *Community Outlook* (June 1990): 14–18.

Furlong, Regina, and Richard Berkowitz. "Intrauterine Treatment: Meeting the Psychosocial Needs of the Family." *Health and Social Work* 10 (1985): 55–62.

Furlong, Regina, and Rita Beck Black. "Pregnancy Termination for Genetic Indication: The Impact on Families." *Social Work in Health Care* 10, no. 1 (Fall 1984): 17–33.

Goodburn, S. F., et al. "Second-Trimester Maternal Serum Screening Using Alpha-Fetoprotein, Human Chorionic Gonadotrophin, and Unconjugated Oestriol." *Prenatal Diagnosis* 14, no. 5 (May 1994): 391–402.

Griffin, Margaret L., M.A., et al. "Genetic Knowledge, Client Perspectives, and Genetic Counseling." *Social Work in Health Care* 2, no. 2 (Winter 1976–77: 171–80.

Haning, R V., Jr., et al. "Effects of Fetal Number and Multifetal Reduction on Length of In Vitro Fertilization Pregnancies." *Obstetrics and Gynecology* 87 (1996): 964–68.

Ilse, Sherokee. *Precious Lives, Painful Choices: A Prenatal Decision-Making Guide.* Maple Plain, MN: Wintergreen Press, 1995.

Johns, Nan. "Family Reactions to the Birth of a Child with a Congenital Abnormality." *Obstetrical Gynecological Survey* 26 (1971): 635–36.

Kenyon, Sara. "Support after Termination for Fetal Abnormalities." *Midwives Chronicle* 101, no. 1205 (June 1988): 190.

Kluger-Bell, Kim. *Unspeakable Losses: Understanding the Experience of Pregnancy Loss, Miscarriage and Abortion.* New York: W. W. Norton and Company, 1998.

Kolata, Gina. "Testing for Infections that Can Harm the Fetus." *The New York Times,* June 8, 1989.

———. "In Late Abortions, Decisions Are Painful and Options Few." *The New York Times,* January 5, 1992.

Leschot, N. J., et al. "Chorionic Villi Sampling: Cytogenetic and Clinical Findings in 500 Pregnancies." *British Medical Journal* 295 (August 15, 1987): 107–10.

Lippman-Hand, Abby, and F. Clarke Fraser. "Genetic Counseling—The Postcounseling Period: I. Parents' Perceptions of Uncertainty." *American Journal of Medical Genetics* 4 (1979): 51–71.

———. "Genetic Counseling—The Postcounseling Period: II. Making Reproductive Choices." *American Journal of Medical Genetics* 4 (1979): 73–87.

————. "Genetic Counseling—Provision and Reception of Information." *American Journal of Medical Genetics* 3 (1979): 113–27.

Llewelyn, S. P. "An Investigation of Anxiety Following Termination of Pregnancy." *Journal of Advanced Nursing* 13 (July 1988): 468–71.

O'Brien, William, M.D. "Midtrimester Genetic Amniocentesis: A Review of Fetal Risks." *The Journal of Reproductive Medicine* 29, no. 1 (January 1984): 59–63.

Olshansky, Simon. "Chronic Sorrow: A Response to Having a Mentally Defective Child." *Social Casework* 43 (1962): 190–93.

Petrikovsky, B. M., and A. M. Ventzileos. "Management and Outcome of Multiple Pregnancy of High Fetal Order." *Obstetrical Gynecological Survey* 44 (1989): 578–84.

Reamer, Frederic G. "Ethical Dilemmas in Social Work Practice." *Social Work* 29, no. 1 (January–February 1983): 31–35.

Rhoads, George G., et al. "The Safety and Efficacy of Chorionic Villus Sampling for Early Prenatal Diagnosis of Cytogenetic Abnormalities." *New England Journal of Medicine* 320 (March 9, 1989): 609–17.

Rothman, Barbara Katz. *The Tentative Pregnancy*. New York: Penguin Books, 1987.

Simpson, J. L., and S. A. Carson. "Multifetal Reduction in High-Order Gestations: A Nonelective Procedure?" *Journal of the Society for Gynecologic Investigation* 3 (1996): 1–2.

Sjogren, Berit, and Nils Uddenberg. "Decision-Making During the Prenatal Diagnostic Procedure: A Questionnaire and Interview Study of 211 Women Participating in Prenatal Diagnosis." *Prenatal Diagnosis* 8 (1988): 263–73.

Spencer, John W., Ph.D., and David N. Cox, Ph.D. "Emotional Responses of Pregnant Women to Chorionic Villi Sampling or Amniocentesis." *American Journal of Obstetrics and Gynecology* 157 (November 1987): 1155–60.

Van Putte, Alison. "Perinatal Bereavement Crisis: Coping with Negative Outcomes from Prenatal Diagnosis." *Perinatal Neonatal Nursing* 2, no. 2 (1988): 12–22.

SECTION III: THE RESPONSE OF OTHERS

Chapter 9: Medical Care When You Lose Your Pregnancy

American Academy of Pediatrics and American College of Obstetricians and Gynecologists. *Guidelines for Perinatal Care*. Washington, D.C.: American College of Obstetricians and Gynecologists, June 1997.

Becker, Rita, et al. "Development of a Perinatal Grief Checklist." *Journal of Obstetric, Gynecologic, and Neonatal Nursing* 14 (1985): 194–99.

Benfield, Gary D., et al. "Grief Response of Parents after Referral of the Critically Ill Newborn to a Regional Center." *New England Journal of Medicine* 294 (April 29, 1976): 975–78.

———. "Grief Response of Parents to Neonatal Death and Parent Participation in Deciding Care." *Pediatrics* 62, no. 2 (August 1978): 171–77.

Bourne, Stanford, M.D. "The Psychological Effects of Stillbirths on Women and Their Doctors." *Journal of the Royal College of General Practitioners* 16 (1968): 103–13.

Berger, Lawrence R., M.D. "Requesting the Autopsy: A Pediatric Perspective." *Clinical Pediatrics* 17, no. 5 (May 1978): 445–52.

Carr, Donna, and Chaplain Samuel F. Knupp. "Grief and Perinatal Loss: A Community Hospital Response to Support." *Journal of Obstetric, Gynecologic, and Neonatal Nursing* 14, no. 2 (March–April 1985): 130–39.

Chez, Ronald. "Acute Grief and Mourning: One Obstetrician's Experience." *Obstetrics and Gynecology* 85 (1995): 1059–61.

Chez, Ronald, et al. "Helping Patients and Doctors Cope with Perinatal Death." *Contemporary Obstetrics and Gynecology* 20 (1982): 98.

Cohen, Lewis, et al. "Perinatal Mortality: Assisting Parental Affirmation." *American Journal of Orthopsychiatry* 48, no. 4 (October 1978): 727–31.

Downey, V. et al. "Dying Babies and Associated Stress in NICU Nurses." *Neonatal Network* 14 (1995): 41–46.

Forrest, G. C., et al. "Support after Perinatal Death: A Study of Support and Counselling After Perinatal Bereavement." *British Medical Journal* 285 (November 20, 1982): 1475–79.

Hall, Lee. "Social Workers Play Vital Role in Perinatal Care." *National Association of Social Workers News* (January 1979): 4.

Jimenez, Sherry Lynn Mims. "Grief Counseling: When Doctors Are Too Distraught, Educators Can Help Grieving Parents." *Childbirth Educator* (Fall 1983): 42.

Kellner, Kenneth, and Marian Lake. "Grief Counseling." In *High-Risk Pregnancy: A Team Approach*, ed. Robert A. Knuppel and Joan E. Drukker. Philadelphia: W. B. Saunders & Company, 1986: 561–74.

Kellner, Kenneth, et al. "Parental Behavior after Perinatal Death: Lack of Predictive Demographic and Obstetric Variables." *Obstetrics and Gynecology* 63, no. 6 (June 1984): 809–14.

———. "Perinatal Mortality Counseling Program for Families Who Experience a Stillbirth." *Death Education* 5 (1981): 29–35.

Kirkley-Best, Elizabeth, and Kenneth Kellner. "The Forgotten Grief: A Review of the Psychology of Stillbirth." *American Journal of Orthopsychiatry* 52, no. 3 (July 1982): 420–29.

Kowalski, Karren, R.N., M.S. "Managing Perinatal Loss." *Clinical Obstetrics and Gynecology* 23, no. 4 (December 1980): 1113–23.

Lake, Marion, et al. "The Role of a Grief Support Team following Stillbirth." *American Journal of Obstetrics and Gynecology* 146 (August 1983): 877–81.

Lehman, Darrin R., et al. "Social Support for the Bereaved Recipients and Providing Perspectives on What Is Helpful." *Journal of Consulting and Clinical Psychology* 54 (1986): 438–41.

Leon, I. "Perinatal Loss: A Critique of Current Hospital Practices." *Clinical Pediatrics* 31 (1992): 366–74.

Lewis, Emanuel, and Anne Page. "Failure to Mourn a Stillbirth: An Overlooked Catastrophe." *British Journal of Medical Psychology* 51 (1978): 237–41.

Morris, D. "Management of Perinatal Bereavement." *Archives of Diseases in Childhood* 63 (1988): 870–72.

O'Donohue, Nancy. "Facilitating the Grief Process." *Journal of Nurse-Midwifery* 24, no. 5 (September–October 1979): 16–19.

———. "Perinatal Bereavement: The Role of the Health Care Professional." *Quarterly Review Bulletin* 4 (September 1978): 30–32.

Quirk, Tina R. "Crisis Theory, Grief Theory, and Related Psychosocial Factors: The Framework for Intervention." *Journal of Nurse-Midwifery* 24, no. 5 (September–October 1979): 13–16.

Rowe, Jane, M.D., et al. "Follow-up of Families Who Experience a Perinatal Death." *Pediatrics* 62, no. 2 (August 1978): 166–70.

Schreiner, Richard, M.D., et al. "Physician's Responsibility to Parents after Death of an Infant." *Journal of Diseases of Children* 133 (July 1979): 723–26.

Whited, Linda. "Helping the Parents of a Stillborn." *Nursing* (May 1985): 63.

Chapter 10: Finding Solace in Your Religion

Biegert, John E. *When Death Has Touched Your Life*. New York: The Pilgrim Press, 1981.

Bramblett, John. *When Good-bye Is Forever: Learning to Live Again after the Loss of a Child*. New York: Ballantine Books, 1991.

Cox, James A. "Aunt Grace Can't Have Babies." *Journal of Religion and Health* 25, no. 1 (Spring 1986): 73–85.

Hunt, Swanee. "Pastoral Care and Miscarriage: A Ministry Long Neglected." *Pastoral Psychology* 32, no. 4 (Summer 1984): 265–78.

Klein, Bert A. "Chaplain's Ministry When a Baby Dies." *Pregnancy Loss: Medical Therapeutics and Practical Considerations*. Baltimore: Williams and Wilkins, 1987.

Kolodner, Anna. "Judaism and Infant Death: A Community of One." *Jewish Review* (September-October, 1989): 6–7.

Kübler-Ross, Elisabeth. *Death: The Final Stage of Growth*. New York: Simon and Schuster, 1975.

Kushner, Harold S. *When Bad Things Happen to Good People.* New York: Avon Books, 1997.

———. *When Children Ask About God.* New York: Schocken Books, 1976.

Limbo, Rana K., and Sara Rich Wheeler. *When a Baby Dies: A Handbook for Healing and Helping.* La Crosse, WI: Bereavement Services, 1998.

Miles, Al. "Comforting a Family When a Child Dies." *Church Educator* (February 1991): 5–6.

Mooney, Bel. "Birth and Death Pangs." *The Guardian,* January 25, 1976.

Petsonk, Judy, and Jim Remsen. *The Intermarriage Handbook: A Guide for Jews and Christians.* New York: Arbor House, William Morrow and Company, 1988.

Schwiebert, Pat, R.N., and Paul Kirk, M.D. *When Hello Means Goodbye.* Portland, OR: Perinatal Loss, 1985.

Seydel, Frank D., M. Div., Ph. D. "Ethical Dilemmas in Perinatal Care: Opportunities for Clergy Assistance." *Birth Defects* 23, no. 6 (1987): 16–24.

Troyer, Ronald. "Funeral Director." *Pregnancy Loss: Medical Therapeutics and Practical Considerations.* Baltimore: Williams and Wilkins, 1987.

Chapter 11: The Response of Your Family and Friends

Beck, Melinda, et al. "Miscarriages." *Newsweek,* August 15, 1988, 46–49.

Berezin, Nancy. *After a Loss in Pregnancy.* New York: Simon and Schuster, 1982.

Hagley, Norman E., D.Min. *Comfort Us, Lord—Our Baby Died.* Omaha, NE: Centering Corporation, 1985.

Ilse, Sherokee, and Susan Erling. *Planning a Precious Goodbye.* Maple Plain, MN: Wintergreen Press, 1994.

Johnson, Joy, and Marvin Johnson. *Children Die, Too.* Omaha, NE: Centering Corporation, 1978.

———. *Miscarriage.* Omaha, NE: Centering Corporation, 1988.

Johnson, Sherry E. *After a Child Dies: Counseling Bereaved Parents.* New York: Springer Publishing Company, 1987.

Moffitt, Perry-Lynn. "Miscarriage: The Baby Who Wasn't." *Parents Magazine,* April 1987. pp. 132–34, 214–17.

Panuthos, Claudia, and Catherine Romeo. *Ended Beginnings: Healing Childbearing Losses.* New York: Warner Books, 1984.

Pizer, Hank, and Christine O'Brien Palinski. *Coping with a Miscarriage.* New York: New American Library, 1980.

Westberg, Granger E. *Good Grief: A Constructive Approach to the Problem of Loss.* Philadelphia: Fortress Press, 1971.

Chapter 12: Helping Your Children at Home

Berger, Terry. *I Have Feelings.* New York: Human Sciences Press, 1971.

Bernstein, Joanne. *Loss and How to Cope with It.* New York: Seabury Press, 1977.

Bluebond-Langner, Myra. "Meanings of Death of Children." In *New Meanings of Death,* ed. Herman Feifel. New York: McGraw-Hill, 1977.

Cain, Albert C., et al. "Children's Disturbed Reactions to the Death of a Sibling." *American Journal of Orthopsychiatry* (1964): 741–52.

———. "Children's Disturbed Reactions to Their Mother's Miscarriage." *Psychosomatic Medicine* 26 (January–February 1964): 58–66.

Cohn, Janice. *Molly's Rosebush.* Morton Grove, IL: Albert Whitman and Co., 1994.

Dodge, Nancy. *Thumpy's Story.* Springfield, IL: Prairie Lark Press, 1985 (available through SHARE).

Elliott, Barbara A. "Neonatal Death: Reflections for Parents." *Pediatrics* 62 (July 1978): 100–102.

Fox, Sandra S. *Books and Films on Death and Dying for Children and Adolescents: An Annotated Bibliography.* Boston: The Good Grief Program, 1985.

Gaffney, Donna A. *The Seasons of Grief: Helping Children through Loss.* New York: New American Library, 1988.

Grollman, Earl A. *Explaining Death to Children.* Boston: Beacon Press, 1976.

———. *Talking About Death: A Dialogue between Parent and Child.* Boston: Beacon Press, 1991.

Grollman, Earl A., ed. *Bereaved Children and Teens: A Support Guide for Parents and Professionals.* Boston: Beacon Press, 1996.

Gryte, Marilyn. *No New Baby.* Omaha, NE: Centering Corporation, 1999.

Hardgrove, Carol, and Louise H. Warrick. "How Shall We Tell the Children?" *American Journal of Nursing* 74, no. 3 (March 1974): 450.

Ilse, Sherokee, et al. *Sibling Grief.* Maple Plain, MN: Wintergreen Press, 1996.

Johnson, Joy, and Marvin Johnson. *Where's Jess?* Omaha, NE: Centering Corporation, 1982.

Kantrowits, Mildred. *When Violet Died.* New York: Parents' Magazine Press, 1973.

Kroen, William. *Helping Children Cope with the Loss of a Loved One.* Minneapolis, MN: Free Spirit Press, 1996.

Lasker, Arnold A. "Telling Children the Facts of Death." *National Jewish Monthly* 83, no. 6 (February 1969). Reprinted in *Your Child* (Winter 1972).

———. "When Children Face Bereavement." *Conservative Judaism* 18 (Winter 1964): 53–58.

Levy, Erin Linn. *Children Are Not Paper Dolls.* Barrington, IL: The Publishers' Mark, 1982.

Martinez, Susan Erling, and Jake Erling. *Our Baby Died. Why?* St. Paul, MN: A Place to Remember, 1994.

Moriarty, Irene. "Mourning the Death of an Infant: The Sibling's Story." *The Journal of Pastoral Care* 32, no. 1 (March 1978): 22–33.

Nagy, Maria. "The Child's View of Death." In *The Meaning of Death,* ed. Herman Feifel. New York: McGraw-Hill, 1965.

Obershaw, Richard J. *Cry Until You Laugh.* Minneapolis, MN: Fairview Press, 1992.

Papenbrock, Patricia L., R.N., and Robert F. Voss, M.A. *Children's Grief.* Redmond, WA: Medic Publishing Company, 1988.

Poznanski, Elva O. "The 'Replacement Child': A Saga of Unresolved Parental Grief." *Journal of Pediatrics* 81 (1972): 1190–93.

Scrivani, Mark. *When Death Walks In.* Omaha, NE: The Centering Corporation, 1991.

Schaefer, Dan, and Christine Lyons. *How Do We Tell the Children?* New York: Newmarket Press, 1986.

Scrimshaw, Susan, and Daniel March. "I Had a Baby Sister, but She Lasted Only One Day." *Journal of the American Medical Association* 251 (1984): 732–33.

Sigal, John J., Ph.D. "Familial Consequences of Parental Preoccupation," paper read at the 125th annual meeting of the American Psychiatric Association, Dallas (May 1972): 53–72.

Smialik, Zoe, R.N. "Observations of Immediate Reactions of Families to Sudden Infant Death." *Pediatrics* 62, no. 2 (August 1978): 160–65.

Chapter 13: For Bereaved Grandparents

AMEND. *Problems that May Be Encountered by Parents after the Death of Their Baby.* St. Louis: AMEND, 1984.

Earl, W. J. H. "Help for Parents after Stillbirth." *British Medical Journal* 1, no. 6111 (February 25, 1978): 505–6.

Friedman, Stanford, et al. "Behavioral Observations on Parents Anticipating the Death of a Child." *Pediatrics* 32 (October 1963): 610–25.

Gerner, Margaret H. *For Bereaved Grandparents.* Omaha, NE: Centering Corporation, 1990.

Ilse, Sherokee, and Lori Leininger. *Grieving Grandparents.* Maple Plain, MN: Wintergreen Press, 1994.

Lifton, Robert J. "Advocacy and Corruption in the Healing Professions." In *Nourishing the Humanistic in Medicine,* ed. William R. Rogers and David Barnard. Pittsburgh: University of Pittsburgh Press, 1979, 53-72.

Smialik, Zoe, R.N. "Observations on Immediate Reactions of Families to Sudden Infant Death." *Pediatrics* 62, no. 2 (August 1978): 160–65.

SECTION IV: SPECIAL CIRCUMSTANCES

Chapter 14: The Impact of Pregnancy Loss on Your Career

Herz, Elisabeth. "Psychological Repercussions of Pregnancy Loss." *Psychiatric Annals* 14, no. 6 (June 1984): 454–57.

Maranto, Gina. "Delayed Childbearing." *The Atlantic Monthly* (June 1995): 55–66.

Tanouye, Elyse. "Late Childbearing Is Found to Raise Risks." *The Wall Street Journal*, August 19, 1992.

Chapter 15: Pregnancy Loss and Infertility

Batterman, Ronni. "A Comprehensive Approach to Treating Infertility." *Health and Social Work* 10 (1985): 46–53.

Bombardieri, Merle. "The Twenty-Minute Rule—First-Aid for Couples in Distress." *RESOLVE Newsletter* (December 1983): 5.

Carter, Jean, and Michael Carter. *Sweet Grapes: How to Stop Being Infertile and Start Living Again.* Indianapolis, IN: Perspectives Press, 1989.

DiGiulio, Joan Ferry. "Self-Acceptance: A Factor in the Adoption Process." *Child Welfare* 67, no. 5 (September–October 1988).

Galst, Joann Paley. "Male-Female Differences in the Emotional Experience of Infertility." *Fertility Research Foundation Newsletter* 8, no. 1 (Winter 1987): 9–11.

Gilman, Lois. *The Adoption Resource Book.* New York: Harper and Row, 1984.

Glazer, Ellen Sarasohn, and Susan Lewis Cooper. *Without Child: Examining and Resolving Infertility.* Lexington, MA: Lexington Books, 1988.

Gold, Michael. *And Hannah Wept: Infertility, Adoption, and the Jewish Couple.* New York: The Jewish Publication Society, 1988.

Harkness, Carla. *The Infertility Book.* San Francisco: Volcano Press, 1987.

Ilse, Sherokee, and Linda Hammer Burns. *What Next?* Maple Plain, MN: Wintergreen Press, 1982.

Jacobson, Mark. "The Baby Chase." *Esquire* (May 1987): 49–50.

Lalos, Ann, et al. "The Psychosocial Impact of Infertility Two Years after Completed Surgical Treatment." *Acta Obstetrics and Gynecology Scandinavia* 64 (1985): 599–604.

Lasker, Judith, and Susan Borg. *In Search of Parenthood: Coping with Infertility and High-Tech Conception.* Boston: Beacon Press, 1987.

Mazor, Miriam D., and Harriet F. Simons. *Infertility: Medical, Emotional, and Social Considerations*. New York: Human Sciences Press, 1984.

Menken, Jane, et al. "Age and Infertility." *Science* 233 (September 1986): 1389–94.

Menning, Barbara Eck. *Infertility: A Guide for the Childless Couple*. Englewood Cliffs, NJ: Prentice-Hall, 1977.

Peoples, Debby, and Harriette Rovner Ferguson, C.S.W. *What to Expect When You're Experiencing Infertility: How to Cope with the Emotional Crisis and Survive*. New York: W. W. Norton and Company, 1998.

Salzer, Linda. *Infertility: How Couples Can Cope*. Boston: G. K. Hall and Company, 1986.

Smith, Jerome, and Franklin I. Miroff. *The Adoption Experience*. New York: Madison Books, 1987.

Valentine, Deborah P. "Psychological Impact of Infertility: Identifying Issues and Needs." *Social Work in Health Care* 11, no. 4 (Summer 1986): 61–69.

Viguers, Susan. *With Child: One Couple's Journey to Their Adopted Children*. San Diego: Harcourt Brace Jovanovich, 1986.

Chapter 16: Becoming Pregnant Again

Bing, Elisabeth, and Libby Coleman. *Having a Baby After 30*. New York: Farrar, Straus, and Giroux, 1980.

———. *Making Love During Pregnancy*. New York: Farrar, Straus, and Giroux, 1989.

Cohen, Marion. *She Was Born, She Died*. Omaha, NE: Centering Corporation, 1983.

Creasy, Robert, M.D., and Diane Hales, M.D. *New Hope for Problem Pregnancies*. New York: Berkley Publishing, 1984.

Davis, D., et al. "Postponing Pregnancy after Perinatal Death: Perspectives in Doctor Advice." *Journal of the Academy of Child and Adolescent Psychiatry* 28 (1989): 481–87.

Ilse, Sherokee. *Another Baby? Maybe . . .* Maple Plain, MN: Wintergreen Press, 1996.

Floyd, Cathy Cornwell. "Pregnancy after Reproductive Failure." *American Journal of Nursing* 81, no. 11 (November 1981): 2050–53.

Forman, Michael, and Judi Forman. "After a Baby Dies." *Parents Magazine* (August 1988): 114–16, 184–87.

Glazer, Ellen Sarasohn, and Susan Lewis Cooper. *Without Child: Experiencing and Resolving Infertility*. Lexington, MA: D. C. Heath and Company, 1988.

Hollingsworth, Dorothy Reycroft, M.D., and Robert Resnick, M.D., eds. *Medical Counseling before Pregnancy*. New York: Churchill Livingstone, 1988.

Kirksey, Janet, R.N. "Impact of Pregnancy Loss on Subsequent Pregnancy." *Pregnancy Loss: Medical Therapeutics and Practical Considerations*. Baltimore: Williams and Wilkins, 1987.

Kolata, Gina. *The Baby Doctors: Probing the Limits of Fetal Medicine*. New York: Dell Publishing, 1990.

Lanham, Carol Cirulli. *Pregnancy After a Loss*. New York: Berkley Publishing Group, 1999.

Morales, Karla, and Charles B. Julander. *Take This Book to the Obstetrician with You*. Reading, MA: Addison-Wesley Publishing Company, 1991.

Perloe, Mark, M.D., and Linda Gail Christie. *Miracle Babies*. New York: Penguin Books, 1987.

Poliakin, Raymond J., M.D. *What You Didn't Think to Ask Your Obstetrician*. Chicago: Contemporary Books, 1987.

Schwartzman, Michael, Ph.D. *The Anxious Parent*. New York: Simon and Schuster, 1990.

Schweibert, Pat, R.N., and Paul Kirk, M.D. *Still to Be Born*. Portland, OR: Perinatal Loss, 1989.

Theut, Susan K., et al. "Pregnancy Subsequent to Perinatal Loss: Parental Anxiety and Depression." *Journal of American Child and Adolescent Psychiatry* 27 (May 1988): 289–92.

Williams, Lynne A., M.D., et al. *The Too Precious Child*. New York: Warner Books, 1989.

APPENDIX A: Managing Problem Pregnancies

Berendes, Heinz W., M.D., and Michele Forman, Ph.D. "Delayed Childbearing Trends and Consequences." In *Reproductive and Perinatal Epidemiology*, ed. Michele Kiely. Boca Raton, FL: CRC Press, 1991.

Berke, Richard L. "Plans for Births Are Seen to Shift." *The New York Times*, June 22, 1989.

Berkow, Robert, M.D., ed. *The Merck Manual of Diagnosis and Therapy*. Rahway, NJ: 1992.

Blatt, Robin J. R. *Prenatal Tests*. New York: Vintage Books, 1988.

Brody, Jane E. "Prenatal Sonography: A Vital Diagnostic Tool That Can Provide Vital Data in Managing Pregnancy." *The New York Times*, November 1, 1990.

Cross, Philip K., and Ernest B. Hook. "An Analysis of Paternal Age." *Human Genetics* 77, no. 4 (December 1987): 307–16.

"For Pregnant Athletes, Reassurance on Exercise." *The New York Times*, January 18, 1990.

Eisenberg, Arlene, et al. *What to Expect When You're Expecting*. New York: Workman Publishing, 1991.

Goodburn, S. F., et al. "Second-Trimester Maternal Serum Screening Using Alpha-Fetoprotein, Human Chorionic Gonadotrophin, and Unconjugated Oestriol." *Prenatal Diagnosis* 14, no. 5 (May 1994): 391–402.

Greene, Michael F., et al. "First-Trimester Hemoglobin A1 and Risk for Major Malformations and Spontaneous Abortion in Diabetic Pregnancy." *Teratology* 39, no. 3 (March 1989): 225–31.

Hansen, John. "Older Maternal Age and Pregnancy Outcome." *Obstetric and Gynecological Survey* 41 (November 1986): 726.

Hilts, Philip J. "Growing Concern over Pelvic Infection in Women." *The New York Times*, October 11, 1990.

Kelly-Buchanan, Christine. *Peace of Mind During Pregnancy: An A-Z Guide to the Substances that Could Affect Your Unborn Baby*. New York: Dell, 1988.

Laros, R., Jr., et al. "Outcome of Very-Low-Birth-Weight Infants Exposed to Beta-Sympathomimetics in Utero." *American Journal of Obstetrics and Gynecology* 161, no. 6 (part 1) (June 1991): 1657–61.

Leary, Warren E. "Premature Births Tied to a B Vitamin Deficiency." *The New York Times*, April 17, 1996.

Leschot, Nico J., et al. "Chorionic Villi Sampling." *British Medical Journal* 295 (August 15, 1987): 407–10.

McGregor, James A., et al. "Antenatal Microbiologic and Maternal Risk Factors Associated with Prematurity." *American Journal of Obstetrics and Gynecology* 163, no. 5 (part 1) (November 1990): 1465–73.

Mills, James, M.D., et al. "Incidence of Spontaneous Abortion Among Normal Women and Insulin-Dependent Diabetic Women." *New England Journal of Medicine* 319, no. 25 (December 22, 1988): 1617–23.

Schrotenboer-Cox, Kathryn, M.D., and Joan Solomon Weiss. *Pregnancy Over 35*. New York: Ballantine Books, 1989.

Wilkins, I. A., M.D., et al. "Efficacy and Side Effects of Magnesium Sulfate and Ritodrine as Tocolytic Agents." *American Journal of Obstetrics and Gynecology* 159 (1988): 685–89.

Wurtzel, D. "Prenatal Administration of Indomethacin as a Tocolytic Agent." *Obstetrics and Gynecology* 76, no. 1 (October 1990): 689–92.

APPENDIX B: Rituals

Anderson, Vienna Cobb. *Prayers of Our Hearts*. New York: Crossroad Publishing Company, 1991.

Hagley, Norman E., D.Min. *Comfort Us, Lord—Our Baby Died.* Omaha, NE: Centering Corporation, 1985.

Ilse, Sherokee, and Susan Erling. *Planning a Precious Goodbye.* Maple Plain, MN: Wintergreen Press, 1994.

Lamb, Jane Marie, OSF. *Bittersweet . . . hellogoodbye.* St. Charles, MO: SHARE, 1988.

Osgood, Judy. *Meditations for Bereaved Parents.* Sunriver, OR: Gilgal Publications, 1983.

Schweibert, Pat, and Paul Kirk. *When Hello Means Goodbye.* Portland, OR: Perinatal Loss Project, 1985.

APPENDIX C: Pregnancy Loss and the Environment

Altman, Lawrence K. "Some Who Used VDT's Miscarried, Study Says." *The New York Times* (June 5, 1988).

Aschengrau, Ann, et al. "Quality of Community Drinking Water and the Occurrence of Spontaneous Abortion." *Archives of Environmental Health* 11, no. 5 (September-October 1989): 283–90.

Bentur, Y., and G. Koren. "The Three Most Common Occupational Exposures Reported by Pregnant Women: An Update." *American Journal of Obstetrics and Gynecology* 165, no. 2 (August 1991): 129–37.

Blatt, Robin J. R. *Prenatal Tests.* New York: Vintage Books, 1988.

Brent, Robert L., M.D. "The Effect of Embryonic and Fetal Exposure to X Ray, Microwaves, and Ultrasound: Counseling the Pregnant and Nonpregnant Patient about These Risks." *Seminars in Oncology* 16, no. 5 (October 1989): 317–68.

"Cocaine-Using Fathers Linked to Birth Defects." *The New York Times,* October 15, 1991.

Deane, Margaret, et al. "Adverse Pregnancy Outcomes in Relation to Water Contamination, Santa Clara County, California." *American Journal of Epidemiology* 129, no. 5 (May 1989): 894–904.

Goldhaber, Marilyn K., et al. "Spontaneous Abortions after the Three Mile Island Nuclear Accident." *American Journal of Public Health* 73 (July 1983): 752–59.

Hatch, Maureen, Ph.D., and Michele Marcus, Ph.D. "Occupational Exposures and Reproduction." In *Reproductive and Perinatal Epidemiology,* ed. Michele Kiely. Boca Raton, FL: CRC Press, 1991.

Hawkins, M., and R. Smith. "Pregnancy Outcomes in Childhood Cancer Survivors." *International Journal of Cancer* 43, no. 3 (March 15, 1989): 399–402.

"Infants More at Risk in Poor Rural Areas, New Study Indicates." *The New York Times,* December 8, 1988.

Jankowski, C. "Radiation and Pregnancy: Putting the Risks in Proportion." *American Journal of Nursing* 86, no. 3 (March 1986): 260–65.

Kallen, Bengt, Ph.D. *Epidemiology of Human Reproduction.* Boca Raton, FL: CRC Press, 1988.

Kelly-Buchanan, Christine. *Peace of Mind During Pregnancy: An A-Z Guide to the Substances That Could Affect Your Unborn Baby.* New York: Dell, 1988.

Lewin, Tamar. "Miscarriages at USA Today Are Under Review." *The New York Times,* December 10, 1988.

Liberatos, Penny, M.A., and John L. Kiely, Ph.D. "Selected Issues in the Evaluation of Prenatal Care." In *Reproductive and Perinatal Epidemiology,* ed. Michele Kiely. Boca Raton, FL: CRC Press, 1991.

Morgan, Robert W., et al. "Fetal Loss and Work in a Waste Water Treatment Plant." *American Journal of Public Health* 74 (May 1984): 499–501.

Murphy, M. J., et al. "Past Pregnancy Outcomes among Women Living in the Vicinity of a Lead Smelter in Kosova, Yugoslavia." *American Journal of Public Health* 80, no. 1 (January 1990): 33–35.

Neel, J. "Update on the Genetic Effects of Ionizing Radiation." *Journal of the American Medical Association* 265, no. 5 (August 7, 1991): 698–701.

Pollack, Andrew. "San Francisco Moves to Regulate Video Terminals." *The New York Times,* December 11, 1991.

Rogers, Bruce D., and Richard V. Lee. "Drug Abuse." In Burrow and Ferris, eds., *Medical Complications During Pregnancy.* Philadelphia: W. B. Saunders Company, 1988.

Rosenthal, Elisabeth. "When a Pregnant Woman Drinks." *The New York Times Magazine,* February 4, 1990, pp. 30, 61.

Selevan, Sherry, Ph.D. "Environmental Exposures and Reproduction." In *Reproductive and Perinatal Epidemiology,* ed. Michele Kiely. Boca Raton, FL: CRC Press, 1991.

Stevens, William K. "Major U.S. Study Finds No Miscarriage Risk from Video Terminals." *The New York Times,* March 14, 1991.

"Study Links Cancer in Young to Fathers' Smoking." *The New York Times,* January 24, 1991.

Tilyou, Sarah. "Three Mile Island—Ten Years Later." *Journal of Nuclear Medicine* 30, no. 1 (April 1989): 427–30.

Tucker, J. M., et al. "Etiologies of Preterm Birth in an Indigent Population." *Obstetrics and Gynecology* 77, no. 3 (March 1991): 313–17.

"The VDT Miscarriage Scare," editorial, *The New York Times,* March 19, 1991.

Wrensch, Margaret M., Ph.D., et al. "Hydrogeologic Assessment of Exposure to Solvent-Contaminated Drinking Water: Pregnancy Outcomes in Relation to Exposure." *Archives of Environmental Health* 15, no. 1 (July–August 1990): 210–16.

Yamazaki, J., and W. Schull. "Perinatal Loss and Neurological Abnormalities among Children of the Atomic Bomb." *Journal of the American Medical Association* 261, no. 5 (August 1, 1990): 605–9.

Index